THE HEBRIDES

BOOKS BY

W. H. MURRAY

Mountaineering in Scotland

Undiscovered Scotland

Scottish Himalayan Expedition

The Story of Everest

Five Frontiers

The Spurs of Troodos

Maelstrom

Dark Rose the Phoenix

Highland Landscape

The Hebrides

*Companion Guide to the
West Highlands of Scotland*

The Real MacKay

THE
HEBRIDES

W. H. Murray

HEINEMANN : LONDON

William Heinemann Ltd

LONDON MELBOURNE TORONTO

JOHANNESBURG AUCKLAND

First published 1966
Reprinted 1966
Reprinted with revisions 1969

© W. H. Murray, 1966

SBN 434 48200 5

Printed Offset Litho in Great Britain by
Cox & Wyman Ltd,
London, Fakenham and Reading

CONTENTS

ILLUSTRATIONS

MAPS

By Adam Arnott

THE ISLES ON THE EDGE OF THE SEA

AN archipelago of more than five hundred islands curves in a double line down the west coast of Scotland. It shields the mainland with an Atlantic barrier nearly two hundred and forty miles long from the Mull of Oa in the south to the Butt of Lewis in the north. Most of these islands are tiny, uninhabited by man, given mass by the twenty or thirty larger islands that form the bulk of the Inner and Outer Hebrides. In the second century A.D. they were named Hebudes or Ebudae by the geographer Ptolemy. The word is considered by students of Norse to have been a slight corruption of *Havbredey* (pronounced Haubredey), which in the plural means 'Isles on the Edge of the Sea'.

When first seen from the sea, the islands appear like bare mountain tops riding the waves, and that is what they are. It greatly helps us to understand them if we bear in mind a few fundamental facts – which have the fabulous ring of saga. The original mountain chain that covered the northern Highlands heaved out of the sea three hundred million years ago. Certainly of Alpine scale and possibly of Himalayan, it was reduced to a sea-level plain by erosion. Twenty or thirty million years ago, 'Scotland' rose again, this time as a solid block. Out of that plateau, ice and water carved our present mountains. The Hebrides were part of that plateau for the land mass extended far beyond them. A huge western subsidence caused their separation. The broad channel of the Minch, which divides the Outer Hebrides from the Inner, is thus a rift valley, and the flooding of the sea into the western glens gave the Highlands that wildly serrated coastline, with fiords running deep into the hills, and that host of islands, which are together the foremost charm of the West Highland scene and the despair of transport authorities.

The Hebrides fall naturally into four main groups. The two southernmost lie off the coast of Argyll: Islay, Jura, Colonsay, Oronsay, and Gigha, which flank the Kintyre peninsula and lie within sight of Ireland; and Mull, Iona, Coll, and Tiree, just north of the Firth of Lorn. The two northernmost groups lie off the coasts of Inverness-shire and Ross: Skye and the Small Isles, the latter meaning Rhum, Muck, Eigg and Canna; and the Outer Hebrides, divided from the others by the Sea of the Hebrides and the Minch. The Outer Hebrides are much the biggest group, extending a hundred and thirty miles through two degrees of latitude, hence often called the Long Isle. Its northern half, Lewis and Harris, lies thirty miles off the nearest mainland coast; the southern half, Berneray, North Uist, Benbecula, South Uist, Eriskay and Barra, lie off fifty miles. Scores of other islands, big and small, lie scattered around them. The farthest flung is St. Kilda, a hundred and forty miles west of the mainland. The lonely spike of Rockall, at three hundred miles, is not strictly a Hebridean island.

The Outer Hebrides are sometimes called the Gneiss Islands. They are constituted almost entirely of Scotland's most ancient rock, Lewisian gneiss, which is one thousand five hundred million years old and extends south-east even to Coll and Tiree, and to the west side of Iona. Exposed over long miles of sea-cliff, the rock's delicate pink hue delights the eye. Affectionate geologists call it 'The Old Boy'. The rocks of the other islands offer wide variety: gabbro and granite hills in Skye and Rhum circled by table-lands of red Torridon sandstone, which again appears far south in Colonsay; basalt through Skye and the Small Isles to Mull; schist, quartzite and slate in Islay and Jura.

In character, the Hebrides are Atlantic islands ravaged by sea and wind. A grey seal on a skerry might be their badge, and the rain-cloud their banner. But never do we find in the isles the gloom that foul weather can bring to even the most splendid of mainland glens, like Glencoe or Glen Affric. Desolation, yes, but not gloom, for here the skies are too wide, the land too low and open, the winds too free, for weather to depress our spirits though it may scourge our bodies. Always the air has a clean tang. Colours in the Isles seem more fresh and true, all life appears simpler and stripped down to essentials. Especially is this true of the Outer Isles. Even if seen from far distance, say from Skye or the mainland coast, their long low line stretching blue-black or palest lilac from Barra Head to Lewis, marks the edge of the world. From their own shores the idea is repeated, for beyond lies a waste of seas like outer space made visible, apparently limitless. A great part of the fascination of the Hebrides lies in that 'edge of the world' atmosphere: they are the last lands, the gateways – beyond them nothing is known (one feels). Thus they appear as the symbols of the frontier; appear thus to the islanders themselves, to whom Tir nan Og, the Land of the Ever-young, has always lain west across the horizon.

Apart from the excellence of their setting, among broad and winding waters, whose colour can change daily or hourly from gun-metal to a blue more brilliant than Aegean seas, the Hebridean islands on close approach can disappoint a first visitor – or at least instil a pang of misgiving. Their outer aspect from close-to is often so stark that one can hardly believe they sustain life at all, apart from those brown patches of heather that cling precariously to naked rock. This aspect of elemental sterility is by no means universal to the islands, some of which are green and fair to look upon from seaward, like Mull, or mountainously interesting like Eigg or Rhum, but is notably true of several of the most beautiful of all, such as Colonsay, Coll and Harris. The reason for this apparent barrenness is that approach from seaward is made from mainland ports, that is, from the east, to which most of the isles present their backsides. Their fair faces are more usually turned to the west.

With few exceptions, the island harbours are set in their rocky eastern shores, which are suitably indented. The western shores, besides being fully exposed to Atlantic gales and hammered by huge seas, tend to be gently curved and much less indented. Here are found the great beaches of shell-sand, backed by flat machair floodlit all summer long with wild flowers.

Any first impression of unmitigated bleakness is changed after we make our landing. Revealed to us now are green fields tucked away in the hollows of the land, flowers strewn thick along stream and ditch; the lochans dimpled by rising fish or circled by snowy bog-bean and waterlilies; neat croft-land and cattle, sea-cliffs and sandy bays alive with multitudes of birds (except in Skye); glens filled with brawling rivers, or quiet with sheltering woods; even wide straths where the corn stands golden and gardens open to the public are enriched by tropical plants.

In the Isles there is something for everyone, but before and above and surrounding all is the extraordinary quality of light. The air is luminous in a way rarely known to the mainland: for the islands are low-set in the midst of a light-reflecting sea; clouds pass over unobstructed by high hills; the northerly latitude gives a long summer day, with no more than a midnight twilight in June – larks and cuckoos still singing. And that Atlantic air has a cleanness hardly known to the mainland save on its mountain tops. To be bathed in light and aware of it is a happy experience. But to be strictly practical, every man not already tanned should take sunburn lotion and dark glasses to ease his first introduction. There is always the chance he might find good weather, and the ultra-violet rays of the Isles are unfiltered.

Spring, summer, and autumn, Hebridean weather is no worse than elsewhere. Average rainfall is 40–60 inches, but more in Mull and South Skye. Wind can be relentless, rainclouds ever-renew themselves from the west, but hours of sunshine are normally high, reaching their peak in April,

May and June. Tiree, the flattest Hebridean island, has the best record for the United Kingdom. Its long-term average for May (Scotland's driest month) is 234 hours – nearly eight hours a day. Fairer examples might be northern Skye with 200 hours, or Lewis with 195 at Stornoway. Impressive as these figures sound, the truth is that Scottish weather is uncertain, and the visitor's fate a matter of chance. Prolonged drought or continuous rain are not equally probable in a given month, say the statistics, but they are in my own experience. 'A year in the Hebrides,' declared an Island seaman, 'can bring us six months of winter and six months gey bad weather.' Island rain comes in horizontally on a big wind. One does not argue with the inevitable: the only argument available in Island rain is rubber boots and oilskins from head to foot, or else shorts and bare legs, holey sandshoes and a hooded waterproof smock for the top half of the body.

Snow is rare in winter, and frost though common enough lacks mainland severity. Warmed by the Gulf Stream and by south-westerly winds, the Islands enjoy a mild winter climate, even if it rarely feels like it. We should be nearer the truth if we said that extremes were absent – extremes of temperature, but not of wind. The winds of winter roar in with a ferocity un-dreamt of by the townsman, and persist. The Long Isle is the worst hit: a gale blows one day in three at the Butt of Lewis.

The Isles are treeless in consequence. Despite the palms of Colonsay and Gigha, and the clumps of tree that can be found on nearly every sizeable island if we look for them, these exceptions prove the rule by the very interest they draw from us. Those plants best thrive that lie low to the ground. The very wonder we feel at the richly fertile but narrow lazybeds between ribs of rock, at the tiny, well-fenced crofts, and our admiration for the men and women whose hard work and patience made them, are recognition that here life is something wrested from warring elements. Our delight in massed irises yellowing a burn, in fields deep-drifted in daisies, in purple and gold honeysuckle scenting a hedge, or a vast machair drenched in dew and loudly abounding in larks at half-past three in the morning, is here made intense by its unexpectedness. That lives so delicate should be so tough enlivens our wonder, for tough they are to survive in this land, where the sea-wind is merciless. The weak go to the wall. Anything that lives is strong. Recognizing this, we take especial delight in all things small, apparently fragile, and in beauty so numerous. The Hebrides throw them up in high relief.

The land then is harsh and clean. Sea and sky are fashioned on the majestic scale, terrible in storm, in clarity of light blinding at the sunrisings, riotous at settings. And when soft grey clouds steal in upon the moors with misty drizzle, they come like a drawing of curtains to grant respite, needed by all living things. In the Islands even more than the Highlands, man lives in the close company of elemental nature. The Highlander gets more shelter and comfort than he knows from his hills. The Islander has almost none but his cot. Living so close to the skies and seas, and until recent years of air travel so isolated from the centres of industry, political power, arts and sciences, of society and fashion, he has over the fleeting centuries been more shaped by his environment and heredity than has almost any other community of the United Kingdom.

Large scale emigrations from the Hebrides to North America, Australia, and the mainland have been forced in the last two centuries. In several islands of the Inner Hebrides, incomers from the mainland have replaced them, by no means equally in number, but strongly in ownership and tenancy of land. But the Hebrides are still to the Gael. His language is alive, spoken in his own home and community. A thousand years of geographical isolation have allowed him less admixture of blood and communication with other races than all but a few British groups have known, such as those of Orkney and Shetland. Hence a broad outline of Island history from earliest known times is peculiarly useful to our understanding of the Hebridean people as they are now.

2

WEST OVER SEA

No one knows who were the aboriginal people of the Hebrides. But the Isles present to the archaeologist an immense wealth of prehistoric remains. Between the sand-dunes and grass along some island coasts are mounds, often called 'sheeans' (the fairy knowes of Gaelic legend). When excavated, these are most often found to be burial grounds, but a few to be kitchen middens of a Stone Age people. Five such sites have been excavated in Oronsay and three in Colonsay. The bulk of the mounds are of limpet shells, once dumped in hollows and now left high by the shifting of surrounding sand-dunes. The evidence shows that these men had reached the Azilian stage of culture, midway between the Paleolithic and Neolithic periods. No accurate date can be assigned; the best conjecture is 7000–5000 B.C. Their arrival would follow the break-through of the Strait of Dover and the sudden change in climate from arctic to warm.

The mounds have revealed among the bone-debris a range of bird-life unchanged to the present day: cormorant, goose, sheld-duck, ringed plover, tern, gull, razor-bill, guillemot, gannet, merganser and great auk. Bone pins suggest the use of clothing, and pierced shells of ornament. Wild animal remains are of grey and common seal, otter, red deer, and pig, but show no trace of domestic animals. The men were huntsmen, using tools and weapons of bone, stone and deer-horn, fashioned as gougers or knives, harpoons with barbs, and hammers.

The primitive Azilians were followed by a new Stone Age people of profoundly different outlook and way of life – the Neolithic. In a cave at Kiloran Bay in Colonsay have been found the flint tools and bones of such a community, which had reached the pastoral stage. Their animals were ox, sheep and horse. Four great advances had been made by Neolithic men, to whom the word 'civilized' begins to be appropriate: (1) domestication of animals, (2) agriculture, (3) tool-making by grinding and polishing, which would allow carpentry (the Azilian chipped edges would be too brittle) and (4) pottery.

The descendants of these aboriginal inhabitants were probably over-run by the first Celts (pronounced Kelts). Many of the earliest Celtic tribes named themselves from the weapons they used. It seems more than likely that the first Celts to penetrate Alban (Scotland's ancient name) used the heavy spear called the pike (pic in Gaelic) and would call themselves Pic-daoine (pronounced Peektowny), or pike-men. Nennius renders the Latin form as Pictones. Research is disclosing that the earliest Picts were very much the same people as the later 'historic' Picts. Tacitus, writing of the latter in A.D. 93, expressly contradicts the later notion that Picti meant 'Painted'.

The Gael, or Celts of the Bronze Age, entered Britain around 1300 B.C. – a thousand years before the Britons of the Iron Age. They colonized Ireland and later Alban. At the time of Agricola's invasion of Alban in A.D. 79, the Romans described the principal tribe as Caledonians, red-haired and large of limb. They later called them Picti, applying the name to a large confederation of tribes of which the Caledonians were the chief. United by the need to oppose Rome, the tribes adopted the name and became the sole nation north of the Lowlands until the Scots arrived in the sixth century.

The Scots were a powerful race of Gael who had colonized northern Ireland before the Picts arrived in Alban. When the Romans abandoned Britain, the Scots and Picts swooped down on the prosperous Britons, plundering them as far south as London. The Scots were always wanderers, under King Cairbre Riada they had begun to colonize Argyll *circa* 258 A.D., naming it Dalriada ('the portion of Riada') after their Kingdom in County Antrim. In A.D. 500, Erc, the Scottish King of Irish Dalriada, died. By Celtic law his kingdom went to his brother. Thereupon his three sons, Angus, Fergus, and Lorn, crossed the sea to Argyll intent to carve out kingdoms of their own. They came several thousand strong. This settlement, dated 503, marks the first Scottish landing backed by a full-blooded drive to expansion.

Under Celtic law, a king had to possess not less than three duns (forts). Angus took the islands of Islay and Jura, Fergus Kintyre and Cowal, Lorn the northern part of Argyll, which has ever since borne his name. Fergus survived his brothers and joined all three kingdoms in one. The Scottish Dalriada now stretched from the Firth of Clyde to Ardnamurchan.

The Scots were soon in conflict with the Highland Picts, the Angles of Lothian, and the Britons of Strathclyde. The wars between them all filled three centuries while a very different battle was being fought on another front by the Celtic Church. Unlike the Picts and Angles, the Scots were Christian. Since the year 400 and earlier, Scottish missionaries of both the Celtic and Roman Churches had been spreading over the Highlands and Lowlands. The best known is St. Ninian, who converted the southern Picts. A greater was to come. In 563 St. Columba with twelve companions sailed from Ireland to a tiny island off the Ross of Mull, called Iona.

Prince of the reigning Irish house most closely allied to Dalriada in Argyll, he was now in the prime of life. His mother was Eithne, princess of Leinster. When to these high connections we add his higher personal gifts – inborn leadership of men, commanding presence, great ability and passionate devotion – we begin to understand his immense influence.

Once established in Iona with church and monastery, he took up his formidable task, the conversion of the northern Picts. These ferocious warriors had broken Roman hearts and never yet been conquered. Their lust of plunder and strife had taken them far into England. Their Druid priests were powerful. No less promising task could be conceived. Columba journeyed up the Great Glen to Inverness, put the Druids out of countenance before the face of their own King Brude, whom he converted, and thus won for his monks access to Pictland. That country was well organized in seven provinces under the king's control. Columba established a hundred monasteries and several hundred churches, many of them in the Hebrides. His conversion of the people was completed. New ideals were presented to the Picts, re-presented to the Scots, and shown to be practical by the monks in their own lives. Such standards, once seen, appear never to be lost, in the sense that even long periods of cruelty and disorder may intervene as lapses from a standard to which a return is finally made. A demonstration is seen in Hebridean history.

For nearly two hundred and fifty years after Columba's death in 597, the history of Alban is unrelieved Picto-Scottish strife. The islands off the Argyll coast were over-run by the Scots, the outer and northern isles by Scandinavian pirates in their Long Ships. Recent evidence has been found that the first Norse invasions of the Hebrides had occurred as early as 100 B.C. to A.D. 210 (see *The Foundations of Islay*, published by Domhnull Gruamach, Isle of Islay). The main assault came six hundred years later.

In 795, Viking invasions of the mainland and islands extended south to Ireland. Three times in eleven years they sacked the abbey of Iona, the third time in 806 when they murdered sixty-eight monks on the shore. Incessant depredations by the Norse on the west coast and Danes on the east caused a revolution in Alban. The Picts had suffered most, and by 843 were so weakened that Kenneth MacAlpin, King of Scots, overthrew their power and united the two kingdoms. His descent from Pictish royalty on his mother's side and (thanks to St. Columba) the absence of religious difference, aided his conquest. The joint kingdom was renamed Scotland.

Meantime, the Vikings continued to play havoc with the Highlands and Islands. Around 880, Harold Fairhair had made himself the first king of all Norway. This revolution led to permanent Norse settlement in the Scottish Isles, first by his bitter opponents who from there raided the Norwegian coast. King Harold was then forced to make an expedition 'west over sea', as the sagas call it. He seized the Hebrides, Orkneys and Shetlands. For the next two hundred years they were ruled for Norway by a succession of warring princes, who usually acted independently of the Norwegian crown. At the height of their later power the whole North of Scotland down to Inverness lay in Norwegian hands.

In 1093 and 1098 King Magnus Barefoot (he earned the nickname by assuming the Scottish kilt) felt obliged to make new expeditions west over sea. The development of the Kingdom of Scotland had become alarming. He devastated the Hebrides and forced King Edgar of Scotland to acknowledge his right to them.

The Hebrides were then governed from the Isle of Man. Meanwhile there had appeared on the Scottish scene the most famous of her warrior chiefs, Somerled. Descendant of Irish kings, he was the progenitor of Clan Donald of Islay, and of chiefs destined for three hundred years to be Lords of the Isles. As a youth, he succeeded his father as king of Argyll around 1130, and won renown by driving the Vikings out of Morvern. The Norse king of the Isles was Godred, a tyrant whose sister was Somerled's wife. The men of Islay invited Somerled to lead them against this harsh oppressor. He realized that Norse supremacy at sea over the last three centuries had been given them by their dragon-prowed Long Ships, with which the relatively frail Scottish boats could not compete. A new conquest of the Isles must depend on new naval power. Secretly, he began to build a fleet of small powerful warships of new design, called Nyvaig, meaning Little Ship. They were shorter than the ships of the Vikings but more manoeuvrable in close combat. The Long Ships had the old steering oar, but hinged stern rudders had recently been invented. It is believed that Somerled now used them.

On the night of Epiphany, 1156, his fleet of Nyvaigs joined battle with the full force of Godred's sea-power off the west coast of Islay. By the close of the following day, 7th January, the Long Ships had been routed. A division of the Hebrides now took place. By agreement with the Norse king, Somerled ruled all the islands south of Ardnamurchan Point and took up his seat in Islay.

Somerled and his successors held their large mainland possessions from the king of Scotland, and their islands from the king of Norway. But the growing power of Scotland could not long allow the Hebrides to remain thus dependent. North Scotland was wrested from the Orkney Jarldom in 1196. Alexander III tried to persuade King Hakon to cede the Hebrides. When he failed, the mainland chiefs made systematic attacks on the Isles, probably instigated by their shrewd and able king. Goaded into an expedition, King Hakon sailed west over sea in 1263. With a hundred and twenty ships he retook lost islands and harried the west coast to the Firth of Clyde. The forces of Scotland and Norway met at the battle of Largs, which finally decided the fate of the Hebrides. The land battle was indecisive, but a fierce October storm shattered the Norwegian fleet. King Hakon withdrew to the Orkneys and died. Alexander swiftly seized the Hebrides, which Norway formally ceded in a treaty of 1266.

The Norse occupation of the Hebrides had lasted wellnigh four centuries. It left a permanent mark on the whole way of life and character traits of the Celtic people, who, at the close of the occupation, still predominated, except in districts like Ness in Lewis. The mixture of Celtic and Norse blood was effected at an early stage in the Outer Hebrides and must have greatly strengthened the ability of the native people to live on these sea-girt ridges. It made them skilled and daring seamen. The evidence of the Norse occupation remains to this day in the preponderance of Norse place-names, in the physical features of fair hair and blue eyes, still abundant throughout the west, and in the great numbers of men who enter and win distinction in the Royal Navy and Merchant Navy.

The harsher Viking traits, in turn, were qualified by the

courtesy and generosity of the Celtic people, and their inborn love of learning, song and poetry. Their impetuous bravery in land-battle, which had become as legendary as that of the Norsemen at sea, coupled with their passionate nature, which leads them to extremes, brought disaster on them when misdirected in later centuries.

The next five hundred years of Island history cannot be properly understood unless at the outset the high place and power of the Clan Donald is realized. Somerled and his first five successors all held rank as *Righ*, or King of the Isles. His grandson, Donald of Islay, gave his name to the clan (from two old Gaelic words, *Domh* meaning House, and *Nuall*, Noble). Donald's grandson, Angus Og MacDonald, firmly buttressed the family fortunes by supporting his friend Robert the Bruce, first by sheltering him in early adversity, then with his Nyvaigs harrying the English fleets prior to Bannockburn – a prime cause of the Scottish victory, in the opinion of an English naval historian – and finally supporting him with eighteen hundred men of Islay on the right wing of his battle array. A grateful king granted him the islands of Mull, Jura, Coll and Tiree; Bruce's son, David II, granted Angus's son, John MacDonald, the farther islands of Gigha, Scarba, Colonsay and Lewis. Two years later, John won by marriage the islands of Uist, Barra, Eigg and Rhum, and assumed the title of Lord of the Isles, thus modified in deference to the wish of his father-in-law, King Robert II of Scotland. Islay remained the principal seat of the family.

The Donald territory remained practically a separate kingdom, and the chiefs virtually sovereigns in their own right, negotiating treaties with England, Ireland, France and Scotland. The clan grew huge and intermarried with other powerful clans of the west, many of whom were Donald descendants. The Kings and Lords of the Isles granted land to vassal clans of two kinds: those of direct Donald descent, and those of other name.

The principal Island clans of direct descent were the Mac-Donalds of Sleat in Skye, holding also Uist and Benbecula; the Clan Iain Mhor of Islay; the Clan Ranald of Knoydart, who later came to possess Uist and Benbecula; and the Clan Iain of Ardnamurchan, who held lands in Islay, Jura and Mull.

The principal clans not claiming direct male descent from Clan Donald were the MacLeans of Duart, holding a great part of Mull, Coll and Tiree, and lands on Islay and Jura; the Clan Leod in two branches, under MacLeod of Lewis, holding land also in Skye, and under MacLeod of Harris, holding much of Skye including Dunvegan; the Clan Neil in two branches, under MacNeil of Barra, also with land in South Uist, and under MacNeil of Gigha; the MacPhees of Colonsay; the MacKinnons of Mull and Skye; and the MacQuarries of Ulva and Mull.

The Lords of the Isles enjoyed long reigns. They held powerful castles, notably at Dunyvaig on the south coast of Islay, to protect the fleet on which their power was based. Their administrative headquarters was sited on the islets of Loch Finlaggan in northern Islay. There the council of Hebridean chiefs met annually to debate problems and administer justice. To this council all serious disputes were referred. Trial and judgment were given by hereditory judges (Brehons) at the Judgment Knoll near the river Laggan, south of Bowmore. This was done in the open air before all people.

The first three hundred years of the Lordship gave firm rule and settled conditions to the Island people; it brought them prosperity; the arts of music, poetry and sculpture flourished. This was a period of peace relative to the centuries before and after, punctuated by the rebellions of the Lords of the Isles against the crown. The true basis of the Donald distrust of the Scottish kings was the latter's introduction from England of the Norman feudal system. This had begun in Somerled's day, when David I, after a boyhood in England, came to the throne in 1124 followed by a thousand Anglo-Normans to whom he distributed land. Thenceforward the feudal system developed on the Scottish mainland.

The Celtic people were freemen, virtually classless, unbound by the principle of primogeniture in selecting a chief (a principle that destroyed the Stewarts), and they loathed the stratification of society into classes, which feudalism entailed. A clan's land was not owned by its chief or ruled by force. It belonged to the clan who maintained the chief and gave the free allegiance of a family to its head. A living descendant of Somerled justly observes that in forcing feudalism on the Lords of the Isles, and then deploring their reaction, the Scottish kings spoke like the Frenchman decrying the lion: 'This animal is a very dangerous beast. When you attack it – it defends itself!'

The Lords of the Isles frequently flouted the royal authority and several times were able to shake the throne, but the very fact that they could do so meant in the end that their power must be shorn. James IV was the first Stewart king strong enough to carry out the task. In 1493 he succeeded in bringing to trail John II, ninth chief of the house of Islay and fourth Lord of the Isles. His lands and title were declared forfeit. Promptly thereafter, James visited the Isles in person and granted royal charters (irreverently called 'sheepskins') to the chief land-holders.

This drastic action by James IV brought the people of the Isles a century and more of dire misfortune. His break-up of the Donald Lordship followed by his own death at Flodden, left the Island chiefs with no supreme head, no kind of common interest or of loyalty. Mainland kings and parliaments were too remote and weak to enforce a rule of law. During the first half of the sixteenth century, three full-scale rebellions and six clan feuds were in process. Chief plotted with chief and they fought each other with ruthless ferocity, often in total disregard of the welfare of the people they ruled, who had to endure appalling sufferings – homes burnt, cattle and livestock killed or driven off, crops destroyed. The burden of maintaining retinues of warriors in the castles fell on the Islesfolk, who themselves were called from their jobs in spring to attack neighbouring clans. Autumn harvest and winter storms brought temporary peace, but the rest of the year was often hell let loose. Lawlessness encouraged 'sorners' who lived by quartering themselves where they could on defenceless people. Many of the clergy were driven away and churches burnt. Christianity fell to low ebb.

Evils tend to force their own cure in the end. James VI succeeded to the English crown in 1603 and to new resources. The state of the Hebrides had become the scandal of his realm. He sent Lord Ochiltree on an expedition west over sea in 1608. Ochiltree seized the castles of Mull and summoned the Hebridean chiefs to a council at Aros Castle in Salen Bay. The chiefs came almost to a man, were invited to dine aboard his flagship *Moon*, then were made prisoner and conducted to Edinburgh. They were well treated and released on condition of ratifying statutes to be drawn by Andrew Knox, Bishop of the Isles (Reformed Church) at a council in Iona.

At this council, held in Iona in July 1609, the chiefs approved nine statutes, which briefly were: (1) They should accept the discipline of the Reformed Kirk, maintaining the clergy and churches. (2) They should establish inns to relieve the people of burdensome hospitality. (3) They should support their households themselves, not by tax on tenants, and allow no man to live in the Isles without a trade or personal income. (4) Sorners should be punished as thieves. (5) To curb excessive drinking, men might brew drink for their families but not import it. (6) Every man having sixty cattle must send his eldest son to a Lowland school. (7) The use of firearms was forbidden. (8) Bards who glorified war should be discouraged as idlers. (9) Enactments to enforce preceding Acts.

Bishop Knox had unerringly detected the weak spots in the social and economic life of the Hebrides. His statutes could not expect immediate success in attaining all objects. New insurrections broke out, notably in Islay, but were short-lived – Islay and Kintyre falling to the Campbells of Argyll in reward for services to the crown and countless treacheries to neighbours. The statutes of 1609 had struck a decisive blow to clan feuding,

which diminished in number. The Isles gradually won peace.
More and more disputes went to law-courts. Trade increased
and a prosperity long unknown returned.

Martin Martin, in his Island survey of 1695, was able to
write: 'If a man had a mind to retire to any of these isles there
is no place of the known world where he may have products of
land and sea cheaper, live more securely, or among more mild
and tractable people. . . . The islanders enjoy health above the
average of mankind, and this is performed merely by tem-
perance and the prudent use of simples. . . . In religion and
virtue they excel many thousands of others who have greater
advantages of daily improvement.'

The Islanders' last big fling followed the landing of Prince
Charles Edward on Eriskay in 1745. The clans rose for the
great rebellion, crushed at Culloden a year later. It was the last
military battle fought in Britain. If it brought the Highlands
and Islands no other good, it made an end forever of clan
warfare. The men were disarmed and the chiefs' heritable juris-
diction abolished, transforming them to landlords and their
clansmen to tenants. Henceforth men of fighting instinct joined
the Royal Navy or the Highland regiments.

The manufacture of kelp had started in the Isles in 1746.
When collected and burned, seaweed produced a brittle substance named kelp containing soda, potash, bromine and iodine,
valuable in the manufacture of glass and soap. The big demand
for kelp by English and Lowland industries gave most re-
munerative employment to many thousands of islanders in the
seventeen-sixties. At the same time the herring fisheries throve
on teeming seas, the export of black cattle increased as prices
rose, potatoes added a new, cheap and abundant food, while
other new crops and methods of agriculture were brought to
forfeited estates by the government. More ominously, at Tyn-
drum in Argyll, an innkeeper had made the discovery that
sheep need not be folded at night. In the Isles, unused grazings

were now exploited. All these developments brought an un-
precedented prosperity to the Hebrides. In 1798, Dr. Jenner
disclosed the efficacy of vaccination. Freed from the checks of
war and of smallpox, the population grew – and grew
dangerously.

The first blow fell at the close of the Napoleonic wars. The
removal of import duty on Spanish barilla, a sea-shore plant
yielding carbonate of soda, depressed the market for kelp,
which was finally killed by a still cheaper production of soda
from salt, and by the entry of German potash.

The blow was the more severe in coming at a time when the
rapid increase of population was causing the division of crofts
among crofters' families, more and more people occupying
smaller and smaller holdings. The crofters had no security of
tenure. The land was owned by a 'laird', or else held on long
lease or 'tack' by a tacksman or gentleman farmer, to either of
whom the crofter owed rent and services (at the peats, or fenc-
ing, or harvest, or spring sowing). He had no protection from
burdensome demands or from rack-renting. Thus he was quite
defenceless when the clearances began in the first half of the
nineteenth century.

The destruction of the clan system had disintegrated a social
system. The lairds had been drawn into metropolitan life and
wanted cash. Their link with the common islesman was broken.
They, and their tacksmen who came to predominate, discovered sheep-farming. There was great demand for wool, big
profit in meeting it. Sheep could be raised with small labour,
whereas cattle needed many men.

Cattle had enriched the land. Their grass grazings ran far
out into present moorland, for their cropping of coarser grass
gave life to the finer. But now the cattle were cleared and sheep
brought in. Big rents could be wrung out of Lowland farmers
for ground that formerly had required say a score of men and
now but three. Since the surplus population could not be gain-
fully employed they were evicted from the farms on to waste-
land by the shores, there to live off the sea if they could, or

forced against their will to emigrate. Like the cattle before them, entire communities of crofters were mercilessly cleared off the land with hardly a word of denunciation from the clergy.

Famine struck in the potato blights of 1846 and following years. Mass emigration then became a necessity to be subsidized by government. From around 1842 there thus began that steady drain of population, which all efforts since have failed to halt.

The social upheaval and miseries caused by these mass evictions brought further disintegration of the Gaelic way of life. Religious observance again fell to low ebb, but the spiritual springs of the Gael run deep. When the Scottish Church disrupted in 1843, the Free Church emerged with missionary fervour to recapture the Isles, save for Barra and South Uist, which remained Catholic. The austerity of its preaching sprang from the extremity of the times and persists to this day.

A few chiefs still honoured the old link with their people. MacLeod of Dunvegan, Lord MacDonald of Skye, and MacLean of Coll, spent almost all their fortunes on relief work. The government of the United Kingdom declined involvement. Elsewhere, the factors of absentee landlords rack-rented the people. Sheep-farming had not continued to yield the rich rewards of its first twenty years. The ground had become impoverished. Sheep, uncontrolled, crop the sweet grass too short, leaving rough grass and bracken to spread. At the finish came deer, for the recreation of late nineteenth-century industrialists.

In 1882, warships had to be sent to Skye to intimidate riotous crofters. Once again the intolerable condition of the Isles provoked partial remedy. A Royal Commission reported on the crofters' plight, resulting in the Crofters' Holdings Act of 1886, which gave them security of tenure, grants for improvements, and fair rent. The 'black houses' shared by man and beast were gradually replaced by 'white houses', mostly built by the crofters themselves, aided later by loans and grants. Electric and water supplies have only recently followed.

In the First and Second World Wars, the Hebrides had given more men to the Navy and Army, in proportion to their population, than any other part of the United Kingdom or Commonwealth. Casualties were exceedingly heavy. When the men returned, the crofters' lack of land provoked outbursts of land-raiding and squatting, causing the intervention of the Department of Agriculture and the Land Court, who bought more land both for new crofts and enlargement of old. The fishermen found on return that the quays and their laid-up boats had gone derelict. They lacked capital for repair and replacement and had to face growing competition from east coast and foreign trawlers, which over-fished the Hebridean seas, poached within legal limits, swept the inshore banks and destroyed the gear of line-fishermen. European markets closed. The government allowed 'dumping' of cheap Norwegian herring. In consequence the Hebridean fishing industry shrank to a fraction of its former size; once numerous curing stations vanished; emigration proceeded apace.

In more recent years, the government has contributed a dozen fishing boats to an Outer Isles Fishery Training Scheme as a start in rebuilding the industry and training new crews, and as nucleus of the much bigger fleet required. In 1964, the Minch was at last closed to foreign trawlers – but not to our own east coast pirates, whose poaching on inshore waters continues. With the new fishing methods now in use the Hebridean industry might greatly develop – granted accessories like new quays where needed, new refrigerating and processing plant, new coastal houses for men drawn from inland, and more and faster fishery protection cruisers.

The crofters too have been helped, both by further subsidies and by expert advisers. But too few holdings are large enough to be in themselves economically viable. Most Island crofters depend for their livelihood on so-called subsidiary industries, like tweed-weaving and lobster-fishing, which are both booming and which together with prawn and herring fishing are in fact their principal money-earning jobs. Much other work is

given by the revived seaweed industry, road-work, and in
some of the Inner Isles distilleries and afforestation. In Skye
and Lewis, but especially Lewis, extensive moorlands are
being re-seeded for grass. Cattle rearing is reviving in Skye.
The growth of tourism has come most strongly to Skye and
Islay, and with new car ferries now operating will extend to
the Outer Isles and Mull (when accommodation is provided).
Hovercraft ferries started on the Clyde in 1965. If these prove
safe and efficient, their extension to the Hebrides could revolu-
tionize island travel.

The population of the Inner Isles has dropped but little in
the last six years compared to the Outer, which continue to lose
heavily – Barra and Uist 25 per cent of their populations, the
others 10 per cent. Yet throughout the Hebrides, and most
markedly in the Outer Isles, a new and vigorous spirit is most
apparent. There is every hope that it will prevail, and every sign
that prosperity may be regained, this time on a firmer basis.

3
ISLAY

THE islands of Argyll are the most exposed of the Inner Hebrides. Unshielded from the Atlantic Ocean, which stretches two thousand miles to Labrador, they are, like the Outer Hebrides, outer isles. There comparison ends. Strange though it may seem, the Islay group are the palm-tree islands of the west, and Islay (pronounced Ila) is the greenest of them all – like a slice out of Ireland, which lies in full view twenty-three miles to its south, nearer than Scotland's nearest port of West Loch Tarbert in Kintyre.

MacBrayne's steamer sails daily on its round of Islay, Jura, Colonsay and Gigha, calling at one of Islay's two ports day about: Port Askaig on the east coast, Port Ellen on the south. An efficient and much cheaper service to Port Askaig is run by Western Ferries Ltd. The eastern approach is the more dramatic on a first visit, up the long narrow channel of the Sound of Islay, whose racing tides divide Islay from Jura. The mountains rise high on either side, shapely to the Paps of Jura; on the Islay side, monotonously brown and bare. Port Askaig is seen suddenly and surprisingly – a tiny niche in the hillside, ringed by rock walls, yet flanked above by the fine woods of Dunlossit House.

An alternative approach is by the daily air service from Glasgow. This way at once discloses Islay's shape and size. Its name is from the old Gaelic I Lagh, meaning The Island bent like a Bow. Twenty-five miles long from north to south, and fifteen broad, its western side is nearly split from the main mass by two sea-lochs, Loch Indaal running up from the south, and Loch Gruinart down from the north. The isthmus between, just two miles wide, links Islay with its huge wing-like peninsula, the Rhinns. Tree-bare and windswept, it takes the brunt of westward storms and partially screens the heart of Islay. Down at the island's south-west extremity juts another rock-bound peninsula, the broad and squat Mull of Oa (pronounced O), which screens the wooded south coast.

Behind the wings of the Rhinns and of Oa nestle the main villages and townships: Bowmore and Bridgend towards the head of Loch Indaal, Port Charlotte and Bruichladdich under the lee of the Rhinns itself, Port Ellen tucked in its harbour under the Oa.

Our plane loses height. We can see these white village houses sparkling like scattered salt at the sea's edge. Far back to eastward stand the big hills of Islay, high-backed to Jura, but sloping gradually west to long sandy flats at Loch Indaal and Laggan Bay, and Gruinart. Between lies the island's strength, the five hundred farms that dapple the moors with Irish green and keep the people in work. The plane banks to the six-mile sands of Laggan Bay and lands on wide flats between Bowmore and Port Ellen.

Fair as the face of Islay seems, there are deserts too, which coincide with the quartzite rock in its skeleton: the north-east peninsula and the south-east mountains, alike empty and road-less. The central fertile area between Port Askaig and Oa is mica-schist and limestone with mica-schist again on the wooded south. At the head of Loch Indaal is Torridon sandstone, at the foot of the Rhinns, archaean gneiss. This geological mixture gives the island a peculiar landscape value – inexhaustible variety and a richness of bird and plant life. Our delight and interest need never flag from one small part of Islay to another.

Like almost every other island of the Hebrides, Islay completely alters character from east to west. The difference is a double one: the hills, whether low or high, turn their backs to the east and open their arms to the west; and secondly, that fair Atlantic side is for most part swept of its trees and shrubs by wind, but granted in their place spray-salted grass, short, and sweet, and green – a delight to grazing cows.

Bowmore is the island's centre. It clusters round a bay washed clean by sea and sky. Here are the administrative head-quarters, the principal shops, the hospital, police, and a new school for three hundred children. Like Port Ellen, its popula-tion is approximately eight hundred. As seen from the seaward side, it teeters on the brink, so that some houses have their garden walls breached in storms. From the pier a broad main street runs uphill to a white church, made round 'with no corners in which the devil can hide'. All is neat and cared-for. The church was built in 1767 by new lairds, the Campbells of Shawfield. They also built the villages, which for good appearance have few rivals in the Inner Isles and none in the Outer.

Islands must be seen at every season before they can be known, especially those western coasts, and more especially in spring. In high summer the road winding round sandy bays between Bowmore and Bridgend may not notably take the eye with colour, but once I walked along it in Maytime: massed banks of golden whin, such as can be seen nowhere else in the Hebrides, flared against green fields. They made a conflagra-tion. Crowds should have come as to a city fire. I stood alone, but close inshore black and white eider drakes idly paddled the bays, still waiting patiently for the ducks to hatch the young. High across the arched back of Islay peeped the cloud-gather-ing Paps of Jura – a sight to be seen when the moon is full, and those twin spires pale against night skies.

At Bridgend in spring it can be hard to believe that we are still on a Hebridean island. A sprinkle of houses lies at the foot of a long glen, which gives the eastward pass to Port Askaig. Down it flows the river Sorn. The glen spreads wide near the river's mouth, giving a flat floor at Bridgend for woods of beech and chestnut and sycamore. Across that floor April spreads a thick carpet of daffodils, May a sea of bluebells. One can stand long on the bridge over the Sorn watching the sun

JURA
Village of Keils

By Tom Weir

GIGHA
North end from
Creag Bhan

By Tom Weir

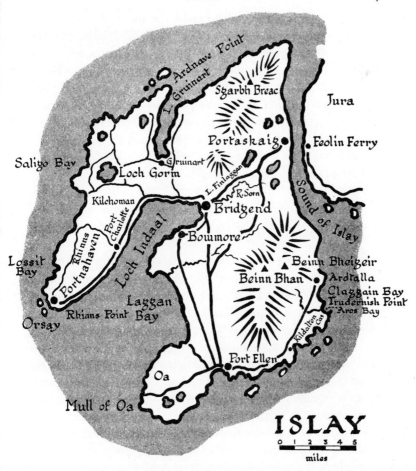

ISLAY

0 1 2 3 4 5
miles

filter through the branches to fall in a rain of light over lagoons of wild hyacinth. They wash in a blue haze deep into creek-like recesses. Yellow celandines and primroses add bright islands to the sea, most densely under the beech-trees. Slow and wide alongside flows the peat-brown Sorn, with white ducks rummaging under the banks.

For the sharpest contrast of scene we have only to round the head of Loch Indaal to the Rhinns. The approach along its

B

more sheltered eastern shore breaks the blow of change. Between its sandy bays and banks of whin are little close-cropped
fields, in their springtime green lively with lambs and dairy
cattle. The gaiety of colour is maintained through the villages
of Bruichladdich and Port Charlotte, whose painted walls and
houses, eye-catching as they are, harmonize with the natural
scene and seem to confirm its prosperity. Two of Islay's lobster
boats work from Port Charlotte, each sharp sterned and high
in the bows. The men set their creels among weedy reefs, and
reckon a fair catch to be ten dozen lobsters a week.

Beyond Port Charlotte comes the main change in scene.
The land rises higher out of the sea; the moorland spreads, not
peat-covered like the eastern moors but bare and windswept,
very much the Atlantic promontory. The Rhinns scene is
lightened and relieved by the green fields of farms and crofts.
Even at the southernmost tip, the roadsides approaching
Portnahaven (one can smell the peat-reek) are heavily verged
with marsh marigolds and bluebells, still backed by golden whin,
which in a site so exposed is strangely unstunted.

At the bitter blunt snout of the Rhinns lie those peculiar
twin villages, Port Wemyss and Portnahaven, divided only by
a burn. A long narrow creek runs into the rocky butt. Lining
its walls on either side, Portnahaven's row of cottages face each
other across the water. Beneath them, rock falls sheer to the
creek. They all have one door and two windows, but no other
conformity. Each has a different roof-level; all doors and windows are of different colour, green, yellow, blue, white. On the
north side, many of the cottages are in ruins. The general effect
is most quaint: clean, bright, yet not gay like Port Charlotte.
The creek has a sinister appearance in bad weather. The village
is most exposed to the south-west winds, and would not be
habitable were it not for two islands close inshore. The bigger
is Orsay, which has a lighthouse. When the tide-race allows, it
is possible to cross to Orsay in a local boat. The view from the
lighthouse shows the rocky coast of the Rhinns, and of the
Mull of Oa across the wide mouth of the bay.

Portnahaven used to be a fishing village, but the trade has died. The boats are not big enough, say the people, and they have no capital to compete with mainland fishing industries. It is a tale one hears throughout the Isles. The land around Portnahaven carries a small crofting community. The security of tenure given by the Crofters' Holdings Act will be most important in Islay: land is readily let to incoming farmers.

The whole west coast of the Rhinns forms a breakwater of solid rock, relieved by a few sandy bays which at Lossit and Saligo come close to perfection. The hilly interior swells into unnumbered hollows, where farmland enlivens the brown moors. The northern third of the Rhinns is quite different country. From Kilchoman it fans out to Loch Gruinart in five miles of almost sea-level flats. At the south edge lies Islay's biggest freshwater loch, Loch Gorm. The huge moor between the two is every conceivable shade of brown, and gold, and green, like a patchwork quilt.

Set on such open ground, and being a mile and a half in diameter, Loch Gorm makes instant response to every mood of the sky: at one moment a full royal blue as the clouds part, at the next grim-grey as they close over, black where a wind-line hits, or flashing steel to a sunburst. This loch and the flats around are the annual winter scene of a vast migration of geese. Every autumn, in late September and early October, Greenland white-fronted and barnacle and grey lag geese begin to arrive until the land is occupied by many thousands. Five other species have been recorded. The tide-line at Loch Gruinart is a favourite feeding place for the barnacle geese, but a close approach is difficult, and likely to cloud the sky and deafen the ear with clamour, when the gruff yapping of the barnacles and the musical *kow-yow* yelping of the white-fronts are easily distinguished. The winter scene here is one of the great sights of the Hebrides, especially at sundown when the gaggles fly in against lemon skies. Migration begins again at Easter, when the geese fly out to their northern breeding grounds.

In winter, too, wedges of whooper swans come down on

Loch Gorm, with wings thrashing and their call sounding far over the moor. As many as fifty have been counted in the air together. To this and most other lochs the mute swan returns to breed in spring, after the whoopers, whom they loathe, have headed north, bound like the geese for Greenland and Iceland.

On the high ground immediately south of Loch Gorm stands the church of Kilchoman. The original cell or chapel (Cill Chomain means Cell of Comman) was pre-Norse and has long since vanished. Of the present nineteenth-century church, the best I can say is that when the door is opened the wind soughs through like a howl of organ pipes. Nothing else commends it. The great historical interest of the place rests on two things, first, that the Lords of the Isles had their summer palace on the grassy plateau to its north-west (the extensive foundations were only recently discovered), and secondly, that in consequence the churchyard has one of the three most beautiful Celtic crosses in the Hebrides. (The others are the Kildalton Cross on Islay's south coast, and the St. Martin's Cross in Iona.)

The cross was set up in the fourteenth century by John, the first Lord of the Isles, traditionally in memory of his second wife Princess Margaret, daughter of the first Stewart king. It stands eight feet high, and because it is thinner than the others appears more elegant. The engravings are of floral design filling the whole of one side, and of Christ on the other. They are much clogged by lichen. On its square base lies a rounded wishing stone, to be turned by expectant mothers who want their babies to be sons. Deep hollows have been worn by the turning of the stone over six centuries.

Beyond the Gruinart flats, Islay thrusts a long finger out into the Atlantic. Ardnave Point is the place to go when windy rain covers the rest of Islay. I discovered that in foul weather the high ground in southern Islay and Jura draws the rain, while the clouds tend to fly across the low Ardnave Point without precipitating. I went out there on one such day, five miles along the shores of Loch Gruinart, a strand where a mile-wide sea runs in across four miles of sand. It came in farther in former days, for the bay steadily makes land.

A battle was fought at the loch's head in 1598. MacLean of Duart landed an army at the point and tried to seize Islay from the young chief, Sir James MacDonald, whose clever tactics routed MacLean's force. But MacDonald fell with an arrow through his thigh. Wrongly thinking him dead, his men went mad. At Kilnave chapel, two miles from the point, thirty men of Mull had taken refuge. The Clan Donald set the building on fire and killed them all. Standing at the lonely ruins by the strand, I felt glad of the high wind.

A gale was raging that day out of the north-west. A shallow loch spread four hundred yards out from the track. The wind was whipping the water to froth and spraying it far over the road. All round the near edge it had built up a deep collar of foam, out of which projected ranks of marsh marigolds, like choir-boys golden-headed in linen.

I walked a further mile and a half over the dunes, rabbits scurrying through the marram grass, out to the point. Here is one of the few stretches of genuine machair in Islay, dry under-foot when all the moors are wet and boggy. The sea was surg-ing into the mouth of Loch Gruinart in rollers of monstrous size. Where they broke on the central shallows the gale ripped off the crowns in white pennons several hundred yards long. The wind was charged with the smell of seaweed tangle.

One must go out to one of the great promontories to see a sight like this. Another such place is the headland at the Mull of Oa. The Oa is most easily reached from Port Ellen, which shelters behind it. The town is of much the same size as Bow-more, but more distinctively a holiday resort, curving round a shapely bay with quick access to a good golf course at Machrie strand, to a most lovely beach of yellow sand nearby at Kil-naughton, a recreation ground, gaily enterprising hotels, an active pier, boats – in short, a tourist trap, in which holiday makers are glad to be caught. Despite all this, it wears a shabby look compared with Bowmore. Something is lacking – paint certainly, when I last saw it, and perhaps some central building to give it heart.

The road out west to the Oa, rising and falling across moor- and farm-lands, goes nine miles to a lonely croft-house at Upper Killeyan. The last mile of road is unusually bad. Beyond, one walks the moor half a mile to the Mull. Its whereabouts would be hard to find were it not for the tall tower of an American monument, whose blunt point projects above the final hill-ridge.

The monument stands close above tall sea-cliffs. It has been strongly built in stone of varied hue, and commemorates Americans drowned at sea when the transport ships *Tuscania* and *Otranto* were sunk by torpedo in March and October 1918. The bodies came ashore along this coast.

The Mull of Oa is the farthest south cape of the Hebrides. It looks straight to the Antrim hills in the original Scottish king-dom of Dalriada. They seem no distance: one can better under-stand why the Scots named the new kingdom from the old, and why Somerled chose Islay for his seat of government.

I first came to the Mull on a loud shouting day of sun and high winds. The air was calm on top, for the wind, baffled, struck upright from the cliffs. I could walk safely at the brink on flat turf, cropped short by sheep. All this day long the sea was a light sharp blue like the Himalayan poppy. Larks sang overhead, and high up in among their invisible selves floated big puffs of white, down-like substance. I might have guessed in vain what they were had I not remembered Ardnave Point – froth no less. When I looked over the sharp edge I could see light-grey cliffs plunge three hundred feet to jagged reefs, which ran far out into the sea. Great waves smashed over their spines, seething white. The froth piled up high on a thin strip of stone shore, there to be frisked by wind. Countless puffs kept floating vertically up the cliff-face to the top and on – till again the wind pounced.

Along the shore's rocky ledge a troop of brown wild goats picked their way daintily, seeking heaven knows what edible

oasis. I began to search for my own quarry, the elusive
chough. One of the rare birds of Britain, it breeds only on
rocky coasts. The Mull of Oa is now one of the few places
where it can be found in Scotland. Glossy blue-black like their
cousin the raven, but slightly smaller, choughs are embellished
with red beak and legs. I searched in vain for half an hour –
until suddenly a couple were there, on either side of the
monument, their beaks showing brilliant red in the sunshine. The flight was extremely graceful – a few beats, then a
long glide on outstretched pinions, outer primaries held wide
apart; suddenly the wings close, it plummets seaward, then
with a couple of beats more, up it soars to former level, and
flies on.

I judged they might be breeding in a big rock-fast bay east of
the Mull, named Port nan Gallan. I walked a mile along the
cliff-tops and found a way down. More truly it was two bays,
at one time divided by cliffs now eroded out into two isolated
stacks, each pierced by natural arches. The rocks sheltered wild
gardens, and even the stacks were brightened with sea-pink
and white campion. Between the stony shores and the red cliffs
curving behind lay flats of green grass, speckled over with
yellow celandines, marsh marigolds, and spring cinquefoil, blue
milkwort and dog violets, and white marsh flowers, scurvy
grass, and daisies. Port nan Gallan made an ideal home for
choughs, and there they were, perched on top of the stacks. I
saw one dart into a cave in the second bay and followed. I could
hear the chirping of young, invisible in niches overhead. The
date was mid-May. Since they could not be seen, there could
be no certainty that the chirping was not from rock-doves,
which would probably share the cave.

Above the tide-level, a small colony of herring gulls was
nesting on a rib of rock splashed yellow by lichen. A dozen
hollows held three eggs apiece, olive-coloured with brown
spots. The bright red spot on the herring gull's yellow beak
serves an important purpose: the young tap it when they want
mother to disgorge a meal. If captured, they will refuse food

from any other source unless a red spot (say on a stick or finger) is first given them to tap.

Islay's greatest contrast to the Mull of Oa is the southern coast, extending eastwards nine miles on the farther side of Port Ellen. The ground is well sheltered by both the Islay hills and the Oa, therefore wooded. The screaming clamour of gulls is replaced by the land-birds' song, and by the soothing call of springtime cuckoos. A dozen small bays and a score of islets give continual interest and change of scene along every mile of road and shore.

The bays nearest Port Ellen have four distilleries: at Port Ellen, Laphroaig, Lagavulin and Ardbeg, each with its own pier. Good supplies of water and peat explain their presence here. Islay whiskies are more fumy and heavy-bodied than those of Speyside. In the old days whisky was free of duty on Islay, which had a bad social effect, say the clergy. Temperate habits now prevail, but no true Islayman will disdain his dram. When the steamer *Lochiel* struck a hidden shoal in West Loch Tarbert a few years ago, and sank, the islanders aboard had the presence of mind instantly to demand the re-opening of the bar, so that all might go down in good spirits. This was done and no life lost.

The distillery bay most worth a visit is Lagavulin. In this bay Somerled moored his secret fleet of Nyvaigs in the twelfth century, and here, a century later, Donald I built Dunyvaig Castle to protect them. The ruins stand on a crag surrounded shore-wards by green meadows. The lower walls are fallen and grass-covered, but the stump of the main keep still stands, perched on rock falling sheer to the sea and graced along its battlements by huge puffs of sea-pink. Swans sail in the rounded inner bay.

I shall never forget my first visit to Lagavulin, for it gave me my introduction to sheld-duck. A pair were close inshore – the most gorgeous of the sea-birds, white of plumage but with a broad orange band across the chest and shoulders, a dark green head, black wing-tips and crimson beak. They are numerous in Islay and in most of the Hebrides in spring, but migrate in

July to Heligoland and the Bristol Channel, thus are often never seen by holidaymakers.

Two miles farther along the coast I discovered Kildalton Castle. It lay buried in the woods of a little peninsula. The lodge at the roadside first drew my attention – a building entirely of white quartzite stone, perhaps the only one in Scotland. Cold and nasty in appearance, it was crowded about with overgrown laurel. I walked up a long wooded avenue to the empty castle, in fact a big house of grey stone with castellated tower. Cattle grazed the lawns. All views to seaward had been blocked by tree-growth. The place gave a vivid sense of eeriness, desolation and disaster.

Next day I heard from an Islayman that the original owner, John Ramsay, M.P., had carried out clearances from the Mull of Oa last century to make way for sheep. When criticized in the House of Commons, he had replied that emigrants' passages had been 'assisted' – as indeed they were, but the people had not been given a choice. One old woman, on the boat carrying her off to America, had laid a comprehensive curse on the Ramsay family and Kildalton. Ramsay had died prematurely. His wife met a bad end, and his successors no good fortune with Kildalton. This castle and lands are now in the hands of a property company, who are proposing to sink a million pounds in developing the site as a tourist resort. Independently of such developments, Messrs. David MacBrayne plan a car ferry service to Islay of the kind recently provided for Mull and the Outer Hebrides. If the plans can be realized simutaneously they seem likely to break the curse. Seventeen thousand inquiries for accommodation by tourists are said to have been turned down in Islay in 1964.

Two miles up the road from Kildalton Castle stands the principal art treasure of Islay, and perhaps of the Hebrides – the Kildalton Cross. A few hundred yards off the road a ruined chapel is sheltered by stunted birch and hazel. To its side stands the cross, nine feet high. The whole has been cut in one piece, elaborately carved, and carries a green patina. The arms do not form a perfect right-angle within the big open circle at centre, but this does not matter. As a work of art, I think it far superior to any other Celtic cross known to me, and movingly beautiful. It probably dates from the late fourteenth century.

Nearby, at Ardmore farm, fallow deer often graze in the fields. The bay below is a natural bird-sanctuary. A maze of islets fill its mouth, and the sandy shore is divided into outer and inner flats by a tumbled wall. This inner part is semi-circled by emerald grass and carries a shallow lochan teeming with birds – sheld-duck at centre, with curlews, oyster-catchers, herons and a host of other waders at the sandy fringe. Binoculars here are essential. So clear was the light when I came that even at a quarter-mile's range I could see an oyster-catcher's reflection on the wet sand where she pecked, so that she and it seemed to be kissing beak to beak.

The two best-known bays on the south-east coast are Claggain and Aros. Claggain once rejoiced like its neighbour in half a mile of perfect sands. A few years ago, one night of storm raised over it a high beach of rounded pebbles. But sand lies there still, nearer the sea, where ringed plovers and dunlin feed together, for the two commonly pair. The Aros sands are flanked by small crags massed with bluebells, and adorned at the head by green fields and cattle.

Trudernish Point divides these two bays. On a hillock jutting into the sea stands a dun. The Hebrides can number dun-sites by the thousand, for inhabited islands maintained a continuous chain of headland sites around their coasts, both as advance warning posts and for quick refuge. They signalled each other by beacon, and for this reason are set back a little from the highest ground. The duns have long since crumbled and few are worth visiting for their own sakes, but almost all for their vantage points. They invariably command the widest prospect available on any given stretch of coast. The dun at Trudernish is such a place.

I came here on a breezy afternoon, and found that I could see

far up the sound of Jura to its craggy isles and points, and eastward straight across the tops of Gigha and Kintyre to the hills
of Arran, thirty miles away. Between the dun and the Kintyre
coast the sea was changing colour with extreme rapidity as
clouds flew over. Near the shore, its pale green, which spoke of
sand, merged quickly into mid-strait blues, where a dull pink
streak fell surprisingly, then turned abruptly to violet off Jura.
Next moment a mop of cloud would wipe the slate to grey, and
then the colours would spread again in new patterns. Across
the moors behind me a curlew was crying – surely the most
beautiful of all the bird-calls.

Examining the low circular wall of the fort, I found chunks
of vitrified rock, and discovered later that I had happened on
the only known vitrified fort of the Hebrides. There are some
fifty of these in Scotland, but none in England and Wales. The
stones of the walls have been fused by heat, probably in the
mid-British Iron Age. Modern experiments show that vitrifaction is produced by fusion of siliceous rock-rubble. When
peat, kelp and wood, in which sand and soda are present, are
burned with the rubble in strong wind, a slag-like cement is
formed. At the duns, rock fragments were thus aggregated to
form ramparts that could not be breached in night attacks. That
vitrifaction was deliberate is shown by the uniform strengthen-
ing of the ramparts along the top edges of defensive slopes.
Continuous, double and concentric vitrified ramparts are found
on the mainland. An old theory that the vitrified duns throughout Scotland were caused by attackers firing the wooden supports in the walls, thus giving accidental vitrifaction, appears
to be discredited by the evidence.

On the farther, northern point of Claggain Bay, stands
another dun, and just beyond it lies the most entrancing bird
and seal sanctuary in Islay. The south coast road ends at Ardtalla just above it. Screened from sight by a bluff below the
farmhouse lies a long bay. Its narrow sands stretch out in a
series of curves with rocky points between each, thus forming
separate and smaller bays. Each one is backed by low crags

glowing with bluebells. Stretched out below them, between rock and sand, are narrow carpets of grass. When I first found the bay they were crowded with primroses, biting stone-crop, marsh marigolds, and celandines, with much honeysuckle and iris still to bloom. A pair of orange-collared sheld-duck occupied the first beach; as I moved in they flew off to the second, then to the third and fourth. I was moving quietly, and surprised a roe-deer emerging through a breach in the crags. It froze, big brown eyes startled, then dashed back to the woods above.

A hundred yards offshore curves a string of islets like a coral reef, a score of them thus forming an inner lagoon. On one tiny rock hardly bigger than itself roosted an eider duck. Along the humped back of the central skerry stood a row of twenty black shags, heads up and motionless like a squad on parade. The farthest isle, called Eilean Liath, bore a colony of gulls all sitting snug on their eggs. On every other isle without exception basked one seal. They basked in every posture, each to its own islet; some tummy-upwards, or head and tail raised in bow-shape on islets smaller than themselves; others just flopped anyhow. A dozen more popped black heads out of the pale blue lagoon, noses pointing vertically up. Nowhere did my presence cause any commotion: the secret is to move slowly. If large parties came from a new Kildalton resort, they would make an end of this sanctuary.

Few beaches on Islay are plagued with humans, not even the greatest of them all, the Traigh Mhor (Big Strand) of Laggan Bay. I have gone there on a perfect day and walked and run along the six-mile sands under skies of unblemished blue, and had its whole length and breadth to myself. Here is no still, calm shore like Ardtalla of the sheltered south. Atlantic rollers thunder up the beach and race far in over the flats. Blue skies then lay across the wet sands the pearly blue sheen that we see in the lining of mussel shells.

The sea can sometimes be too much with us on islands, and the shores seem windy and cold. But always on Islay we can withdraw to the hill-moors. Among their hollows heat and sun can really be felt – a pleasure often denied us at the coast by unceasing breeze – and the warm moor scents yield sensuous delight after the sharper sea-tang. We still have the larks and cuckoos on the moor, but the gulls' cry is exchanged for the grouse-squawk and the hard *korr-kok* of pheasant. I have called Islay a palm-tree island, since a few palms can be found around Port Askaig, but more truly it is a land of pheasants. They are everywhere, even in the Rhinns, hence tend not to be mentioned.

Peregrines, kestrels and merlins are not uncommon on the moors, but may be hard to identify. Blackgame survive. Last century, Islay had both white-tailed eagles and ospreys, but the golden eagle has driven off the former, and a keeper shot the latter 'by mistake'. Islay is more richly stocked with birds than any other island. More than a hundred and eighty species have been recorded, and nearly a hundred stay to breed.

Among the sixty sizeable moorland lochs (many with good trout and salmon fishing) the most honoured is Loch Finlaggan. It lies high above Port Askaig. From its two little islets the Lords of the Isles administered the Hebrides. The stump of their old castle sticks up from Eilean Mor like a molar tooth. Alongside is the Council Isle, only a small round pancake, yet on this islet the fourteen lords of the Hebrides used to meet to rule the kingdom. Now a scene of utter desolation, the contemplation of it should be obligatory for every new laird of Islay, to remind him *sic transit gloria mundi*.

After the downfall of the Lords of the Isles, Islay was governed by the Donald chiefs of Dunyvaig, until Machiavellian intrigues between the Campbells of Argyll and King James VI, coupled with treachery, secured Islay for Sir John Campbell of Calder in 1615. In 1726 the Campbells sold Islay to Daniel Campbell of Shawfield, a Glasgow merchant, whose family held it till the nineteenth century. The greater part of Islay is now owned by a small number of Lowland and English landlords. Some still disapprove the encroachment on the moors by farmland, since that is bad for the shooting. Nearly all the farms are tenanted from the big estates, only two or three being owned by the occupiers. Some three hundred are of good size, and the tendency is for gradual amalgamation of smaller units with larger. The crofting areas give a low production. Almost two-thirds of the land is now in the hands of incomers. The original Islaymen have become employees in the several industries.

Unlike most of the islands, and despite the big fall in population, Islay has maintained its cow-stock at nearly 4,000 by turning to dairy farming. A creamery was set up in Port Charlotte in 1939 and absorbs the milk supply. It produces an excellent Islay cheese. The sheep-farms carry 60,000 head. Beef cattle number 6,000.

Islay has no less than seven distilleries: two north of Port Askaig, one at Bruichladdich, and four on the south coast. They are alleged to pay annual tax of more than fifteen million pounds, but for all this they give relatively small employment locally – about two hundred men. In the nineteenth century Islay grew its own barley for the whisky. Nowadays it is all imported: a most strange situation when barley can not only still be grown but yield a cash-crop alongside the industry using it.

The population of Islay reached its peak in 1831 with a figure of 15,000, since when it has steadily declined to 3,850 in 1964. Of the larger islands only Mull has suffered a worse depopulation. The truth is that remote areas near to large cities lose their people most heavily. Glasgow draws men from Islay especially to the merchant navy, in which such a large number rise to high rank that Islay is called 'The Captains' Nursery'. Success induces them to settle on the Clyde coast, whereas in the Outer Isles the men go home both between voyages and to retire.

There is no unemployment on Islay. Any big development of the tourist industry, such as could follow a Kildalton plan, might arrest the depopulation by new immigration. But the seafaring tradition is strong in the blood and bone of Islaymen.

4

COLONSAY AND ORONSAY

It was six o'clock on a wet morning, twenty miles out from the coast of Kintyre. Heaving gently, the *Lochiel* stood off Colonsay, while a small ferry boat struggled out from Scalasaig harbour, which (until 1965) had no pier that could take a steamer. Drizzle was smirring out of a grey sky. The island stared through its veil, hard and hostile. Its whole eastern flank looked to me like rock unadulterated by anything green or growing. South of Scalasaig headland, one brief smile of sand broke its grim eight-mile length.

The passengers climbed down into the ferry boat. Soon it was filled to the gunwales, for a large party of Colonsay folk, were returning from a Mod (Gaelic festival) in Bowmore in Islay. The drizzle thickened. Not even a cup of tea had been obtainable on the ship, and hardly a word been spoken by anyone. Then, as we cleared the *Lochiel*'s side, the islanders looked up at the departing ship and suddenly started to sing. They sang in the Gaelic. Hebridean songs owe much in their mood of composition to the Island sea and sky and weather. Hearing this one out in an open boat, I was more fully aware of its haunting beauty, and most deeply moved.

The air of hostility lifted from the rocky shore. I was among friends. The far-offness of the mainland was forgotten. Colonsay became one of a community of islands, only six miles north of her neighbour Islay, and nine west of Jura. Even the Americas seemed to come closer when a day later I found sugar-cane washed up on a western beach.

We landed at Scalasaig under clearing skies, and from that day I came to know one of the best of all Hebridean islands.

Colonsay is just three miles wide by eight long – or ten if we include Oronsay at the south end, from which it is cut off only at flood-tide. It is thus small enough to retain a full oceanic flavour, yet not so low as to be unrelievedly windswept.

Colonsay was born with a silver spoon in her mouth. The rock is Torridon sandstone, not of the classic upper strata that gave name to the rock, but of lower strata containing lime, which gives better soil. Many thousands of years ago Colonsay was four islands, for the sea-level was a hundred and thirty feet higher than now. The two main valleys, between Scalasaig on the east coast and Machrins on the west, and between Kiloran Bay and Port Mor both on the west coast, were then straits. Oronsay would be marked only by its hill-top. A later shore line at fifty feet above the present appears at seven or eight 'raised beaches' spread along the west coast. These raised beaches of Colonsay, Jura, Islay and other islands were caused by the withdrawal of polar ice. The ground below, depressed by its weight and now released, 'sprang' back to position in three widely separated but equal movements of isostatic recovery, which left beaches at 100 feet, 50 feet, and 25 feet above present sea-level. When man first lived in Colonsay, the sea-level was down to twenty-five feet above today's and the four islands were two. Trees grew well.

The former strait of Kiloran, little more than three miles long, is now the true heart of the island. It has a highly privileged position. To the west, south and east, and again to the north-east, it is flanked by hills that rise between three and four hundred feet, yet are set well back and sloped gradually inwards, not shutting out the sun. One would have to go to Gigha, close in to the Kintyre coast, to find a comparable site so well-sheltered from savage westerlies and searing easterlies. It gives Colonsay what no other island has in such full degree – a plant, bird and animal life that covers the double range of Atlantic mildness and Atlantic exposure. Peaches and figs ripen in the open air, given good sites, and the grey Atlantic seal breeds on remote skerries.

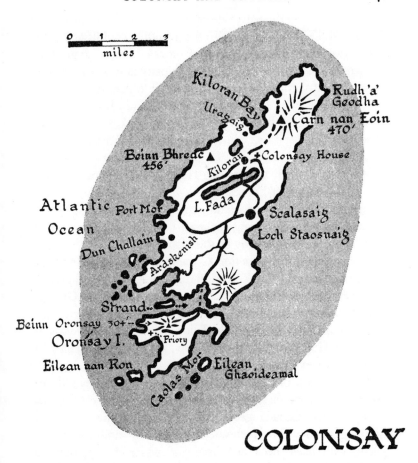

0   1   2   3
miles

Kiloran Bay

Rudh 'a' Geodha

Uragaig

Carn nan Eoin
470'

Beinn Bhreac ▲
456'

Kiloran   +Colonsay House

Atlantic   Port Mor   L.Fada

Ocean   Scalasaig

Dun Challain   Loch Staosnaig

Ardskenish

Strand-

Beinn Oronsay 304'-

Oronsay I.   Priory

Eilean nan Ron   Eilean Ghaoideamal

Caolas Mor

COLONSAY

Seventeen crofts lie scattered across Colonsay, which is stocked with 500 head of cattle and 6,000 sheep. The 200 inhabitants are mostly concentrated at three villages. Scalasaig has the only harbour, shop, hotel, post office, and a pier recently built by the county council at a cost of £150,000. It had to be made unusually strong. To allow a winter service at that open site a fendering system had to be designed able to absorb blows of a hundred tons. The two other villages, Upper and Lower

Kilchattan, lie on the west side of the island at the south end of Kiloran valley. At the north end, roughly equidistant from these two main groups, stands Colonsay House amid full-grown woods, with a home farm and justly famous gardens. A ring road of eight miles round the middle part of the island links all three, with offshoots north to Kiloran Bay and south to Oronsay strand. It is a great pleasure to walk this road in the absence of motor-cars, which are not worth bringing for so small a mileage.

Most visitors stay at Scalasaig Hotel. A new alternative is at one of several croft-houses, which having fallen empty have been modernized by the island's owner and are let during the summer months. Scalasaig makes a convenient centre, but it does lie on the wrong side of the island.

The very best introduction to the real Colonsay is the hard way across its rocky back. An old road behind the hotel gives a stiff climb of three hundred feet to a pass on Beinn nan Guidairean, then drops a hundred feet down the far side to a lochan set in a little bowl of the hills. The Kiloran farm and the woods of Colonsay House are now in full view, and the whole valley lit by the three-mile waters of Loch Fada.

A short drop of a hundred feet leads to the valley's floor. Near the head of the loch, on the fields beyond the fringe of reeds, several Canada geese will be seen feeding, or heard honking as they fly overhead. They are not unlike barnacle geese, with black neck and head and white cheeks, but are much bigger with plumage of browner grey. They are bred here by Lord Strathcona. In former years they numbered a hundred, but ate too much young grass. Also bred this century were black swans and flamingos, but only one black swan survives – it may usually be seen at the head of the loch. Several hundred wild geese fly in for wintering in October.

The far side of the valley is flanked by the range of hills, rising to Beinn Bhreac at 450 feet, which once formed a separate island. Its coast line is three miles of riven cliffs projecting slightly west of the rest of Colonsay. Big numbers of sea-birds nest there, especially fulmars, which have spread remarkably through the Isles in recent years. There are several caves. The most famous is Uamh Phiobaire or 'Piper's Cave', south of Beinn Bhreac. The legend is that an exploratory piper playing MacCrimmon's Lament led his dog into the cave in hope of discovering hell. That was the last ever heard of the piper, but his dog emerged from a cave on Beinn Eibhne, four miles away at the south end of Colonsay, with its coat singed off. Variations of this same tale are told in several other islands, notably of MacKinnon's Cave in Mull.

The cliffs are breached by a number of broad gullies, some of which give good grazing at their upper ends. The best known lies north of Beinn Bhreac at Aoineadh nam Muic, or 'Sows' Terrace', used in former days as summer grazing for pigs. A Scalasaig hotel owner renamed it 'Pigs' Paradise', thus encouraging visitors to inspect the gorge plunging through cliffs to the shore.

The range comes to an abrupt end in the north at Uragaig, a headland raised like a big platform above Kiloran Bay. Stormy seas have gouged creeks and caves out of its cliffs. Uragaig makes a fierce scene in winter. When a gale springs out of the south-west, the sea-gulls' wild crying mingles with the full-throated bellowing of the sea, now louder at one place, now lower at another. The wind howls across the crags and drives the breakers' spray far over the Uragaig crofts. In early summer it can look almost like a rock-garden: huge clumps of rose-root and sea-pink sprout from crags yellowed by lichen, while innumerable flowers speckle the gully-beds, including the purple northern marsh orchid.

North and south of the Beinn Bhreac range, the west coast of Colonsay is scooped by a series of sandy bays, one for every day of the week and no two alike. The Hebrides have such wealth of sand and rock formation that a bay to be ranked as one of the two or three outstanding bays of the Isles must needs be fabulous. But Colonsay has the Traigh Ban of Kiloran.

The approach road from Kiloran farm to the bay is only a

mile long, but there is no mile like it anywhere else in the Hebrides, at least in the month of May. The roadside hedge is snowed with hawthorn. Bluebells and primroses spread among the woods. The chestnut trees carry big candles. Every strip of ground or hollow holding water is brimming with marsh marigolds. The rhododendrons bear rich red blossom. From the gardens of Colonsay House there wafts across the road a delicious, sweet and heavily scented air, vibrant with the hum of bees, the calling of cuckoos and pheasants, and the rattle of corncrakes.

On passing through this scented mile we come out quite suddenly on open fields that merge into machair and marram dunes at the edge of the Traigh Ban. *Ban* means white or fair, and the latter applies here: the sand is a golden colour, curving half a mile from the Uragaig cliffs to the cliffs of Carn nan Eoin on the far side of the bay. Carn nan Eoin, 470 feet, is the highest hill of Colonsay. The bay's two arms run out half a mile northwest, in perfect proportion to the Traigh Ban. The sands are spotlessly clean, free of the tar-like globules that mar so many big beaches. Towards the north end, the sharp prow and stern of a wrecked fishing boat project out of the sand, the rest of the hull buried gunwales-under. It came ashore some years ago in a big storm with just a man and boy aboard, who were miraculously saved.

Beyond the wreck, black fingers of rock thrust out to sea, creating a small cove adjoining the north cliffs. This often has sheld-duck, which love small secluded bays, and I have watched black guillemots, distinguished by their white wing-patch, diving alongside them. At the opposite end of the main bay are three offshore islets, on which shags stand sentinel.

The marram at the back of the bay belongs to the larks. Judging by the sheer volume of sound, one cannot imagine room left in the sky for any other bird. They sing on and on, eighteen hours a day in May and more in June. Ringed plovers run along the sands among the oyster-catchers, but shore-birds are few compared to some Islay beaches. From the woods below Uragaig cuckoos call day-long. And day by day the green turf edging the bay slowly puts out its flowers in methodical annual order, daisies first, buttercups soon after, then blue speedwell, and yellow bird's-foot trefoil; a score of others following till the green almost vanishes under the summer blossom.

At both sides of the bay are caves. On the Uragaig crags is the Uamh Uir (Cave of the Grave) or the Crystal Springs Cavern where the flint tools of a Neolithic people were found. At the north side is the Uamh Bantghearna (Lady's Cave) and Uamh Shiorruidh (Endless Cave) which has an ancient kitchen midden. On the sand-dunes the grave of a Viking warrior has been found, buried in his ship with sword, spear, axe, shield and horse, and a half-farthing dated 831–854.

One day in May I scrambled along the cliffs at the north side, aiming for a sharp edge that fell from a cliff shaped like a cock's comb. I reached a spur of grassy rock, and was stopped there facing a huge overhanging cliff. It towered out of a circular cove deep-filled by the sea. A flock of rock-doves suddenly flew out from its face and vanished. I looked more intently. Then I saw them: ledges packed with birds. Most obvious were the grey-backed fulmars, all on grassier ledges towards the top of the cliff. One was ejecting oil to repel a boarder (probably its own mate, for the birds sit by rota), which was trying to oust it from the nest. With tubular nostrils and gaping beaks they looked savagely ugly, but elegant in flight with white head and silver-grey wings outstretched. The invading bird, bigger and even uglier than its mate, came in determinedly time and again to the same nasty reception. It persisted, and finally the sitter flew off. The relief-bird settled on the single egg.

Below the fulmars were dozens of black razor-bills, their white underparts partially hidden. Their most striking feature is the bill, flattened vertically with white stripes at right-angles to a clear white stripe running from bill to eye. Despite my presence, none flew off its ledge like the doves and fulmars, but their occasional stirrings showed that each (like the fulmar) had one egg only, laid direct on the rock without grass or other padding. The eggs were grey with big black and brown speckles, and as large as a duck's. On a ledge beside the razor-bills stood another member of the auk family, a common guille-mot – a much milder-looking bird with brown head and back, a big white 'shirt-front', and a long beak. It was not sitting on its egg, but there were many other birds nestling so closely into niches that I failed to identify them. It may be that these, or some of them, were guillemots.

This great cliff formed part of the base of Carn nan Eoin (Hill of the Birds), so I later climbed to the summit from the south side. It gave me a bird's-eye view of all the nearer islands – Mull and Iona, Scarba, the apparently vast length of Jura, and the gleam of the Gruinart strand on Islay. The hills of Donegal appeared like islands to the south-west. On a very clear day, such as I have never enjoyed on Colonsay, it is possible to see the Skerryvore lighthouse forty miles north-west. Close below, the green strath of Kiloran spreads out to Kilchattan and the hidden south.

Being the geographical heart of the island, the strath has a public hall near Kiloran farm, and a school and church (Church of Scotland) at Upper Kilchattan. There are no thatched cot-tages. Many of the houses have been reconditioned and new ones built. An electricity supply has been provided by the owner, but cannot be taken to remote houses. The villages look in thoroughly good condition, both here and at Scalasaig. For more than two hundred and fifty years the island has been blessed with energetic and generous lairds. A factor, minister, schoolmaster, and doctor all live on the island, and in case of need the doctor's patients can be flown out by plane to hospital.

An easy three miles' walk leads through the strath to the coast at Port Mor. The most delightful walk on the island is then to leave the road and follow the west coast to Ardskenish Peninsula. Port Mor is a big double bay with raised beaches. Immediately beyond is one of the widest real machairs of the Argyll islands. In the upper corner the maps mark a golf

course, which no longer exists. The land is grazed from the
farm at Machrins, but the true possessors are the peewits.
Unless for the larks, no bird seems to enjoy a machair so much
as they, tumbling, crying and frolicking across the broad acres.
Pheasants are here too. As on Islay, they are daily seen everywhere except on the cliffs and beaches.

The shore-line of this machair has two deeply indented bays,
Tobar Fuar (Cold Well) and Port Lobh (Port Stink – from
decomposing seaweed), full of white sand. A high point runs
out between them, bearing on top the remains of Dun Challain.
The site gives excellent views far up and down the jagged coast.
The fort is almost certainly named after an early chief, Colin,
for that name in ancient Gaelic is Colla, in later, Cailean, and in
the genitive Chailein. It is thus most probable that he also gave
his name to the island: the later Vikings would add the öe or ey
termination (meaning Island and usually spoken as 'a') to give
the modern Colonsay, or Colin's Island.

From behind Port Lobh we can follow a track leading over
low hills into the Ardskenish Peninsula. Where it descends to
the coast it skirts the bay of the Plaide Mhor. The beach is
white shell-sand. Beyond it, serried ribs of black rock jut into
the sea, giving a pleated plaid appearance, and a black and white
tartan effect when the sea whitens across the ribs. The track
then strikes into the middle of the peninsula through a wilderness of sand-dunes and marram, probably with a bigger lark
population than any other part of the island, until it ends at
Ardskenish farm. The fields about the house are heavily grazed
by sheep and cattle, but this ground is the most fearsomely
exposed part of the coast, open to all sun and wind. The house
looks across Oronsay to the Paps of Jura, and is occupied only
in summer.

The marram desert of south-west Colonsay is matched by
the rock-heather-bog desert of the north-east extremity. North
of Kiloran Bay, at Port Sgibinis, there is an excellent example
of a raised beach. On top of it I found the jaw-bone and vertebrae of a whale. The vertebrae were huge, like the bollards on a

pier, and the jaw-bone, which I measured, was eighteen feet long.

These bleak out-lands of the north, south, and west are crofted, but production is necessarily low. They also serve by standing there: without them there would be no Colonsay gardens. Nor could the gardens have come without lairds of vision.

The most ancient known proprietors of Colonsay were the MacPhees, but after the fall of the Donald Lordship, Colonsay passed to the Campbells of Argyll. In 1701, the first Duke of Argyll sold the island to Malcolm McNeil of Knapdale, who built Colonsay House in 1722. He used for this purpose the stones of Kiloran Abbey, which had been founded by St. Columba in honour of St. Oran (hence the name Kiloran). The first big plantations were made by the McNeils early in the nineteenth century. Ten years passed before they made good enough cover for strong growth. Rhododendrons followed in 1850, again as cover. The deciduous trees that came to full growth included beech, elm, ash and sycamore. The conifers were silver fir, spruce, larch and pine.

Gardens at last became possible. Lord Strathcona bought the island in 1904 and developed the gardens as we see them today, with large numbers of exotic rhododendrons, azaleas, magnolias, eucalyptus, acacias and maples, until it became one of the most splendid gardens of the Scottish west coast.

It should be seen in mid-May. At the entrance drive, massed banks of azaleas take the eye by storm. Many of the rhododendrons have red trunks and creamy, wax-like blooms of great size. There are numerous palm-trees (excellent shelter in rain), but above all I admired the trees with fiery red blossom, which I call flame-trees but are properly named *embothrium longfolia*. The garden has a burn flowing through it, ponds full of water plants, enclosures covered by a lake of forget-me-nots, and so much to delight the eye and nose that a full day must be spent by anyone who would see everything. The creation of this garden is a triumph of man's persistence in face of long discouragement, and a living memorial to the value of imagination. The men who planned it could never hope to see the fruition.

St. Columba's foundation of Kiloran probably gave Oronsay its original name of Eilean Orain. The Norsemen would later drop Eilean and substitute öe or ey. Oran was one of Columba's disciples, who accompanied him from Ireland. Columba is said to have landed on Oronsay in 563, but on climbing the hill found that he could still see Ireland and so moved on north to Iona. Some writers have argued that Oronsay must derive from a Viking word meaning 'half-tide island', for a score of such islands off the Scottish west coast are so named. Despite the latter evidence, there is no such Norse word, ancient or modern. But there is a Norse word Orn, meaning Eagle. It may well be that the white-tailed sea-eagle, which nested in the Hebrides prior to its extinction in the period 1879–90, favoured the tidal islands.

The high road from Scalasaig to Oronsay goes three miles along the heathery back of the island, then falls through a broad gully to the strand. The strand is a mile wide and covered five feet at high tide. One must carefully time one's arrival or pay the forfeit of a long wait – but need not wait till full ebb. It is easy to wade across two hours before and after the ebb, or more if one is long-legged. A Land-Rover from Scalasaig can be used by the decadent. I speak virtuously, having waded.

At first sight it seems hardly credible that one should ever be able to wade at all. The water looks (and is) very deep. But I learned. First, the crossing can be halved by walking round the grassy fringe of the bay to a low rocky point. From there it is just half a mile to the road-end on Oronsay. This road is not seen – it lies hidden behind a rocky point, but the point is cairned. The time to wade has arrived whenever weed is seen to float on the surface – a sign that the water is knee-deep at the deepest, and half that for most of the way. I could make straight for the cairn. The best way is easy to find as soon as one ventures out. At no point is there danger of any kind.

The road when found, circles round the south side of Beinn Oronsay to the thirteenth-century Priory of St. Columba, and to Oronsay farm. The priory is built on the site of a sixth-century Celtic monastery, thought to have been a dependency of Kiloran Abbey. The Celtic monks were later succeeded by Augustinian canons from Holyrood. The priory is now in ruins and roofless, yet in good condition. The rooms seem tiny and the cloisters small, but with arches and pillars most beautifully shaped. In a square niche behind the altar I noticed human bones, and more in a niche to one side. They had been dug up by archaeologists. Outside to the south-west a Celtic carved cross stands twelve feet high. This again is a work of high art, but not equal to the Kildalton Cross of Islay. In a recently roofed building alongside the chapel, twenty-seven tombstones are laid out on the floor, each six feet long and slab-shaped, carved with long swords (a Donald emblem), armed knights, a bishop, an old woman, and monks. These figures are framed in floral designs.

The priory has a sun-smitten site on a wind-blasted isle, but the farm is too close and spoils all. The stones from the priory had been used to build the farm, just as the stones of Kiloran Abbey had been used for Colonsay House. One would imagine the sacrilege to be Campbell work, but in fact it was done by McNeil.

The whole of Oronsay is let as one farm. Trailing out into the sea to its south spreads a broad apron of skerries, the biggest at centre named Eilean nan Ron (Seal's Island). On this wild spot an old house stands bleak and ruinous against the sky. It was used by a man gathering kelp, probably a hundred and fifty years ago. Every year sheep are put out to graze on these seemingly barren rocks, because the barnacle geese that come in winter fertilize the grass. In September, grey Atlantic seals haul out to pup. Their colony is a thousand strong.

My happiest recollection of Oronsay is one of the great

strand. Far out across the sands at the sea's edge, three herons stood black and motionless against bright, pale light. The priory may be ruined but the island still breathes peace. Not unconnected with that is the chief impression I bear from Colonsay. The old people of the island, who have lived there all their lives, have the hall-mark of the true Celt – a dignity of eye and bearing that one no longer expects to meet in great cities, save once or twice in a lifetime.

5
JURA

I F a man knew only Islay and Colonsay, he might well glance at a map of Jura and exclaim, 'Why, here is a favoured island! – screened by the Islay hills from the south-west, by the coast of Argyll six miles east, and partially from the west by Colonsay. Jura must surely have splendid woods, luxuriant gardens, rich grazings, tall crops – especially on that west coast where Loch Tarbert bites the island nearly in two: perfectly sheltered under the lee of the Paps!'

He would be wrong. If Colonsay got the silver spoon, Jura got the wooden. Her skeleton is fine-grained quartzite: the largest expanse of the poorest rock to be found in the High-lands. Not only Loch Tarbert area but the whole west coast is uninhabited by man and trackless. On the east side, a narrow strip of schists runs down the twenty-seven miles of coast. Here all farms and villages are sited, and the only road. Outside the schistose strip all is moor, peat-bog and mountain.

Seen from near and afar, it is the mountains that dominate Jura, rising to over 2,500 feet in the three Paps, all in the south half. They have high, distinctive character when seen from the right angle, but the rain-clouds make straight to them like iron filings to a magnet. The lochs abound in trout, but the island being only eight and a half miles wide at widest, the rivers are too short and steep to give much salmon fishing. Red deer are the principal stock, and have been since Viking days. Jura's name comes from the Norse *Dyr Öe* (pronounced Jooruh), meaning Deer Island, and her early history was mainly that or a hunting ground.

It remains hard to believe that two islands lying so close as

Islay and Jura can be so different, the one so green, the other so brown. The Sound of Islay splits them apart by half a mile at the narrowest point. It helps understanding to remember that where Jura's quartzite extends south into Islay it gives her the two brown deserts we noted earlier. But deserts can give men pleasure if not profit, and Jura is well fringed with oases.

The island's population of 200 is mainly housed in six villages. The chief township is Craighouse on the south-east coast within Small Isles Bay – so named from its outer screen of eight islets. Over two miles wide, the bay is fringed by strips of grass, by sand at the north end, and by clumps of trees. The houses form a line fronting the sea for half a mile, and some have a pleasing appearance. But Craighouse, as a village, cannot be praised. The prime culprit is an ugly new distillery facing the pier, and the pier itself has a raw look. To its south stands the only hotel, on a good site overlooking the bay. It keeps a high standard of service, food and courtesy.

The other villages are spread widely along the east coast: at Keils, a typically Highland clachan on the hill-slopes above Small Isles Bay; at Knockrome and Ardfernal on the north point of the bay; at Lagg Bay, where the south island dips to the north; at Tarbert, on the mile-wide isthmus in the middle of Jura; and at Ardlussa in the north. All these villages are tiny – there are only eighty houses on the whole island and fourteen of them holiday homes. Craighouse has now the only school with two teachers and twenty-five to thirty pupils. As on Islay and Colonsay, all the natives speak the Gaelic (which on Jura does not get a place on the school's curriculum). The island has a doctor, but no police. Crime is unknown.

The Empty Quarter of Jura is that long west coast. It has two remarkable features. There is no other mainland or island coast so rich in big caves, nor with so many raised beaches over such long stretches. The exploration of that coast on foot would be a tough undertaking. The most rewarding area is the mouth of Loch Tarbert, therefore much help can be had if a canoe, dinghy or motor-boat is towed or carried to the head of

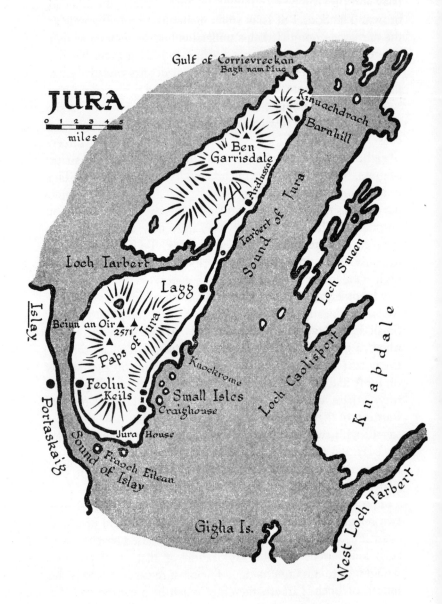

JURA

Gulf of Corrievreckan
Bagh nam Muc
Kinuachdrach
Barnhill

Ben
Garrisdale

Ardlussa

Sound of Jura

Loch Tarbert

Lagg

Beinn an Oir
2571'
Paps of Jura

Islay

Loch Sween

Tarbert of Jura

Loch Caolisport

Knapdale

Knockrome

Small Isles
Craighouse

Feolin
Keils

Jura House

Portaskaig

Fraoch Eilean
Sound of Islay

Gigha Is.

West Loch Tarbert

the loch. Two of the best examples of raised beach are found at the north shore of the outer loch, at Bagh Gleann Righ Mor and Rubh' an t-Sailein, and another three miles north at Shian Bay. The rounded quartzite pebbles, each as big as a cricket ball, shine snow-white in the sun.

The caves are countless, big and small, dry and spacious, many with finely arched roofs and level floors. They have been used over the centuries for many purposes. They were and are still much frequented by red deer seeking shelter in wild weather, and in former days by the men hunting them. Later, when cattle gave way to sheep-farming, shepherds folded their flocks in the caves at clipping time. In the old days, when the Jura people carried their dead across the island for burial in Oronsay and Iona, they rested the coffins at sites called corpachs. The caves near the corpachs were used for overnight shelter, and some had rough altar-stones. One such cave is called Uamh Muinntir I, or cave of Iona folk.

Perhaps the most interesting cave in Jura is one at the Gulf of Corrievreckan. The gulf is the northern strait between Jura and Scarba, and site of the most notorious whirlpool of the British Isles. The name is properly Coire Bhreacain. There are several widely differing stories of this Breacan, some that he was a Norwegian prince, others an Irish merchant trading to Scotland, but all agree that his ships were engulfed. The whirlpool, by one account, cast his body up on the north shore of Jura. He was buried in a cave known ever after as Breacan's Cave. A letter written by John Campbell, an early school-master of Jura, states that a stone coffin had been dug out of the floor with dust in it, but that similar remains had been found in other caves of the Jura coast.

In 1960 I spent several days on Scarba studying the whirlpool from a camp by the shore. Now, in 1964, I went to explore the Jura side and to find the cave. Martin Martin, writing in 1695, declared that the cave had Breacan's stone, tomb and altar. John Campbell had thought it might once have been used as a fort: at the mouth were the ruins of two thick walls, one within the other, while outside lay a scatter of tombstones. No writer explained how to find the cave. My only clue was an Admiralty chart, which marked Breacan's Cave in a bay called Bagh nam Muc, but gave no indication of the site.

The motor road up Jura stops at the woods of Ardlussa House. Thereafter it continues as a motorable track for eight and a half miles to the croft of Barnhill, which is little more than two miles from Bagh nam Muc. Ardlussa marks a great change in the character of Jura. Southward all is high moorland; northward, low and gently swelling, pleasing to the eye by way of change. Yet in human habitation this is the emptier half, being so remote from Craighouse.

I took to my feet at Barnhill and walked through birchwoods to the most northerly croft-house of Kinuachdrach, then northwest over low hills. From the high ground I looked down on the Gulf of Corrievreckan. Half a mile wide, the tide race sped between rocky shores till it whitened at the great whirl, which showed clearly at a mile and a half's range close to Scarba. I descended a narrow glen to the Bagh nam Muc.

It formed a double bay with an island filling its mouth. I went first to the northern half, where clean grey sand enticed me to swim out to join a big Atlantic seal. A herd of wild goats appeared on the beach – big brown beasts, long-bearded and shaggy; I came out and followed them round to the second bay. No cave could be seen. I scrambled almost half a mile along the rocks of its farther arm, passing several shallow caves and overhangs, until at last I saw it. When seen, it is unmistakable.

The cave bores into a tall crag standing well back from the true rock-shore. In front spreads a broad stretch of turf. Three rock walls (not two) ring the entrance, the outer low, broken, grass-grown. Sixteen yards in from it stands the second wall, then the first within the overhang of the cliff.

The cave is sixty yards deep by fourteen wide. I entered to find a red deer hind at the back. She stood petrified. I flattened myself against one wall to give her a clear run, and out she

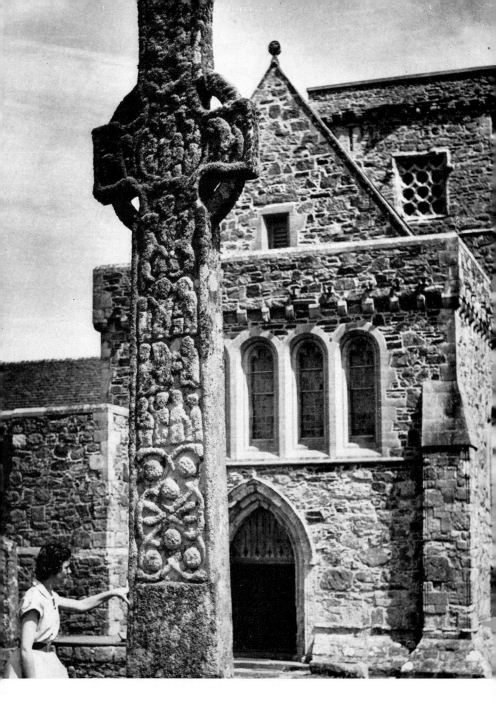

IONA   St. Martin's Cross

By Tom Weir

IONA
St. Columba's Bay

By Tom Weir

went, like a ball from a cannon. The earth floor was covered
with deer-droppings and a deer's skeleton lay in a corner.
There is no longer any trace of the altar mentioned by Martin.
Small stalactites hang from the roof. The outward view is to a
jagged claw of Jura projecting into the seething water of the
gulf.

This north shore of Jura is the most savage of the whole
island. I contrast it with another day that I once spent camping
on the Corran sands of Small Isles Bay. My tent stood on a
strip of short green machair, spotlessly clean, at the very edge
of the beach. A heat haze lay over the sea. The mainland
vanished but Gigha stayed on view as a long low shape with a
series of humps on its back like the Loch Ness monster. The
sands were quietly busy. Ringed plovers and oyster-catchers,
both with chicks, ran around close to the tide-level. Two sheld-
duck with four chicks paddled a few yards out. The drake, I
noticed for the first time, had an orange splash under the tail.
A little farther out were the eider ducks, their soft and soothing
ooee sounding like the perfect expression of bliss.

That night the sun set orange behind the Paps, which stood
knife-sharp and black. Between them glowed Venus, seeming
huge till the moon rose full behind Kintyre. It rose yellow,
pouring between the Small Isles in a golden, dancing track.
Where it struck the beach it floodlit oyster-catchers, still trot-
ting the wet sands in search of supper at 11 p.m. The dry sands
near the machair were shining white through the dusk, for the
sky was still a pearly grey-blue. Dew had come on the machair,
where the rabbits were out, tails bobbing. They would suddenly sit alert, one paw up, as if watching the lighthouse flashing on the sound, or listening like me to the waves whispering
up the beach. Then they were off, determinedly, but still
questing.

Next day I climbed the Paps. No matter where one goes in
the neighbouring isles, the Paps are always there too, either in
full view or peeping unexpectedly over hill-ridges. It becomes
necessary to climb them, if just to work them out of one system.

c

There are three Paps, forming a horse-shoe around Loch an t-Siob. The nearest (or most easterly) is Beinn Shiantaidh, the Holy Mountain. The highest peak behind it is Beinn an Oir, the Mountain of the Boundary (usually mistranslated as Mountain of Gold) 2,571 feet. The south peak is Beinn a' Chaolais, the Mountain of the Sound (of Islay).

I climbed Shiantaidh first by an easy walk up to its eastern saddle, where eleven lochs wink in the sun, nine of them swimmable. This makes a good route on a hot day. At this level there is no sound of water, no bird-song. The utter silence comes on the mind with a touch most soothing.

The Paps are often maligned for their truly enormous scree-slopes – and no scree is worse than quartzite. Both on Shiantaidh, and later on the slopes of Beinn an Oir, I found that the screes could be turned by long strips and zigzags of grass. A few hundred feet under the top of Beinn an Oir, on the east side, a spring of clear water bursts out of the velvety moss. The isolated, western position of the summit makes it a superb view-point, embracing the whole of the Inner Hebrides from the Cuillin of Skye to the Isle of Man – but only in the clearest of weather. The farther islands were lost in haze. Islay was revealed in full, so nearly severed by Loch Indaal. Loch Finlaggan gleamed on the brown hills above it, two dots on the surface marking its famous islets. Close below me stretched the vast empty moors of Jura's west coast, bearing the long rock scar of Sgriob na Caillich, the Witch's Scrape.

When I came down to the lower moors the curlews were calling. There are still a few blackcock on Jura, and larger numbers of snipe, plover, woodcock and pheasant. The golden eagle is here, though I saw no sign, and the chough has been reported breeding on lonely cliffs. Barnacle geese used to come in October only in small numbers, but have increased of late years until they can now be seen in flocks of two hundred.

A good place for watching sea-birds is down at the south coast between Jura House and Claig Castle. The House, surrounded by full-grown woods and rhododendrons, has one of

the best sites in Jura. It overlooks the entrance to the Sound of
Islay. Below lies the island's best beach. The long arm of an
offshore island protects its eastern side, and Fraoch Eilean,
bearing the ruins of Claig Castle, guards the west. Oak and
sycamore screen the landward side, where a long bank, dropping from trees to beach, is crowded with bluebells, irises,
fuchsia and montbretia. These bluebells in May give a dense
carpet and strong scent. Under the bank stretch pure white
sands fringed by yellow silverweed. I had imagined that the
only 'singing sands' in Scotland were those of Eigg. To my
surprise, the sands of this Jura bay sang well and truly when
scuffed with the heels.

The shore from here to the Ardfin jetty, opposite Claig
Castle, is often teeming with sea-birds, but not necessarily in a
wide range: sandpipers, tern, eider and sheld-duck, and the
normal waders. It is much favoured by eiders, who enjoy it as a
nursery. In the last week of May, six or seven duckling may be
seen scuttering along at mother's tail as she dashes out to the
safety of deep water.

There are usually swans around Fraoch Eilean (Heather
Isle). The castle is now just a stump on a jutting crag. It must
have been impregnable before the days of cannon. Sea-girt on
three sides, it is trenched on the fourth or island side by a
natural moat fifteen feet wide. Somerled built it to guard the
Sound, which was of great strategic importance to his fleet at
Lagavulin Bay. The Lords of the Isles exacted tribute from all
ships passing through. The island gave Clan Donald its war-
cry of 'Fraoch Eilean!'

About a mile beyond Ardfin, and within three hundred yards
of the road, there is an unusually good standing stone. There
are so many throughout the Isles that, as with pheasants on
Islay, one tends to make no mention. But this Jura stone is a
fine example. It stands twelve feet high on an open site facing
the Sound. Green with lichen, it is thousands of years old. The
erection of these stones by man began in the later Stone Age
and continued to early Christian times. The accepted dating of

Stonehenge is around 1850 B.C. The stones of Islay, Colonsay and Jura are thought to be later, probably around 1600 B.C.

Much less obscure is the later history of Jura. On the fall of Clan Donald, it went to the Campbells of Argyll in 1607. They sold it in 1938. The island now has five landowners, including the Forestry Commission.

After the Forty-five there came a great trade in black cattle. Cattle throve in the mild winter climate of the Inner Isles, and their export was then the only realizable wealth. At Feolin, where a ferry boat still plies across the narrow sound to Port Askaig on Islay, the ferry records show that between 1801 and 1807 an average of 2,640 cattle were exported annually from Islay by way of Jura. They were then driven to Lagg Bay and ferried again to the mainland.

The population reached its peak in 1841 at a figure of 1,320. When sheep displaced cattle there were no open evictions in Jura. Rising rents were used to force out tenants whose families had held the land for generations. Large emigrations followed to America and the mainland, and to the seafaring life. The once wide cattle-grazings deteriorated under the sheep, profits fell, and more and more land went over to deer. There are now 200 people on Jura and 4,000 deer.

The old life and climate of Jura seems to have favoured longevity. At Inverlussa graveyard there stands a memorial stone to Mary MacCrain who died in 1856 aged 126. More remarkable still is the stone erected in Keils graveyard, Craighouse, in 1964. It commemorates another member of the same family and bears a bronze plate inscribed: 'Gillouir MacCrain, who lived to spend one hundred and eighty Christmasses in his own house, is buried here. He died about the year 1645.' This was the original inscription, now renewed, as recorded by Thomas Pennant in 1772.

Farming and crofting are still the chief means of livelihood – almost the only means. The old breed of Highland cattle has been kept pure and not allowed to die out. The annual export of both Highland and cross-bred cattle amounts to 300 head, and of sheep 500, from a stock of well over 1,000 beef cattle and 10,000 sheep. Jura could support a much larger population: many thousands of acres, which once raised stock and crops, lie unused. But some ground has recently been reclaimed from moor, and proprietors have been improving their farms. In Jura, as in all Hebridean Islands, the people are finding that a most serious handicap to prosperity is high freight costs.

The new distillery at Craighouse gives (as yet) little employ-ment locally. The barley is brought in already malted, hence needs no men to turn it on the floors, and no carters of peat. The skilled labour required is brought in from the mainland. The distillery company plan to establish an airstrip at Corran, which will be of great benefit to all Jura.

Most promising for the future is the work of the Forestry Commission. They have recently bought land in south Jura and the first plantations are being made between Craighouse and Jura House. The work employed only six men in 1964 and has come rather late, in the sense that local labour has to be drawn from other necessary work, for there is no unemploy-ment in Jura. But in forestry there is promise of growth – for more than trees.

Neither farmer nor forester has ever been a friend to deer. Yet Jura has ever been *Dyr Öe*, and still is. Can the leopard change his spots? Or Deer Island her red-brown skin?

6

GIGHA

THE long, low, lean, and lumpy Island of Gigha, all set about with rocky seas, could make even a baby elephant happy – palm-trees sprout in the village street of Ardminish and tropical bushes in plenty at Achamore House – but, please, only a baby elephant: the island measures just six miles by one and a half.

Gigha (pronounced Geea, with the G hard) lies three miles off the coast of Kintyre. The name is thought by some to mean God's Island, from missionaries of the Celtic order Gille Dia, or Servants of God, who might have settled there in the eighth century. The thirteenth century MS of The Hakon Saga names the Island Gudey, which could mean either God island or Good Island. The latter would still be appropriate today. 'A land flowing with milk and honey!' I never thought to hear such words of a western isle, but I heard them of this island Canaan – from a farmer's wife. And I found them to be literally true.

We have two ways of access to Gigha, either from West Loch Tarbert by steamer, which plies day about to a pier at the south end, and to the northern point where it stands off to be met by ferry boat, or else from Tayinloan on the Kintyre coast, whence a regular ferry-service takes passengers (not cars) to Ardminish Bay at the middle of the island.

A view from seaward presents Gigha, like the other isles of the group, as all hilly moor with a featureless coast: none of which is true. The worst way to see islands is to sail round them. 'Land and explore' must be our motto. Gigha like the others abounds in green, colourful and beautiful bays and hollows, which one would not anticipate from long distance.

A long spinal ridge of epidiorite runs through the island from north to south. The surrounding land is of sandy, lime-free loam, nourishing twelve farms and six crofts. All but two of the farms lie under the shelter of the spine. Unluckily for them, Gigha's three lochs are all on the west side of the water-shed, so that eastern farms, which have to rely on springs, go short of water in drought. The best ground is on this eastern side – an exception to the general rule, like Jura. If a traveller should arrive here after visiting any other western isle, even Islay, he will be startled by the greenness of Gigha's land, by the rich soil, the well-kept farms and good gates (no iron bed-steads here), and the many different crops on her nine hundred acres of arable land. Acre for acre, Gigha is the most productive island of Scotland in terms of exports.

Ardminish is the only village, and very small, for the island's population of 190 is well spread. It stands well back from the shore with school, hotel, village store, and a stone church with good stained-glass windows, where services are still preached in the Gaelic. Although it lies so close to the mainland, Gaelic is still the daily language of the people. Only one road runs up and down the island, but many side roads, all in good order, lead off to the farms and crofts. Since nearly every household has a car or van, tractor or lorry, the main road can be busy. There is a nurse, but no resident doctor.

The most excellent vantage point for viewing Gigha is the top of her highest hill, Creag Bhan. It is only 331 feet and lies on the northern part of the spine. I went up there one day from Ardaily farm, and found the summit to be ice-ground slabs of rock. Although there are many outcrops along the spine there are no big crags or cliffs, and almost no heather. Instead, much of the top is covered in clumps of dwarf whin, growing tight and close to the ground, and thick with blossom that gives off a heavy scent. Bluebells are here too, and pale lilac orchids. Bumble-bees were plundering the blossom that day, and I can

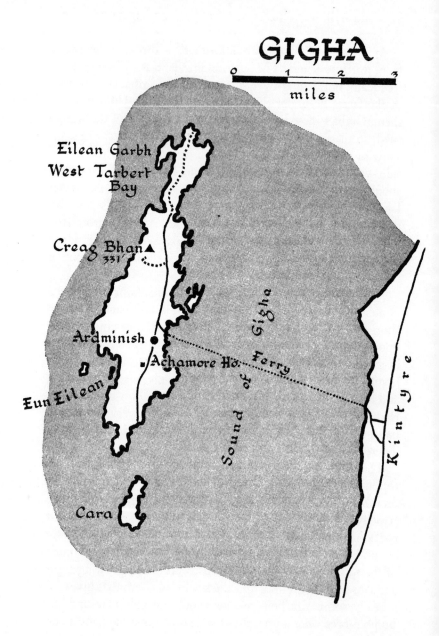

truthfully say that there is no other summit like this in the Isles.

Islay and Jura were lost in blue haze – normally one can expect to see Rathlin and the Irish hills. But I had come to see Gigha.

Both sides of the island are bitten out in rocky bays, many with sand. Each west coast bay has a croft-house above it, and the holdings are relatively small with mixed sheep and cattle and tiny areas of crops. The eastern farms are much bigger – still more so farther south, where Achamore farm is queen of all. That south end cannot be properly seen, but the northern quarter is in full view and quite different from the rest of Gigha, being flat and narrower with the green fields of three farms at centre. The extreme north end is heavily gouged by big bays, leaving a far-western peninsula, Eilean Garbh, linked to Gigha only by a narrow strip of sand. 'Garvilan', as it is usually called, has a huge gullery. Guillemots and eider ducks breed on its western ledges.

South of Creag Bhan, Gigha's three lochs lay on the moor like blue eyes on a peacock's train. I crossed over to them and watched mallard and teal. The lochs were rimmed with white bog-bean, which filled one bay with a broad crescent like soap-suds, for the petals have a feathery edge. Another loch had three islets, one packed with rhododendron and ringed by bog-bean, which formed a lace-like cravat for the red bloom at centre.

Cattle were grazing round the lochs' shores, for this was no Jura moor. In Lewis they might count it grass. The 'rough' hillsides were dappled with large and luscious orchids, thyme, spring cinquefoils, bluebells, speedwells, stitchwort both white and starry, and a host of others, but more especially primroses, which grow in profusion throughout Gigha. Cotton grass would come later, and big yellow irises on the lower ground.

Herons fish the upper lochs, and a few wigeon and pochard. Snipe and grouse breed. Unlike the rest of the Islay group, Gigha has no migration of geese, which arrive only if storm-driven. On the lower ground there are pheasant, a very few woodcock, and a plague of hoodie-crows and jackdaws. There are no deer on Gigha, nor is there a fox, hare, stoat or weasel. In consequence the island was a paradise for rabbits until smitten by myxomatosis.

The road from Ardminish to south Gigha is lowland-type country, flanked by lowland hedges, and by masses of golden whin between the road and the Sound of Gigha. On passing the magnificent woods of Achamore House it emerges on open farmland, and so to the southernmost point where the pier stands alone. A Campbeltown fishing boat comes into the bay to set creels and nets. Gigha has only one boat of her own, but not so many years ago had renowned cod-banks, and lobster fishing on which eight boats were engaged in the years following the Second World War. Many people were thus employed. Great lines, set with a thousand hooks, were used on the banks, but one day a poaching trawler sailed within the three-mile limit and scooped all the gear, which the men were unable to replace. The lobster boats made big catches, but these dwindled, perhaps through over-fishing. The people say that they are discouraged from any resumption of line and lobster fishing by heavy freight charges.

A mile south of the pier, the lonely island of Cara lies out in the sound. It belongs to MacDonald of Largie but has not been inhabited for thirty years and the house stands empty. It has a fifteenth-century chapel in ruins. Bare and treeless, it is grazed by sheep, goats and rabbits. A hill shaped like a coffin gave it the Norse name of Karöe, or Coffin Island.

On Gigha, the main grazing is by 600 dairy cattle and some 80 beef cattle. There are less than 500 sheep. On most days of the week, close on a thousand gallons of milk go into the creamery at Achamore farm for cheese-making.

If one keeps to the eastern side of the watershed, Gigha seems quite untypical of a western island. To redress the balance, one need only walk through Achamore farm and cross the fields down to Eun Eilean Bay (Bird Island Bay) on the west coast. It is best of all to come here of an evening. The bay is a bird sanctuary. A score of rocky islets lie close inshore; from the sands of a double bay ragged points stick out seaward. Sheld-duck may be seen in their season, a couple of scoter if one is lucky, and mergansers, tern, fulmars, eider duck and black-throated divers. I last went there when a setting sun was flooding colourless behind Islay and Jura. The rocks jagged black into the dying light – a wild scene, as true to the Isles as the mild east is anomalous.

Prior to the battle of Largs, Gigha made a favourite anchorage for the Viking fleets. It was ruled by Clan Neil under MacDonald aegis, until in the seventeenth century it passed to the Campbells, who sold it back to the Neil family in the eighteenth century, who again sold in the nineteenth. Thereafter it frequently changed hands and is now the property of Colonel Sir James Horlick.

When Martin Martin visited Gigha in 1695, he reported no wood in Gigha. As on Colonsay, the normal trend to treelessness has here been reversed. Two big plantations were made at Achamore House, one seventy-five years ago, and the second ten years later. Using that cover, and starting in 1945, Colonel Sir James Horlick has created a woodland garden that can already rank in beauty with those of Colonsay and Inverewe, though quite different from either. He recently gifted the garden to the National Trust for Scotland, who open it to the public.

The main gate is a mile south of Ardminish. A broad curving drive leads in, bordered by lawns, at whose back are massed azaleas of orange and fiery red. Branching paths meander to the heart of the woodland, which is mainly deciduous and spaced to give light and air. Clearings are cunningly planned: they are unexpected, spacious, and shaped to give unusual vistas of the flowering shrubs, trees, and plants. The sunlight makes great play with these, flooding through the tree-tops on to laburnums and flame-trees (*embothrium longifolium*), which then light our ways like torches, or through the leaves palely on to primula candelabra, exploring their many blues with delicate touch.

Remoter tracts of land are left wild to the bluebells, and always somewhere overhead, if rarely seen, wood-pigeons moan.

The making of this garden has been a work of high creative art ('luck' swears Horlick). That it should have been possible in so short a time is no small tribute to the quality of Gigha's soil, which here lies on a raised beach deposit. That soil has allowed her people to take the tide of agricultural prosperity. The big drop in her population has helped. Last century there were nearly 600 people on Gigha. Less than a third remain. Gigha is quite as remote as Islay though lying so near to the mainland and within sixty miles of Glasgow as the crow flies. That sixty miles take nine hours to cover by public transport. Depopulation was thus inevitable in modern times. But the chosen third have arrived in the Promised Land.

CORRIEVRECKAN

The tide race and whirlpool of Corrievreckan, in the gulf between Scarba and Jura, has a reputation legendary in the full literal sense. I had known from boyhood that it sank ships, which were drawn helplessly into the maelstrom and sucked down, despite which I grew to a sceptical disbelief. I thought these excellent yarns to be not based on fact and therefore, like tales of bottomless Highland bogs, legendary in the sense of untrue. My views underwent a radical change when I took to sailing and came to learn something of the Scottish west coast.

In the summer of 1959, when I sailed north of Crinan, out through the Dorus Mor (Great Gate) into the turbulent channels of Scotland's Atlantic coast, I saw tide-white seas peppered with black and craggy islands and heard, four miles to westward, the deep-throated roar of the Corrievreckan. It thundered like an artillery barrage, unceasingly; it must have been audible at double the distance. If so much noise could be heard at so long a range, thought I, the maelstrom must indeed be worth inspecting at close range. Legend must after all be near to the truth. I determined to go at the first opportunity and to find this truth for myself.

Stretching all the way up the coast of Argyll from Crinan to Oban are strings of islands: Jura-Scarba-Lunga and the Isles of the Sea on the Atlantic side; Luing-Seil-Kerrera hard against the mainland, plus a throng of outliers. In the straits between are several notorious tide-races, like the Pladda Narrows between Luing and Scarba, and the Dorus Mor off Craignish Point. At flood and ebb the tides race there at seven or eight knots. Small ships and yachts, unable to make these passages against a foul tide, must time their arrival for fair tide or slack water. One exception is the Gulf of Corrievreckan. There, only slack water permits passage. A fair wind and tide promise no safety. A ship can still be wrecked or founder.

The Admiralty chart shows that flood tide drives north up the Sound of Jura, then sets west through the Corrievreckan strait at nine knots. The gulf runs east and west, is two miles long by a mile wide, and gives deep soundings of forty to a hundred and twenty fathoms. The great overfall and whirlpool form at the west end, near the Scarba shore. They are caused by a rock pyramid projecting from the ocean floor. Its blunt crest lies a full fifteen fathoms under, causing violent upsurge from the lower layers at flood or ebb. At spring tides, which come each fortnight at the change of moon, the current gains tremendous power. The upsurge meets the fast-travelling top layer, ninety feet thick, causing those breaking seas and the vast sucking whirl in which no small boat can hope to live. When a strong westerly blows against a spring flood the commotion is still more terrible. The breakers at the overfall can then be twenty feet high and spout higher still. In a storm the roar can be heard along a twenty-mile stretch of the mainland coast.

What minimum size of ship could expect to win through with the current at mid-flood? No answer is known, for luck plays too great a part. The powerful eddies and cross-currents are likely to seize the ship and spin it round. All response to the rudder being then lost, the boat is more likely to go through the maelstrom stern first than bow first. If struck by a big breaking sea in a high westerly wind, a yacht's crew might be scooped out of the cockpit and drowned, the yacht waterlogged, thrown head to sea, smashed by the next breaker, and sunk stern first. A ship might escape the whirlpool itself to be seized by one of the on shore currents and broken up on the Scarba rocks.

In *Sailing Orders*, Captain J. R. Harvey writes: 'Keep away from the eastern approach to the gulf because the flood or north-going stream directs into the gulf – no place for a yacht.

The gulf in a westerly gale is a fearsome place. A West Highland steamer, laden with a deck cargo of cattle, was in a westerly gale drawn into the gulf from westward. The ship took a big list owing to the cargo shifting, making it necessary to throw the cattle overboard, and she only just managed to steam out before she was actually in the gulf.'

On the other hand, when Vega Productions made the film *I know where I'm Going*, they directed a boat into the gulf with two dummy figures aboard. But in this they reckoned without the Cailleach (Old Woman), which is the local name of the presiding demoness. She perversely refused to sink it, and merely cast it up on Scarba, waterlogged. In 1913, two men were carried through the gulf in a small yacht on the full tide, and only survived by battening themselves down in the cabin and praying hard. She was tossed about like a shuttlecock and spun in all directions, but she won through. The Cailleach was kind. During the Second World War an LCP (Landing Craft Personnel) with a flat bottom and 250 horse-power petrol engine went through the overfall undamaged at mid-tide. In 1946 a lifeboat, towing a dismasted yacht, went through against the flood by hugging the Jura shore. Mr. Iain Rutherford has sailed his eight-metre yacht *Pleiades of Rhu* through the gulf in calm weather on the ebb, but he also narrowly escaped wreck on the Scarba shore when the wind momentarily died. Failing great motor power to give thrust for steering, it can thus be seen that much depends on the luck of the tide-race – that is, on the Cailleach Herself. The gulf is the tub in which she tramps her blankets. Her whims cannot be foretold.

The name Corrievreckan is from the Gaelic Coire Bhreacain, which has long been thought to derive from a legendary hero named Breacan. Early records conflict on the details of his fate, ranging as they do from the plain to the fabulous, but they are unanimous in naming a gulf from his death there. The *Glossary* of Cormac, who in 901–8 was King of Munster and Bishop of Cashel, first describes the whirlpool and then continues, 'Brecan, son of Maine, son of Nial Naoighiallach, had fifty curraghs trading between Erin and Alban. They fell afterwards on that coire and it swallowed them altogether, and no news of their destruction escaped from it.'

The ancient topographical work, the *Dinnseanchus*, differs from Cormac only in detail: 'And it was into this that Brecan, son of Partholan, was drawn and was drowned with his fifty boats when he fled out of Erin from his father.'

These legends, long accepted as referring to the Scottish Corrievreckan, were in fact not told of the Jura strait but of the strait between Rathlin and Northern Ireland. Adamnan, the seventh-century biographer of St. Columba, calls that Irish strait the Charybdis Brecani. He several times mentions the whirlpool of Brecan, notably in one of his stories of St. Columba's power of prayer, which could save friends in peril. The story is headed: 'Of the peril of Bishop Saint Colman . . . in the sea near the island that is called Rechru (Rathlin)'. Then Columba speaks: 'Colman, Beogna's son, has begun to sail over to us, and is now in great danger in the surging tides of the whirlpool of Brecan. . . .'

All the Irish stories refer to the Rathlin strait, for which the name Corrievreckan has long since fallen into disuse. Was the name then transferred to the Jura strait? Not necessarily. Coire Bhreacain in plain Gaelic means Speckled Corrie, and both gulfs would be named thus from their great streaky overfalls. Breacan is not a Celtic Christian name. But the Gael is a born story-teller, and the legends would almost certainly be told to provide a dramatic background to tide-races naturally spectacular.

The Scottish gulf carries a more stirring Norse legend of its own. Breacan, a son of the King of Norway, fell so madly in love with a woman that he swore to perform some great feat in her honour, to show how fearless he could be for her sake. He decided to anchor his galley in the Scarba-Jura gulf for three days and three nights. He had three anchor ropes specially woven: one of wool, one of hemp and one of virgins' hair – this last for dire emergency. He sailed to the Corrievreckan. He threw out all three anchors. On the first night of storm the wool rope parted. On the second night the hemp rope parted. On the third night, the continuing storm intensified. One by one, the strands of virgins' hair gave way. The last held till the last hour but the fury of the storm and maelstrom heightened. The rope snapped. The galley was sucked into the whirlpool and swallowed up. Breacan's dead body was later dragged ashore by his own black dog. He was buried in Uamh Bhreacain, the cave on the Jura shore.

The legend omits to point the moral, which would seem to be that virgins are not all that heroes would like to think.

In September 1960, my wife and I camped for several days on the Scarba side of the gulf. We set the tent abreast the whirlpool on a grass patch among the rocks. This whole south coast, which flanks the gulf, is high, steep, often precipitous, but never sheer. There is no beach, only riven rock indented by narrow guts, which are one moment filled full by the swell of the sea, and the next sucked dry with a fierce gurgle. An occasional breach in the rock escarpment carries a carpet of big shingle, allowing one to bathe at slack water, We swam, but only at waist-depth. Beyond that point, currents ran fast enough to snatch away the most powerful swimmer.

Our tent was ideally situated for watching the whirlpool, which lay two hundred yards offshore. Save for an hour at high and low water, it was never absent. Throughout the five intervening hours, the gulf roared continuously, but not deafeningly, for the wind stayed a light northerly. Outside the gulf, the sea was calm, blue, hardly ruffled; but inside, a seething tumult of white breakers. The overfall raced more than a mile along the Scarba coast and half a mile in breadth.

The moon being full, spring tides were running, but that northerly wind was checking the flood up the Sound of Jura, thus the overfall was not giving its more spectacular performance. Martin Martin, in his description of the Western Isles of 1695, declares that the whirlpools form pyramids, 'and immediately afterwards spout as high as the Mast of a little Vessel, and at the same time give a loud Report.' We could see that in

favourable conditions his words must be true, indeed he under-
stated for westerly gales. In flat calm, the surge and fury of the
flood held us fascinated for hours.

The only visible inhabitants of Corrievreckan were black
shags. They love the sharpest edges of rock, on which they
were lined up in squads of twenty, often standing there for
hours punctuated by brief flights across the tide-race and back.
They did no fishing. We never observed where they fed. The
eastern shores of Scarba and Lunga abound in seals, sunning
themselves on the rocks where they may be closely approached
by boat. In the gulf itself we saw only one, an east to west
traveller coming through fast on the tide – not the least afraid
of the whirlpool, which it narrowly avoided.

At high water on our second day we had the good fortune to
see a big fishing smack go through from east to west. She would
be powered by the usual 88 horse-power Kelvin diesel, and had
in addition set a mizzen sail. A perfectly timed arrival brought
her to the overfall just as it died away. No waves were breaking,
but a strong current was still running and swung her through
at a full fifteen knots. She made straight for the site of the
vanished whirlpool and went through at dead centre. At that
point she plunged and reared like a horse hurdling. There must
still have been a big upsurge at the maelstrom's sleeping heart.
Then she was through, bound for the Sea of the Hebrides, or
perhaps Coll and Tiree.

The Corrievreckan is one of the great sights and sounds of
Scotland. Apart from the tide-race, which alone is sufficiently en-
thralling, we have rock shores savagely wild, a limitless seascape,
and across on Jura serried bays and capes and hill-ridges receding
endlessly southward, dancing with light or suffused by mist, offering beauties of form that hold the eye day-long. Not all men will
want to camp on Scarba at a spot so exposed; for them there is,
abreast the whirlpool, a great cave magnificent enough to have
housed the Cailleach Herself, or Breacan and his Hundred Sailors.

The spell of legend with its tang of the fabulous still lies over
all. And here it is matched by the reality.

8

THE ISLES OF THE SEA

THE Isles of the Sea, often called the Garvellachs, are set in the wide outer arms of the Firth of Lorn, between Scarba and Mull. The ideal place to view them, and the other isles great and small that lie off the north of Jura, is from the top of Scarba's hill, the Cruach Scarba, 1389 feet.

Scarba (Norse Skarpöe, Rough or Sharp Isle) is little more than a circular mountain-top lifting steeply out of the sea, and less than two and a half miles in diameter. It is an island to approach with caution. At the south end is the Corrievreckan; at the north, a notorious tide-race called the Grey Dog, hurtling through a channel only two hundred yards wide between Scarba and the island of Lunga; and eastward, the Sound of Luing, which is the main coastal passage but this too with a race that obliges small boats to await fair tide. A few cattle and red deer are grazed by the owner, who keeps a farmer-gamekeeper at Kilmory Lodge on the east side. To north and west the shores are ringed high by rock, yellow and black and grey.

Access to Scarba is from the Oban road, first through the island of Seil, reached by a humped bridge of single span – famed as 'the bridge that spans the Atlantic', thence by ferry across the Cuan Sound (three hundred yards) to the island of Luing. Scarba is finally reached by hiring a motor-boat from Black Mill Bay; the Isles of the Sea by hiring from Cullipool. The boats belong to lobster-fishermen, one of whom sets his creels in the Gulf of Corrievreckan – at slack water.

I climbed Cruach Scarba on a fine September morning. The sky was congested by cloud, packed loose and galloping across their blue plain like stampeding buffalo. The sun everywhere burst through, lighting the whole long length of the Firth of Lorn, till it faded into the still longer Loch Linnhe, which though itself hidden carried one's eye to the wide Highland fault that splits Scotland by way of the Great Glen to Inverness. The isles below spread an irregular pattern across the blue, some of bare rock lit by sun and shining whitely, some gaily green, seasonally grazed by sheep and cattle though uninhabited, others left darkly purple and cold like the lobsters under their own shelves. Four miles to my north-west, the four small Isles of the Sea stretched four miles in line astern, each sloping up from the south-east to present bold cliffs to seaward.

Between them and the Sound of Luing lay half a dozen islands of the Lunga group, including Belnahua, once heavily quarried for its slate. None were inhabited, not even Fladda lighthouse. These are dangerous seas and many ships have been wrecked. Across the Sound of Luing, a long mainland 'peninsula' swung southward, divided by the narrowest of straits into the islands of Seil and Luing. Like Kerrera and Lismore farther up the Firth, they are not topographically part of the Hebridean archipelago, and therefore I do not deal with them as such. But they have made their contribution to Iona Cathedral. Both are slate islands. When the cathedral was rebuilt it was noticed that the old broken slates had rusty pit-marks, revealing Luing or Seil as place of origin, for the slates there are set with iron pyrites and yellow crystals, which weather out like those of Iona. The new slates needed were therefore quarried from the north end of Luing.

Looking out across this island-strewn seascape to Mull, my eye followed the twenty-mile length of the Ross of Mull to its far western end, where Iona lay hidden behind the butt-end. I could not help marvelling that Columba had been able, amid these isle-infested seas and without aid of British Admiralty charts, to pick an island so well placed strategically for the conversion of the northern Picts. He had pushed north to the utmost limit of Scottish-controlled territory, found a place that no one could easily reach to ravage (for the Vikings were not yet rampant), and there, up the Firth of Lorn to the Great Glen, stretched his highway to the heart of Pictland and its capital.

On his voyage from Ireland in 563, Columba had made brief visits to south Kintyre and Oronsay, then continued to the Isles of the Sea, where he called on monks already living on the southernmost island, called Eileach an Naoimh (the Rock of Saints). A monastery had been founded there by St. Brendan around 542.

In the years that followed, Iona became the centre of the most intensive evangelical work of a practical kind, involving the founding and staffing of monasteries and chapels all over the Western Isles and Highlands. It became essential to Columba to have a place of retreat, to which he could withdraw from time to time to revive, by prayer and meditation, the inner springs from which his works in the world flowed. He found this on an island named Hinba, to which Adamnan (an early Abbot of Iona) constantly refers in his biography. After Adamnan's death in 704, and perhaps through destruction of records in later Viking invasions, the identity of Hinba was lost. This has aroused deep regret in men of all later centuries, for the evidence is clear that St. Columba loved Hinba as dearly as Iona: they must both have come to symbolize in his mind the inner and outer aspects of his life and work, neither complete without the other. The identification of Hinba, say the Celtic historians, 'is the great desideratum of Hebridean topography.'

Majority opinion has favoured Eileach an Naoimh, on the grounds that Hinba was evidently within easy reach of Iona, and the small monastery on the Eileach would always be there ready to welcome Columba. His uncle Ernan had been placed in charge of the monastery. Then an aged priest, Ernan would certainly not be given a monastic charge farther north in Pictish territory when Scots and Picts were still at enmity. Hinba would lie south in friendly country. Adamnan records that when Brendan (at the age of almost 90) sailed from Ireland to visit Columba he found him unexpectedly at Hinba. The one place at which Brendan would be certain to call *en route* for Iona would be his own foundation on the Isles of the Sea.

Minority opinion among historians has favoured Jura and Oronsay, on the grounds that Adamnan states that in Hinba there lay a Great Arm of the Sea (Muirbolc Mar), which is true of Jura (at Lowlandman's Bay) and of Oronsay.

This unnecessary difficulty with Adamnan's Latin script has arisen through translators inserting a comma, thus altering the author's obvious meaning that Hinba was *in* the Great Arm of the Sea – which well describes the position of Eileach an Naoimh within the long arm of the Firth of Lorn.

Equally important has been the academic historians' apparent ignorance of, or lack of research into, classical Gaelic. There is no purpose in seeking a translation of *Hinba* (pronounced Eenba) through Gaelic as spoken today. We must refer to the now obsolete usages of these very old times, which can be found by reference to Edward Dwelly's Dictionary, which is the only reliable glossary. It will be found there that *In* means Island, and that *Ba* (now *Bath*) means the sea, giving *Inba*, Isle of the Sea. Furthermore the unpronounced *H* indicates a plural. The original words would be *Na Hinba*, but the definite article *na* is frequently dropped, which would leave *Hinba*, 'The Isles of the Sea'. This in fact has been their name from time immemorial, although the derivation has not been noticed, is pure and correct Gaelic, and makes complete sense. The relatively new name of Garvellachs, which has been given to the four islands from Garbh Eileach (Rough Island), the name of the largest, should be dropped as a group name in favour of the original.

Eileach an Naoimh appears from afar to be barren rock a mile long. Its south-west end, however, is blessed by a hill of 252 feet, which gives to the south-east side a sheltered seclusion and gentleness in extreme contrast to the cave-punctured cliffs of the Atlantic shore. In springtime cuckoos call from the hollows and little glens of the sheltered side which are bright with bluebells, primroses, marsh marigolds and other wild flowers without number. Larks trill from the rough ground above. Nestling in a green hollow near the landing place are the ruins of the chapel, which show that the walls must have been three feet thick and over twenty long. Close by are the remains of the monastery and outhouses. A little way off to the south is the old turf-covered graveyard, and beyond it at the crest of a swell a single grave where a standing stone slab is roughly incised with a cross. St. Columba's mother Eithne, is declared to be buried here, but that story's only support is its own great age. There is no evidence that Eithne ever moved out of Ireland.

Well away from the monastery are two beehive cells, an underground cell, and an oratory. In 1937 a Ministry of Works party restored one of the beehives, which now stands more than ten feet high. The stones are built inward and overlapping to give a structure like an igloo. These buildings have survived, at least in outline, when so many of St. Columba's original buildings have not, because of their protected site on an uninhabited island. Men living here would long since have used the old stone for new buildings. They are now one of the oldest Christian monuments of the Isles.

The monastery had been set in a haven of quiet, undistracting beauty. To Columba, coming straight from the hectic work of dealing with pagan Pict and colonizing Scot, his short withdrawals to Hinba meant renewal of life and unfailing refreshment. When a man's spirit is burdened or lightened the natural movement of his heart is to lift upwards: nowhere could this be more readily done than on Eileach an Naoimh. Here it would be easy to be still. The island offers what another priest, Gerard Manley Hopkins, sought thirteen centuries later:

> I have desired to go
>   Where springs not fail,
> To fields where flies no sharp and sided hail
>   And a few lilies blow.

And I have asked to be
Where no storms come,
Where the green swell is in the havens dumb,
And out of the swing of the sea.

Perhaps more would have been done in past centuries to protect and preserve these ruins had it been realized earlier that Hinba and the Isles of the Sea were one.

9
IONA

Long before Columba was born, and long before Christ, Iona was a centre of worship by the Druids, whose high motto was *An Fhirinn an aghaidh an t-Saoghal*, 'The Truth against the World'. The island's ancient Gaelic name was Innis nan Druinich, 'The Isle of Druidic Hermits', but we find Adamnan calling it Ioua, one of several spellings (Io, Hia, Hi, and Hii) used by him and Bede and others as if trying to render phonetically a word that certain scholars believe may have been originally Norse (Hia is not Gaelic). There is a traditional story that when Columba's coracle was approaching from the Isles of the Sea the first man to sight Iona cried, 'Chi mi i' – I see her. Columba quickly answered, 'Henceforth we call her I.' This, we must advise, is the incorrigible Gaelic story-teller at work. After Columba's coming, Iona became known everywhere as I-Chaluim-cille, 'Island of St. Columba'. It was known thus for a thousand years until the earlier Ioua, euphoniously changed to Iona, happily crept back into general use.

Every island has its own enthusiasts, and none more than Iona. Its friends number countless thousands, who declare it the most beautiful island of the Hebrides. It would be hard to adjudicate on comparative merits. Every one being different, each can surpass most others on one point or another. Iona has machair, but none to compare with the Uists; delightful sandy bays, but no string of them to match Coll; no woods like Islay, no mountains like Skye. What Iona does have is a purity of light and colour that seems to excel that of other islands. Tiree has equal clarity of air but not of colour, which in Iona invades even her seas. One's first and abiding impression is of greenness and fairness, and of a grace peculiar to the union in one small island of a multiplicity of minor excellencies.

Iona lies a mile off the Ross of Mull. The approach is made from Oban, either by car-ferry to Craignure in Mull, thence by road to Fionnphort at the end of the Ross, where a passenger-ferry plies across the Sound of Iona, or else, in summer only, direct from Oban by steamer.

Iona measures three miles by one. The main mass of its rock is a lower stratum of Torridon sandstone, but the west coast has archaean gneiss. Lying far out from the mountainous body of Mull, Iona must often tantalize Mull-folk, for it rejoices in clear skies when Mull is clouded, and seems to bask in a sun all of its own. Seen of an evening from Fionnphort, as I saw it for the first time, with a sun setting deep orange behind it, Iona looks not at all of this world, but of Tir nan Og.

Iona lies low to the sea, yet is given distinctive outline by the rugged moors of north and south, which dip to a wide central waist-line, and by the fort-like hill of Dun I (pronounced Ee) at the north end. The southern third is entirely uninhabited, its moor peppered with high knolls, purpled by heather and splashed green by bog; all round its coast are cliffs eaten out in a dozen bays, stony-floored bays, mostly with grass at their backs and none with sand until the shores meet the machair of the central belt. The northern third differs from the southern in the absence of cliffs, the abundance of sandy beaches towards the north, and the machairs that lie behind them. The central belt is the island's granary and treasury. Here are the tilled fields and farms, especially on the eastern side and middle part, while over on the west spreads a mile-wide machair, sloping to the one big bay of the island, the Bay at the Back of the Ocean.

Most of Iona's sixteen crofts are spread over the central belt, the rest being on the flat north-eastern coast and near the Village. The permanent population is around 100. Most of the island's fifty houses are concentrated at the Village, twenty of them in a row called The Street. They are built mainly of red granite at the very edge of the road, all with little gardens on the

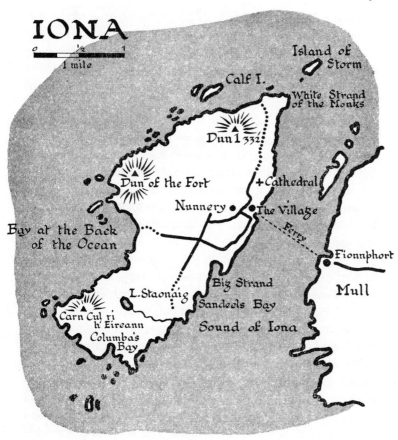

far side. They look straight across the sound to the Ross of
Mull. Three hundred yards north of the Street stands the
cathedral church of St. Mary.

Twenty or thirty thousand people visit Iona every year, yet
the island remains unspoiled. Most of these visitors are day
trippers from Oban or Mull, who walk the half-mile from the
jetty to the cathedral and stray little farther, unaware that the
cathedral buildings are surpassed in excellence by Iona itself.
On a fine day in mid-August, a score of people will visit a

western beach in the course of a day, but I have rarely seen more. In spring I find them deserted. Still more is this true of the moors and cliffs. One need only walk a short distance away from the Village-cathedral axis to be alone. The island's broken surface gives ample scope for the solitude that men still crave as they did in Columba's time.

There are two main roads in Iona. One crosses the island from east to west, the other goes from the Village past the cathedral to the north point. A southward extension of the first holds close alongside a sandy shore, its inland side flanked by crofts, until it ends at the Big Strand, where pink cowries may be gathered at drift level. At ebb tide one may walk the sands a few hundred yards to Sandeels Bay, or else climb a grassy hill and approach the bay from above by a terrace.

Iona has a dozen beaches of white shell-sand, each of different shape and character, and on every coast except the south. Sandeels Bay is very small and extremely beautiful. The terrace sloping in runs below a big cliff thickly covered in ivy, which has given a framework for the intertwining of pink bind-weed and honeysuckle. On top it wears a pink cap of heather, which glows to the morning sun. In August the terrace grows a huge variety of flowers, which thin out at the marram-dunes but extend right into them with harebells and eyebright, and even to the very edge of the beach with clover and bedstraw and tiny-headed daisies and dandelions. The marram grass there produces its very fattest, longest tails of golden seed. Farther back near true grass the seed is absent or negligible.

The bay curves deep, the white sands dazzle, the rocks are silvered and oranged by lichen. Yellow irises and purple thistles fill a broad gully in the crags behind. Here stands a hawthorn tree – the only tree between Sandeels and the south point of the island, and one of the few 'wild' trees of Iona, as distinct from garden trees in the Village or the forty plane trees planted in the grounds of the manse. Close in to the shore are two rocky islets, and far over their backs across the sound stretch mile upon mile of pink granite cliffs edging the Ross of Mull. From these cliffs came the stone for Iona Cathedral and Nunnery, and for many island houses. The quarry lies half a mile north of Fionnphort.

In the early mornings a score of starlings come down to feed on the sands among the seaweed. Apart from two herring gulls, which live here, and the ubiquitous oyster-catchers, there are few birds: the beach is too much frequented by summer visitors. At low tide one may pick one's way south below the rocks to Otter's Cave. The rock pools near it are well worth study: Full of the most delicate and many-hued seaweeds, as delightful to the eye in this extraordinarily clear water as garden rock-plants.

Farther progress down this coast can be made only by way of the cliff-tops and moorland. One place most worthy of exploration is the coast around the marble quarry. It is very hard to find the quarry from above, and easy to make wrong descents through gullies splitting the cliffs. The one certain way is to walk a mile from the main road to the Big Hill of the Strangers, topped by a turf cairn, then descend south by way of a broad grassy gully to the quarry bay. The white marble is streaked by green serpentine, and was used for the great altar in the cathedral church. Although no longer quarried, the stone remains justly famous and is still much used in Celtic ornaments, for its colours are those of Iona's beaches: the white of her shell-sand and the green of her inshore water.

A tiny but remarkable bay, which can be reached only at low tide, lies immediately south of the quarry. Its floor is covered in small pebbles, wonderfully coloured, which have been broken off the surrounding rocks and rolled and polished by the sea: quartz, serpentine, marble, felspar and a variety of semi-precious stones. They include translucent green stones, which are believed to preserve the owner from drowning. Many rock doves may be seen hereabouts. They nest in a cave three-quarters of a mile north up the coast.

Iona has one loch. It lies in the middle of the southern moor and is the source of her water-supply (apart from springs). An easy descent can be made from the loch southwards to Columba's

Bay and the Port of the Coracle. It was here that St. Columba first landed. His ship was of wooden ribs covered by hides, long-shaped and pointed bow and stern. His heart must surely have sunk when he landed on that day in May, and climbing to the ground above surveyed moor and bog stretching far in front, offering no hope of the fertile ground essential to the feeding and sheltering of his company. Not even the heather would be purpling the moor in welcome – for the August scene becomes gay. They must have plodded a cheerless mile till they reached the edge of the central strath. One can imagine the joy with which they first saw it.

The broad beach is heavily covered in big rounded pebbles. Long reefs run seaward, creamed by an everlasting swell. A sloping meadow where cattle graze lifts to the moor behind, and overlooking all to the north-west stands the Carn Cul ri h'Eireann, 'Cairn with its Back to Ireland', 243 feet. It gives the best viewpoint on Iona – better than Dun I, which is the highest point.

Iona, like Mull and Colonsay, and other parts of the west, were in the period A.D. 200 to 250 divided between the Picts of Alban and the Irish King Cairbre Riada. Boundaries were marked (probably by treaty) by twin cairns known as Carn Cul ri h'Alban and Carn Cul ri h'Eireann. The Mull cairns stand to this day in Glen More, a mile or two apart. That Iona was likewise divided is shown by the recorded presence of the two cairns, of which only the Erin cairn survives. The other was probably on Dun I. The tale that the Erin cairn was so named because Columba stood there and turned his back to Ireland, 'in witness of his resolve never again to visit Ireland,' is a romantic fabrication. Columba in fact returned to Ireland to attend a Convention around 575, and probably on other occasions. Likewise it is said that he turned away from Oronsay because Ireland could be seen from the top. If this be true, it is fortunate that he climbed no pre-eminent hill on arriving on Iona – one can see Ireland from them all.

I went to the top of the Cairn with its Back to Ireland during an August heat-wave. The sky was unclouded blue. I should have sworn that the sea was a flat calm had rollers not been crashing over a dozen black skerries that run far out to southward, and whitening more menacingly over submerged reefs that run still farther. When I raised my head I found myself looking straight on to the yellow sands of Kiloran Bay on Colonsay. With binoculars I could even see the croft-houses on the Uragaig platform, and the rock-apron of Eilean nan Ron cleaving the seas towards Islay and Jura. On Iona one does not escape the haunting presence of the Paps, for there they were, as plain as ever.

Beyond Islay and farther to its right were apparent islands where none should have been. I then examined these through binoculars and saw them to be linked: the hill-tops of Ireland. I confirmed the fact by a compass-bearing, which gave 192° true and a map distance of more than eighty miles. Much closer at hand to the south-west, Dubh Artach lighthouse at fifteen miles' range stood clear against the open sea, marking, like a tiny candle, the entrance to Tiree Passage. Tiree and Coll seemed to be one island spreading over a huge arc of horizon. Tiree was so much a sea-level platform that the houses at centre stood clear and square against the sky. Across the Tiree Passage, Mull stretched towards them the arms of its vast western bay, where Staffa sailed as stiff as a man-of-war. Far beyond rose Muck and Eigg and the high hills of Rhum, and beyond these again the Cuillin of Skye, purple-black like a cluster of grapes, appearing at sixty-five miles as one mountain instead of thirty. Ben More of Mull bore a halo of cumulus cloud.

The sea-cliffs encircling the south-west coast are anything but easy of access. Ways can be found with care down to stony creeks. Access to the south-west point is barred by a land-cliff running behind and parallel to the sea-cliff. The way down when found is barely worth the time spent. Reefs and little tidal islands project into tide-streams, which race between them leaving long lines of froth: otherwise this is the least attractive part of Iona's coast-line.

Little more than half a mile of heathery moor separates the south-west point from the central machair. The road to the west across the back of Iona from eastward should be taken slowly, not because it is steep – it rises to seventy feet – but to give ourselves time to see little things that we should overlook if we hurried. Alongside the farms red clover grows in thick matts by the road; sweeter than the white and mingling with mown hay it heavily scents the air. The daisies and dandelions have minute and extremely delicate heads, perhaps through much grazing by sheep and cattle. Near the breast of the hill is a field of barley; silvered by wind it whispers softly and drily, caressing the air with a low sound that communicates mysteriously with our sense of touch. It is important to stop and listen to this most soothing of Iona's voices. The road-side walls are turf-covered and carry a dense bed of harebells. The hill's wide pass, even in summer, offers deep draughts of cool air rising fresh as spring-water from the coast. The island shines, as though its fair fields had an inner light. The broad machair slopes emerald green to the sea, for it carries few flowers, which are cropped by the dairy cattle that graze the whole area. The Bay at the Back of the Ocean is revealed in its entirety.

No marram dunes fringe the machair, whose grass ends abruptly at the beach. Pink gneiss thrusts out near the middle at Otter's Point and divides the bay in two. The left-hand part is shell-sand, the right more rocky and shingly but with sandy patches where waders are at work: oyster-catchers, dunlin, sandpipers, ringed plover and curlew. This right-hand bay is again divided by the long prong of the Island of Protection – a tidal island, grass-backed and rising to a high outer knoll. Sheltering behind it are the coarse shell-sands of Port Ban.

The Island of Protection, which is easily reached at low tide, is one of the best points from which to enjoy the west coast. It sticks out far enough to show the Inner Hebrides from Skye to Islay, and the Irish coast beyond. I last climbed on to its knoll on a day of strong sun, when the sands of Port Ban and the

STAFFA
Fingal's Cave

By George Scott Johnstone

RHUM
and
EIGG
From Moidart

By Tom Weir

Back of the Ocean flashed blinding white like Alpine glaciers, paining unprotected eyes. The sea that day was not the famed Iona green, but the pale, delicate blue of the harebell, and this same shade spread far out towards Coll and Tiree where a great change occurred. Above them hung a long white cumulus cloud of unusual brilliance, which the sea reflected, so that Coll and Tiree appeared to be floating on mercury, buoyed above normal level, dark on the sky yet bathed in pearly light.

This was in August, and nowhere on the sea lay the deep dark blues of June. Below me on both sides were rocky islets, set in water so clear that the tangle deep down could be seen gleaming and glinting as the ribbons turned and twisted on their round stalks, catching and playing with the light.

On the farther, north side of Port Ban, the machair ends against a bigger hill called Dun of the Fort (167 feet). Its top gives a less intimate glimpse of the sea-bed but a better view across the middle strath to Mull and up to Iona's north-west coast. The mile of coast north from Port Ban has no sandy bays. Rough moorland and bog come down to the rocks at the sea's edge until we reach Rory's Creek opposite Calf Island. From here to the most north-easterly rocks facing the Island of Storm, the beaches are continuous shell-sand, narrowly bordered by marram dunes, behind which green turf spreads inland towards the island's highest point, Dun I, 332 feet. The Island of Storm has a most alluring strand but a boat is needed to reach it. The chief delight of this whole north coast is its sea-colouring. The big irregular patches of tangle and sand in deep water give alternating shades of green and mauve or lilac close inshore, blue and purple farther off, and as the eye travels out the general light blue deepens to indigo.

The ascent of Dun I is surprisingly both steep and easy from a farmhouse on its east side. Ten minutes take one to the top. If MacBrayne's steamer is lying off Staffa eight miles northward, one can see the tourists lining the natural causeway on its cliff-face, like a regiment of ants, *en route* to Fingal's Cave. I have been to this summit many times and know that

D

however often I come I shall never tire of its vast sea- and sky-scapes. The southern Hebrides are not seen so clearly as from the Carn Cul ri h'Eireann, but the northern isles more so. The mainland hills throng the horizon as far as eye can reach, in their spring snows like a storm-sea frozen. Best of all in summer is Iona itself: the moors blushed by ling heather, the fields and machair fresh green, the sands shining white upon seas of multitudinous hue. Close below one's feet, the cathedral stands rugged as a great rock, as if left stranded on its meadow by an Ice Age glacier.

No trace has ever been found of Columba's original monastery. The Vikings flattened all. It is thought to have been sited either at the present cathedral or a few hundred yards to its north. The suggestion that it must have been built of wood and a wattle sounds most improbable. In Columba's time and much earlier men built in stone, as we can see from the older and less important monastery of the Isles of the Sea. Columba spent thirty-four years on Iona and died before the altar on 9th June 597. He was then seventy-seven. In centuries to follow Iona was to become a place of pilgrimage for countless thousands of men and women seeking to honour a man who even in his own lifetime was known and recognized as a saint. His true Gaelic name was Calum. This was sometimes rendered Calman, meaning Dove, hence the Latin Columba.

Iona's history became violent in the ninth and tenth centuries, which brought the terrible misfortune of five Viking raids. The first attack came in 795 when the Norsemen plundered and destroyed the abbey buildings. Again this happened in 801, and worst of all in 806, when they murdered sixty-eight monks at Martyr's Bay near the present jetty. Iona had to be temporarily abandoned and a new monastery founded at Kells in Ireland. The next abbot rebuilt the Iona monastery, probably in stone, for it is believed that among the several foundations traceable at the cathedral-site the earliest is one of the ninth century. In 825 came another raid and massacre, followed by a hundred and sixty years of peace until 986, when Norsemen from Dublin fell upon the island and murdered the abbot and fifteen monks on the sands of the northern point. The beach there has since been known as the White Strand of the Monks.

In 1074 the monastery was restored by Queen Margaret (who also built the nearby chapel of St. Oran) not for the Celtic Church but the Roman Catholic Order of Augustine. By the twelfth century the monastery had again become ruinous and around 1200 was completely rebuilt by Somerled's son Reginald of Islay, King of the Isles, this time for the Benedictine Order. The new abbey was dedicated to the Virgin Mary and forms the main part of the present foundations. Reginald in the same year founded the nunnery, which remains to this day as a ruin of exceptional beauty to the south of the cathedral.

Around 1430 a Bishopric of the Isles was created with the bishop's seat in Iona. From 1500 the abbey was raised for sixty years to the dignity of a cathedral, but the Reformation intervened and in 1561 the buildings were dismantled. MacLean of Duart seized Iona in 1574, then it fell to Argyll in 1688. Finally, the Duke of Argyll in 1899 gifted the ruins to the Church of Scotland, who restored the church between 1902 and 1910. The restoration of the monastic buildings was undertaken by the Iona Community in 1938 under the leadership of the Very Reverend Doctor George MacLeod, and was completed in June 1965. It may yet be that St. Columba's prophecy will be fulfilled: 'In Iona of my heart, Iona of my love, instead of monks' voices shall be lowing of cattle, but ere the world come to an end Iona shall be as it was.' That fulfilment means much more than a replacing of stonework.

The Iona Community is a brotherhood of ministers and laymen formed by Dr. MacLeod within the Church of Scotland. The laymen are tradesmen and the ministers are pledged to work in industrial towns and housing estates for a period of two years. The two groups meet every summer at their headquarters on Iona. They have rebuilt the once ruined monastery, their present and future spiritual home; now their principal mission is 'to find new ways of life and witness that will bridge the gap between industrial men in Scotland and the Church'.

The cathedral appears best of·all when seen in sunlight from north or south of west. Its background is then the Sound of Iona, the far distant Paps of Jura, and the bulky surge of Ben More in Mull. Sun is needed to bring out the colour and sparkle of the stone, which combines rose-hued granite with a rock as dark green as a shag, and with a creamy sandstone thought to come from Carsaig on the Ross of Mull. The contrasting stones set each other off. The pink granite would seem dull in so great a mass if unrelieved. At the same time the cathedral is simple in plan and small enough to befit Iona. The church is cruciform with a short square tower. The adjoining cloisters, refectory, chapter house, infirmary (now a museum), and Michael chapel have all recently been restored, and the whole, inside and out, has been done with taste and fine discrimination by the architect, Mr. Ian Lindsay, and the Iona Community.

There are three points of minor detail to regret. In the south transept the white marble effigies of the eighth Duke of Argyll and his lady appear monstrously large in relation to the size of the church. They should be removed to Westminster Abbey. In the chapel of the north transept there hangs on a dark wall a small but superb painting of the crucified Christ by De Maestre, which deserves to be artificially lit. In the Michael chapel, the east wall bears a green dragon and sword-bearing hand, which are crudely made, garishly painted, and offensive to eyes made sensitive to beauty by all else in Iona.

In the cloisters there now stands a remarkable bronze sculpture of the Virgin. It represents in powerful symbolism the descent of the Spirit to embrace Man and the Cosmos. On its back it bears this inscription: 'I, Jacob Lipchitz, a Jew faithful to the faith of my fathers, have made this Virgin for a good understanding among all the people of the earth. That the Spirit may reign.'

Close beside the west door of the church stands the tall cross of St. Martin. The common dating of it to the tenth century is doubtful, for the Isles were under Norse rule. It more probably belongs to the twelfth century at earliest. Splendid though it is, it cannot match the beauty of the Kildalton Cross; these two are the only Celtic crosses with encircling 'glory' still standing in Scotland. Behind the cross and to the left of the west door stands the tiny chapel of St. Columba, where an undying light now burns. The light shines through a little window visible from the Sound of Iona and will be marked henceforth on Admiralty charts.

Farther off to the south-west is St. Oran's Chapel and the burial-place of the kings, called the Reilig Orain. The chapel is of pink granite, very small within and white-walled. Behind the sandstone altar a Celtic cross flashes silver from the wall when the door is opened. On a table to one side are two verses by John Boyle O'Reilly. They speak also for St. Oran:

> The Infinite always is silent:
> It is only the finite speaks,
> Our words are the idle wavecaps
> On the deep that never breaks.
>
> We may question with wands of science,
> Explain, decide, and discuss;
> But only in meditation
> The Mystery speaks to us.

Outside in the grounds of the Reilig Orain (Graveyard of Oran) are buried sixty kings. When Donald Monro, the Dean of the Isles, visited Iona in 1549 he reported that there were three tombs like small chapels in the Reilig Orain. They were engraved *Tumulus Regum Scotiae, Tumulus Regum Hiberniae,* and *Tumulus Regum Norwegiae,* wherein were buried forty-eight kings of Scotland, four of Ireland, and eight of Norway. The Scottish kings included Kenneth MacAlpin, the first of a united Scotland and Pictland, and MacBeth and Duncan. Nearby lie Reginald of Islay, and several of his direct descendants, the Kings and Lords of the Isles, and many Highland chiefs. These tombs have long since disappeared. In outward appearance the Reilig Orain is just an ancient graveyard.

The thirteenth-century Nunnery, which lies immediately behind the village, is one of the most beautiful ruins of Scotland. The stonework is similar to that of the cathedral in its combination of pink, black and creamy rock. Several pointed gables still stand, the connecting walls being here low and there high, forming a pleasing pattern. The floors are of cut grass and the ruins kept as a natural rock-garden. The lowest walls are only a foot high, bearing on top short turf from which spring harebells, eyebright, roses, and innumerable other wild flowers. In corners bloom the tall red flowers of the sidalcea. From every crevice of the pink granite, which is lovely in itself, grow pale blue ivy-leaved toad-flax, bird's-foot trefoil, the delicate lady's bedstraw and abundance of others.

Despite the visitors who flood in during the summer from all parts of the world, the island's life goes quietly on in the background, as though the cathedral did not exist. The population has dropped from 500 in 1842 to its present 100-odd largely through emigration to America and the consolidation of tiny crofts into larger units. There is only one fisherman, and any lobster-fishing is done by men from Mallaig. Thus the principal occupation is still crofting. The island's stock amounts to some 1,500 sheep, 180 cattle and 600 hens. But the main money-earner for many people is the tourist trade. The houses on the Village Street are of two or three rooms and kitchen on the ground floor, and some of two or three upstairs. In summer many people move into garden huts to make room for visitors. There are two hotels. Children get their primary education at the local school and for their secondary move to Oban and Tobermory. The nearest doctor and nurse are six miles away at Bunessan on the Ross of Mull.

When people come to know Iona, they inevitably grow to love it for its own sake. The long history of the cathedral, with its tale of Druids, of Columba's arrival, of his spiritual regeneration of Pictland and Scotland, of Viking plunder and

massacre, of gradual restoration by the Church of Scotland –
all these things then fall into perspective and are not only what
men think of when they think of Iona. For it is the island itself
that has won their regard as it won Columba's.

On summer nights, about 9.30 p.m., I used to walk the track
over the island past the scented clover and hay, stop briefly to
hear the barley whisper, then on to the western machair where
a lonely peewit was always calling and falling out of the sky.
Behind me, the mountains of Mull would crouch black and for-
bidding, but in front the open sea would stretch shining white
to the earth's rim. The sea would be white in fine weather
regardless of violent sky colours or the state of the moon. But
however much a layered sky flamed or faded through orange
and lemon to the palest of greens and to zenith blue, the green
band would always be there and be wide. It was this band that
gave the white light to the sea. The inshore islands, where sea-
gulls were crying incessantly, stood black upon it. Close by the
coast the white water livened to a rippled silver between the
islands, streaming in zigzag channels between the cliffs of the
Isle of Protection and the Dun's dark tower. That was Iona
when I last saw it. And that and a multitude of its other facets
are what one remembers.

MULL

MULL is shaped like a dog, crouched and barking towards the Atlantic, complete with head, body, legs and tail. Three big sea-lochs on the west coast carve the shape. Loch Tuath is the open mouth, Loch na Keal cuts in to the neck, and Loch Scridain separates the foreleg of Ardmeanach from the hindleg of the Ross. On the south coast Loch Buie gives the tail. The island lies in the Firth of Lorn, close in to the mainland coast of Morvern, from which the Sound of Mull separates it by a strait twenty miles long by one and a half to three miles wide. Oban lies seven miles east.

Mull is twenty-five miles long from north to south. Breadth varies from three miles at the neck to twenty at the body. In size it ranks next to Skye as the second largest of the Inner Hebrides. The three main parts have distinct character. The body is mountainous, rising to 3,169 feet at Ben More. The head is gentler and lower country of wide moors, grooved by the long shallow valley of Aros. The hindleg of the Ross is treeless and bare as befits a seaward peninsula, but hilly with sheltered pockets. The climate is extremely mild and rainfall high at eighty to ninety inches. The north and south-west are drier and windier, being farther from the big hills and more exposed.

It is remarkable how few inland lochs there are on Mull – only ten of any size – and how fast drying is the ground despite the rainfall. The underlying rock is Tertiary basalt, which weathers into terraces that give their outstanding horizontal stratification to western hill-slopes. The red granite at the butt of the Ross is only four miles square. Over Mull as a whole, the

ground thus given is more suited for grazing than crops, is
naturally grassy, potentially most fertile (as it was in the past)
and should support a large cattle-stock, which can be out-
wintered in this mild climate with less imported fodder than
most Highland areas require. The high fertility wasted away
last century after the large-scale and sudden move to sheep-
farming, with attendant ills like rough-grass burning – grass
that cattle should have eaten. This policy ruined the land and
with other misfortunes lost Mull 85 per cent of her human
population.

If a visit be made to Mull after one to the Outer Hebrides, a
most startling double impression is made – of fertility amount-
ing to lushness on the one hand, and of emptiness on the other.
If approach is made instead from Oban, either by car-ferry to
Craignure in central Mull, or by steamer to Tobermory in the
north, the first impression is of landscape typically south Highland. This eastern side facing the Sound has a long but narrow
coastal plain of moorland and farmland, with upper hill-slopes
of coarse grass. There is little heather. The natural woods are
of oak, birch and ash, the planted of pine and larch. Indenta-
tions along the coast are shallow, and only the narrow sound is
there to remind us that this is a Hebridean island. The open
west tells a different story, and so does Tobermory at the
north.

Tobermory is the finest small town of the Hebrides, and one
of the safest anchorages. Its foremost asset is Calve Island,
which guards the bay's mouth. The harbour is gracefully
shaped facing east. Steep hill-slopes encircle it and fall to the
water's edge. Sycamores wood the slopes and houses ring the
bay high up, but the main town forms an arc at sea-level. In
1788 the British Fisheries Society tried to develop the port, but
all that remains of the effort are good stone houses on the main
street. They have two or three storeys with pointed attic
windows. The walls are painted white, black, pink or cream,
with windows picked out in different colour. Across the Sound
of Mull are the low Morvern hills, green and wooded. The

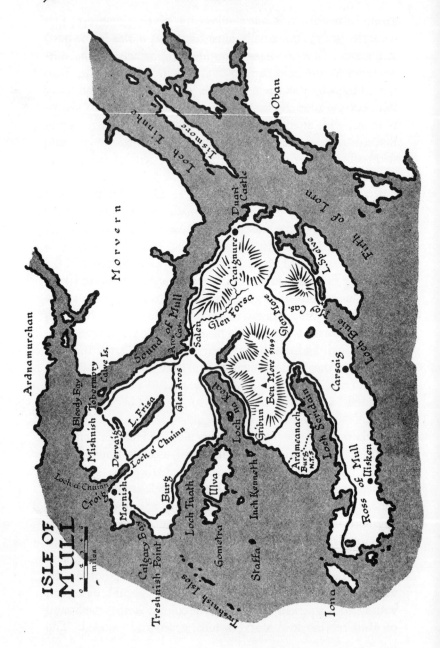

ISLE OF
MULL

miles
0 1 2 3 4 5

Ardnamurchan

Morvern

Loch Linnhe

Lismore

Oban

Duart Castle

Firth of Lorn

Aros Cas.

Scaur of Mull

Craignure

Glen Forsa

Glen More

Loy Cas.

L. Spelve

Loch Buie

Salen

Ben More 3169

Gribun

Loch na Keal

Glen Aros

Loch á Chuinn

L. Frisa

Dervaig

Mishnish

Tobermory

Calve Is.

Bloody Bay

Loch á Chuian

Croig

Mornish

Calgary Bay

Treshnish Point

Burg

Loch Tuath

Gometra

Ulva

Staffa

Treshnish Isles

Inch Kenneth

Ardmeanach
Burg
N.T.S.

Loch Scridain

Carsaig

Ross of Mull

Uisken

Iona

sound sparkles blue, and the harbour scene is enlivened in summer by many yachts and small boats riding at anchor. Although so well sheltered, the town has an oceanic flavour.

Tobermory Bay has a famed skeleton in its cupboard. After the defeat of the Spanish Armada in 1588, the *Almirante de Florencia* put into the bay and anchored there for several weeks. MacLean of Duart, then feuding with kinsmen, borrowed a hundred Spanish soldiers to ravage Coll. This delay to dabble unwisely in local politics cost the Spaniards dear. MacLean demanded blackmail money from the galleon's captain, and when this was refused sent two men aboard to fire the magazine. The galleon blew up and sank. She went down in eleven fathoms about eighty yards offshore with three hundred and. fifty officers and men. She was believed to hold a treasure of £300,000 and many attempts have been made to salvage it, but without success. The first big operation was in 1912, when the galleon was found to be covered by thirty feet of clay. The last was by the Duke of Argyll in 1955. The only items recovered have been a few silver goblets, pieces of eight, gold chain, brass cannon, and other small objects.

A short way to the north of Tobermory is Bloody Bay, so named from a fierce sea-battle between John, the last Lord of the Isles, and his son Angus, who had been infuriated by his father's 'improvident grants of land to Macleans, Macleods, Macneills, and other tribes'. Angus won after great loss of life and the incident weakened the clan.

The population of Tobermory is 634, or half of what it was last century, and makes northern Mull (from the neck up) the most populous part of the island. A road encircles the coast omitting the big northern point of Mishnish, and another drives over the central moors from Salen to Dervaig on the north.

The road south from Tobermory to Salen shows eastern Mull at its best. The high ground above Tobermory gives long vistas down the sound to the mountains of Lorn, which can purple even heavy clouds above them. The sound shines and glints like a python, steely but soft. Farms, fields and crofts look small, for the hills crowd to the sea heavily wooded with conifers. Buzzards, which thrive on woodland voles, perch on the telegraph poles. In August, the roadsides are bright with heather.

Salen has a wide bay facing east to Morvern. The wooded village lies at the south end; on a craggy knoll at the north end stand the ruins of Aros Castle, last used in 1608 when Lord Ochiltree kidnapped the Hebridean chiefs aboard his ship *Moon*. The castle looks far down the Sound of Mull to Ben Cruachan. From here one can see well the division of Mull by its neck, the south brownly mountainous, the north gentler and greener.

Glen Aros running inland from Salen Bay is heavily forested to the head of Loch Frisa. The plantation dates from 1925. Pine and spruce crowd close and will look much better in future years when thinned and matured. The huge moors above it are bare and open, but for all their greenness and freedom from heather, surprisingly empty. From the watershed, one looks down a long low strath to Dervaig at the head of a narrow sea-loch.

The other road over the moors from Tobermory to Dervaig is very different, for it crosses the grain of the country. The first long rise leads over the lip of a pass to the three Mishnish lochs. The moors here are much rougher, golden bronze in August from a wiry grass that in spring is soft green and silvery where the wind blows. I have crossed both these moors in the height of summer and seen no livestock. There are few birds of prey, yet not even larks rejoice on the moors. But Mull abounds in hoodie crows, which presumably kill small birds.

The road corkscrews through the hills down to Dervaig, which is Mull's most beautiful village and the largest in the north. Its forty houses are grouped among woods at the head of Loch a' Chuinn. Heather glows richly pink on the hill-slopes rising close behind. The great Mishnish headland to the north is by contrast the bleakest moor and windiest part of Mull.

It gives a most wonderful view of the sun setting behind Coll and Tiree.

Less than three miles farther up Loch a' Chuinn, at Croig on the Mornish headland, is the finest sea-view on the island. Croig lies in a half-mile inlet of the north coast. In the old days, cattle from the outer isles were landed there and driven through Mull to be embarked for the mainland at Grass Point south of Craignure. Across a foreground of tiny islets, framed by the outer bay, the hills of Rhum, Eigg, Canna and the Cuillin heave out of the sea unexpectedly close and clear. They tower, mountains of the sea rather than isles of the low order to south and west. Immediately ahead, the mainland thrusts out almost to our own line of longitude its most westerly point of Ardna-murchan (meaning Point of the Great Ocean), bearing its tall lighthouse on the last rocks.

On the south-west side of this Mornish headland, Calgary Bay gives the first and only shell-sand to the west coast, to Mull its most famous beach, and to Canada the name of a city. The bay is a mile and a half deep with bold outer bluffs at the Treshnish and Mornish headlands. The white sands, un-marked by rock, curve in to a sweep of machair ringed by wooded hill-slopes. The trees are wind-blasted sycamore and rowan, leafed only at the crown, yet the bay is green and gay in the sun.

The entire west coast south from Calgary is coastal landscape on the grand scale. The great sea-lochs bite deeply in, the mountains swell high at centre, cliffs interrupt the coast-line, and the seaward views across scattered islands change from headland to headland. The road is narrow but quiet even in August. The most beautiful stretch of all is along the starling-infested shores of Loch Tuath, between the Treshnish headland and the island of Ulva. In front of the roadside oak and hazel are masses of meadowsweet and iris; small stone cottages appear at intervals, their garden hedges bearing the most luxuriant fuchsia, weighted with red and purple blossom. At one point the Eas Fors burn crosses under the road, tumbling to either side in splendid waterfalls, and finally plunging in one huge bound to the sea.

If Croig gives the most dramatic sea-view in Mull, Dun Asgain above Loch Tuath gives the best one of Mull itself. Half a mile from Burg village towards the sea, Dun Asgain perches on a craggy headland. The walls of red-brown stone are low and circular: it may once have been a galleried dun or broch. When I went there the waters spread green, blue and purple to Ulva – the large purple areas silvered by speeding clouds, and the whole surface flecked lightly by white horses. The range of Ben More filled the head of Loch Tuath. The broad but finely pointed peaks were also gently purpled, per-haps by shadow cast on their screes, for all were dappled by sun and cloud. Iona basked as usual – even the cathedral was clear to the eye at fifteen miles. Clearer still were the isles of the great western bay: Ulva, Inch Kenneth, Little Colonsay and the Treshnish group.

The hill-flanks of Ulva are horizontally stratified, as are Mull's, but on this northern side are monotonously greened by bracken. The south side carries a big bay filled with islets. The east end has flat ground where hayfields spread, and is wooded around Ulva House. Access may be had if granted by the owner, by means of her own ferry.

The island repeats in miniature the history of Mull. Its popu-lation of 1837 was over 600 and is now only a dozen. In the old days every man had a boat of his own for fishing, now the only boats are the owner's. The people had fathered men like David Livingstone and Lachlan Macquarrie, 'the father of Australia', but the people were cleared for sheep. And the land, which was cattle country ranking with the best in the Highlands, became a jungle of bracken, which in gullies will grow as high as a cow's head. Just before the bracken-plague strikes each spring, the hill-slopes are alight with wild flowers. During the last twenty years the owner, Lady Congleton, has cut a thousand acres of bracken; the island now carries 1,200 sheep and 40 head of cattle bred to championship standard.

South of Ulva, Loch na Keal (Loch of the Cliffs) runs in to the neck of Mull. The slopes of Ben More fall gently to long strips of flat ground by the farther shore, where big banks of whin splash the green with springtime gold. The flats spread at the loch's head to the woods of Gruline estate, but towards the outer loch narrow to a mere ledge rounding the Creag Mhor headland, just wide enough to carry the road between the sea's edge and eight-hundred-foot cliffs. The cliffs are loose. Notices warn the traveller of falling stones, which after heavy rain litter the road.

Round the corner, opposite the island of Inch Kenneth, the flats spread wide again at Gribun, where there is a village of half a dozen houses, but still with cliffs above. Between the first two cottages, a gigantic boulder surrounded by a stone wall is poised on the east side of the road. Last century a young couple came to live here on their wedding night. A violent storm blew up. The boulder fell from the cliff and crushed both house and occupants, who were never seen again.

On the Gribun flats stands the farm of Balmeanach. On the shore less than a mile to its south lies Mackinnon's Cave, even bigger and better than the notorious cave of Eigg, and much longer than Fingal's. It is reached from the cliff-top at the southernmost extremity of the farm-fields, where a small iron gate opens on to a track down and across steep, grassy and muddy slopes. Low tide is needed for entry to the cave, which is hidden until one passes a waterfall tumbling over the cliff-face, and is opposite the south edge of a line of ebb-tide islets.

The entrance is huge. The roof is 100 feet at highest, and the length 200 yards. A torch is needed for exploration. A long passage on pebble leads into the main chamber, which has a floor of sand. A low wall is crossed to a second chamber, which marks the half-way point. The cave then turns sharp right and runs a hundred yards to the inmost chamber, where stalactites hang from a red roof.

The great Ardmeanach headland divides Loch na Keal from Loch Scridain, which runs nine miles into Mull to separate the

Ross. Ardmeanach is a high moor buttressed by great sea-cliffs. Mackinnon's Cave bores into its north shore, but the western butt has a rock feature still more surprising. There is here a long coastal strip named 'The Wilderness' – which probably gave name to Loch Scridain (Loch of the Screes) – a wilderness of stone blocks fallen from cliffs rising twelve hundred feet from the sea. Near its south end a fossil tree forty feet tall is implanted on the cliff-face. The original tree was engulfed by a lava flow of the Miocene age, possibly fifty million years ago, when the Tertiary basalt of the present cliff was formed. The ground belongs to the National Trust for Scotland but access is hard. The approach road from Loch Scridain to Burg cottage is the worst in Mull, twisting, rocky, muddy, and steep for four miles. A walk of more than two miles is then needed to reach the tree over exceedingly rough ground, where, to turn a but-tress projecting seaward, arrival must be timed for low-water.

Ben More is easily climbed from Dishig on Loch na Keal. An ascent in fine weather reveals the isles from Ireland to the Outer Hebrides, and the Highlands over vast tracts beyond naming. Around the summit, clouds boil up with extreme rapidity: map and compass are essential, but the compass should be read well away from the cairn, which is magnetic.

From Loch Scridain's head, Glen More gives a long low pass through central Mull to Loch Spelve on the Firth of Lorn. The glen once formed the boundary between the kingdoms of the Picts and Scots. To its north, on the hill-top of Mam Clachaig, is a cairn called Carn Cul ri h'Alban (Cairn with its Back to Alban); to its south is the counterpart, Carn Cul ri h'Eireann. These are both marked in Blau's map. The glen is a typically bare Highland defile, wooded on the descent to Loch Spelve, where the MacLeans of Duart harboured their war-galleys. The coast here is open country, although so far inland, but immediately westward a narrow glen bearing a forested loch cuts through the hills to Lochbuie village on the south coast.

Loch Buie is a bay open to the south-west. Three miles long

by two wide, its rocky coast-line, pierced by caves, runs out on either hand to far-off headlands. The estate at its head was once known as the 'Garden of Mull'. Much of the lower land has been sold to the Forestry Commission, and the uplands leased to the Department of Agriculture. The 'big estate' appearance prevails. Broad hayfields slope gently to the sea. Although the ground is farmed the houses are mostly residential, well-painted and clean. Their gardens are full of flowers, big-headed hydrangeas being an August feature. A long spit divides the bay. Above the grey sands of the eastern half stands Moy Castle. Square, battlemented, and ivy-covered, it remains in a good state of preservation. Lochbuie House behind it is thickly wooded but open to the sea.

Although Lochbuie passed from the MacLeans last century, they are still established farther up the coast at Duart Point, facing Loch Linnhe. The castle was restored from its ruinous state in 1912. The present chief is the twenty-seventh of his line, Sir Charles Hector Fitzroy MacLean, who is also the Chief Scout. He opens the castle to the public. 'Duart' is from the Gaelic Dhu Ard, meaning Black Height, describing the crag upon which the castle stands high over the sea. The steamers and car-ferry from Oban pass close under it.

The MacLeans in former days also had the Ross of Mull, but the Campbell's seized it in the seventeenth century and the Duke of Argyll still owns. The peninsula is bare and windy like the Rhinns of Islay, most of it hilly moorland grazed by deer and hunted by eagle and buzzard, yet with sheltered pockets where trees, grass and crops grow well. Its coast-line is by far the most interesting in Mull: continuous rock, not only extremely varied in kind from granite to chalk, but beautifully coloured, fragmented by the sea into islets and scooped out into bays innumerable, several of which have fine sand. It is best to find these delights by exploring unguided, for the pleasure of surprise is then greater. A few may be mentioned to whet the appetite.

Six miles from Fionnphort is the chief village of Bunessan,

snug in a hollow with good shops and hotels and a harbour on the north coast. Fishing boats call in from the mainland ports: from Mull no fishing is now done save for the setting of lobster creels when crofting allows time. Bunessan is the best centre for exploring the Ross, and Iona too when no accommodation can be had there.

The longest day's work is the exploration of the Carsaig Arches. At the east end of the Ross, the peninsula is crossed from north to south by a road over grassy moorland, falling steeply through woods to Carsaig Bay. The soil here is perhaps the richest in Mull, the farms and fields and big houses all look most prosperous. The arches lie three and a half miles west at Malcolm's Point, and two hours will be needed to reach them. The shore is too rough for sandshoes, and boots should be worn. One must traverse grass slopes, which fall steeply from an unbroken line of cliffs to the sea, but sometimes walk the stony shore, where the way is occasionally made easy at ebb-tide by long sandstone shelves.

My own journey to Malcolm's Point was made at the tail of a procession of twenty white he-goats. They had the largest horns I have ever seen on goat, barring Alpine ibex. Near Malcolm's Point, which is marked from afar only by a number of high rocky islets, the goats climbed high, and I came on their mates, a herd of twenty she-goats with young. I turned aside to examine the islets from a natural rock-quay. The water was deep. On one of the barnacled islets, which was no bigger than eight feet by three, stood three marooned nannies and four kids. The sun shone through their white hair, clothing them in light. They had barely standing room and with the tide coming in wore a woeful expression of consternation and helplessness – as humans would too on that icy brink. I could not wait to see what became of them; presumably goats can swim.

The arches lie on the farther side of the point. The cliffs above drop seven hundred and fifty feet vertically in columnar basalt. From their base, a grass headland juts steeply down and seaward, finally plunging a hundred feet sheer, still columnar.

This headland is pierced right through by a sea-bore, forming a perfect arch sixty feet high and wide. The rock-columns are intersected by ledges where a host of shags stand with their brown young.

I could not see beyond the arch, and to the shags' annoyance had to cross over it by a goat-track under the lip of the hundred-foot cliff. Great care was needed lest the ledge might be weak at some point. At the far side the cliff fell sheer to a sea-filled cauldron. Beyond rose a great spire, chisel-bladed on top and pierced below by a second arch, shaped high and narrow like a tall cathedral window. Every ledge bore shags. Behind stretched a huge table of isolated rock, the Leac nan Leum (the Slab of the Leap).

A full day from morning to evening should be allowed for this excursion, if leisure be desired. Two shorter ones from Bunessan are south to Uisken or west to Erraid. Uisken has a wide bay of grey sand with many islets offshore. A heavy crop of meadow cranesbill spreads blue over the fringing grass. At the south-west end of the Ross lies Erraid, the most pleasing of Mull's many islands, not counting Iona. David Balfour of *Kidnapped* was wrecked on its west coast at Traigh Geal (White Strand), now known as Balfour Bay, and thought himself marooned till he found the east strand that makes it a tidal island. The sands dry out for two hours on either side of low water, when access can be had from the Ross coast.

Weeks could be spent on Erraid, although it is only a mile square, exploring the coast and its ring of islets. The interior is entirely hilly, rocky and heathery, but the heather is short and grass grows in the glens. The owner keeps livestock but sheep and cattle from two farms on Mull also cross the strand to graze. On the north side stands a row of eight granite cottages and behind them a couple of older houses, in one of which Robert Louis Stevenson is said to have written *Kidnapped*. His father and uncle built Skerryvore and Dubh Artach lighthouses, and the granite cottages for the keepers, who are now housed at Oban.

From the west end of the row, a path climbs to the summit of Cnoc Mor, 246 feet, where there is a round iron shed called the 'Observatory', formerly used to exchange signals with Skerryvore and Dubh Artach. Balfour Bay to the south-west rivals Calgary in the excellence of its white sand, and is much more secluded. The water has Iona's pure green, and the cliffs walling its sides are pink granite. This superb rock used to be quarried both on Erraid and at Tormore, half a mile north of Fionnphort, and was used to build Iona Cathedral, the Albert Memorial, the piers of Blackfriar's Bridge, and the lighthouses of Skerryvore and Dubh Artach. At the back of Balfour Bay, a long meadow is covered with white grass of Parnassus, hare-bells and eyebright, and dips shoreward to a bank packed with blue pansies. On the flat hill-tops there is much white heather.

Thrusting into the main eastern strand, the great bay of Erraid Sound is studded with islands like a castle door with nails. They shelter it from the south, and farther out are thirty more islets of the Torran Rocks. As seen from the Erraid cliff-tops, the sands at the bottom shine green as phosphorous through clear water free of weed. At the northern entrance to the sound, the owner stretches a salmon net between the tele-graph poles on either side.

One of the most famous islands of Mull is uninhabited Staffa, lying seven miles off the west coast. The name is Norse, mean-ing Stave Island. (Norsemen built their stave houses with tree-logs set vertical like the columnar basalt). At the north-east end Staffa shelves up from the sea, but elsewhere jumps up to 50 feet in cliffs, rising at the south to 135 feet. The island is less than a mile long by a third of a mile wide. Giant hexagonal columns of basalt lift up from a tufa basement. The cliffs are riddled by caves. The better known are Clamshell Cave, forty-three yards deep, on the south-east shore in front of the Great Causeway, where a columnar stack emerges from the sea at the ebb; the Boat and Cormorant caves at the south-west; and, at the Great Face at the south point, Fingal's Cave, which is seventy-six yards deep and sixty-six feet high.

The columns of black pillars at Fingal's Cave are almost perfectly symmetrical. On the left-hand wall they rise to forty feet. Staffa is one of Scotland's many geological freaks, and Fingal's Cave unique of its kind. In summer, steamer trips are run from Oban, and motor-boat trips from Iona and Ulva in calm weather. On such occasions the true character and atmosphere of Fingal's Cave are lost. It becomes a show-piece. To know Staffa one must go alone.

The Treshnish Isles, which lie four miles to the north-west of Staffa, are a string of eight islets and a score of skerries. Tiny as they are, they are most important to wild life, and once gave summer grazing for cattle. Sheep are still grazed on Lunga, the largest island at the centre. The four principal islets from north to south are Cairn na Burgh Mor, Fladda, Lunga and Bac Mor or Dutchman's Cap.

Cairn na Burgh Mor has the ruins of a castle, dating from the Lords of the Isles. The MacLeans of Duart were the keepers, and during a clan feud seized the MacLean of Lochbuie, imprisoned him in the castle, and to make sure that he would have no heir gave him the ugliest woman in Mull as servant. Lochbuie rose to that challenge and gave her a son. Mother and child both escaped. In later years the son won back his patrimony.

Half a mile south, Fladda used to be occupied in summer by a lobster-fisherman, whose hut has lain empty since the last war. Lunga, a mile farther south, was once permanently inhabited. The ruins of the houses are still used by shepherds when they come to shear sheep. The island is a volcanic mound, a mile long by four hundred yards wide, rising to 337 feet. All the others to the north are flat-topped, as Lunga is too in its south half, with vertical sides of basalt resting on lava platforms. On these platforms, the grey Atlantic seal hauls out and breeds. The Treshnish stock amounts to more than 300 cow-seals, and 140 calves have been counted on Lunga's south shore. The rich green grass above attracts many winter visitors: hundreds of blackbirds and thrushes, starlings and peewits, and a thousand head of barnacle geese. The nesting sea-birds are multitudes of auks, fulmars, manx-shearwaters, kittiwakes and storm-petrels.

Two mile south of Lunga, the Dutchman's Cap is by its shape the best known of the group. It is the cone of an old volcano, 284 feet high. The wide brim is its lava platform.

Mull was originally granted by the Donald Lords of the Isles to the MacLeans. Clan feuding of the sixteenth century weakened them, allowing Campbell of Argyll to break the power of both. Sheep came, the cattle went, the kelp industry failed and potato famine gave the *coup de grâce*. The population plummeted from 10,600 to its present 2,230, but contributing factors have been the devastation to life and work caused by the First World War, and later the natural desire to share, by emigration, in rising standards of living. The estates of Mull have been frequently changing hands, and most of the owners are English.

Mull's only resource is its own good land. The stock held is approximately 340 dairy cattle, 4,400 beef cattle (the potential is 22,000), and 80,700 sheep. These are spread over 160 crofts and half as many farms. Livestock production has increased by 50 per cent in the last twenty-five years, and autumn exports require the chartering of special ships. The farmers are comparatively prosperous but crofting appears to be difficult.

Fishing never amounted to much in Mull, and there seems little likelihood of any revival except on a small scale. At Tobermory, only a few men send salmon, lobsters and whelks to London. A systematic organization of lobster-fishing in the Ross of Mull could provide a living for several families.

There are twelve primary schools on the island, with some dozen pupils in each, save at Tobermory, which has 120 pupils up to third year secondary standard, after which they go to Oban. English has supplanted Gaelic, which less than a third of the children speak. When parents are bilingual their children tend to use English, and less Gaelic is now used in Mull than in other islands.

Tourism is the principal industry at Tobermory, which has three good hotels, several boarding-houses and numerous private houses that 'take people in', a golf course, and motor-boats for cruising along the mainland coast. Elsewhere it provides many inhabitants with a useful income, notably at Bunessan, but all is on a small scale. It is astonishing how little Mull is prepared for the tourist, although so near to the mainland, and easy of access. The opening of the car-ferry service to Craignure in 1964 brought in four times as many car-owners as in previous years. But the basic needs for accommodation of a tourist influx have not been met.

The Forestry Commission has planted large areas of central Mull, giving employment, especially at Salen, to forty or fifty workers of both sexes. The Commission plan before 1970 to export 8,000 tons of timber a year to the new pulp mill at Fort William. The Department of Agriculture has many holdings in all three parts of the island, gives employment to shepherds, and hires equipment to crofters.

Mull farmers advise that the cure for the island's problem of under-employment and depopulation is expansion of cattle-breeding. Factors against this are, first, the large government purchases of Argentine beef, with which the Scottish cattle-breeder cannot compete; second, the relatively small subsidy given to cattle-breeding; and third, the too large possession of land by absentee landowners, who hold it, not as one might imagine as sporting ground, for little stalking and grouse-shooting are done nowadays, but as holiday wilderness. Nothing is done with it to help the land or employ people. The emptiness of the land is only too obvious to the eye. There is great scope for development by reclamation of moorland and by modern farming methods.

Potentially green acres lie derelict while there is congestion over on Lewis, where men work hard on too little ground. An evolution of government thought and action could resolve the paradox by giving the land back to the Celt, perhaps to the Outer Islesman, whose croft is too small to be economically viable, using a Land Bank to lend him capital, and giving his beef product a market at the expense of Argentinian.

The people of Mull have much to learn from the Skyemen, who now know how to get an income from tourism, and from Outer Islesmen, whose weaving and lobster-fishing give a livelihood. The people of Mull not only need government action, but have to learn how to help themselves by creating subsidiary industries. They have become aware of this truth, and plan at Aros a residential training centre where outdoor activities of many kinds would be taught, from boat-building, sailing and seamanship to hill-farming and agriculture. In 1966, an airstrip was made close to Glen Forsa House Hotel to provide the new hospital at Salen with an air-ambulance service. Next year this was followed by a once-daily passenger service from Glasgow operated in summer by Benmore Flights Ltd. Flying time from Glasgow is 55 minutes, including a stop at Oban. A new luxury hotel is to be opened at Craignure in 1970. These and other plans show that hope for Mull's regeneration is alive.

COLL

THE passage out to Coll from Oban goes fifty-eight miles round the north end of Mull – a voyage unfolding a panorama of wide-away islands and mountains: Loch Sunart leading the eye far inland to the mountains of Ardgour; Rhum, Eigg, Canna and Skye rising dark behind the Ardnamurchan lighthouse; the Treshnish Isles close to the south, standing clear against the dim Mull hills; and far off in the background, but still with us, unmistakably, the Paps of Jura. In such splendid company, Coll looks dull company, low but rugged on the west horizon.

On close approach it looks more positively daunting – bare rock and heather in a long straight line of twelve miles without a single redeeming feature. Even when Loch Eatharna (Loch of the Small Fishing Boats) comes into view, and the steamer turns suddenly to round the guiding harbour buoy, Arinagour village stands close and grim around a bay without colour, apart from one green field. The hinterland is all grey and dull brown. A ferry takes one ashore.

Coll has several likenesses to Colonsay, and this east coast is one of them. Another is the people, a friendly, helpful, smiling people, whom it is good for any man to meet. A third is the island's extraordinary beauty.

Coll is shaped like a sea-trout, complete with tail, nose to the north-east. Standing two or three hundred feet high out of the sea, and three or four miles wide, the skeleton is archaean gneiss, the flesh peat, and the skin heather. But the soft belly facing west is shell-sand and machair. Gneiss does not break up into well-drained soil like the basalt of Mull. Its characteristic form is like the low rocky hills of Sutherland, bespattered with lochs. The same rock in Lewis carries boulder-clay under the peat, but not here. Coll is made inhabitable because a full sixth of the surface is covered thinly or thickly by blown shell-sand, which counters acidity and grows the flowers and grasses of calcareous soil. The grazing on the machairs is no less than excellent.

Rainfall is nearly half that of Mull at 40 to 50 inches. The climate is mild and the frosts of winter light. Hours of bright summer sunshine are higher than at most parts of the West Highland coast. But there is much wind. Ask anyone in Coll, even a housewife, what today's weather will be, and the answer is never 'Dry', or 'Wet', but a figure from the Beaufort scale – 'Force 9', or 'Force 3'. Islanders listen to the Shipping Forecast rather than the mainland Weather Forecast. Wind is what matters here, and the rest discounted. There are no trees on Coll.

Arinagour at the middle of the east coast is the only village and has nearly half the island's population of 130. The harbour faces south-south-east and is unprotected. There is a pier, but without water deep enough to take the steamer alongside, although suitable for cargo boats. In 1964 work was started on a new deep-water pier several hundred yards south of the old – a long-delayed need for rehabilitation of the island's life and economy. Alongside the old pier will often be seen wooden boxes floating on the water. These hold lobsters waiting for the Oban steamer. Arinagour brightens at close quarters. The pale grey rocks are greened by grass between the ribs. Rightward of the pier, the main street is lined on one side by a dozen white-washed cottages, on the other by their tiny gardens full of purple fuchsias and blue hydrangeas. Beyond the cottages are two good shops, and farther still, on the other side of a little bay, the church and hotel. Behind the sea-front cottages, the county council has built on top of a hill a double row of modern houses. Here lives the District Nurse, with bikes to hire and caravans on the west coast dunes.

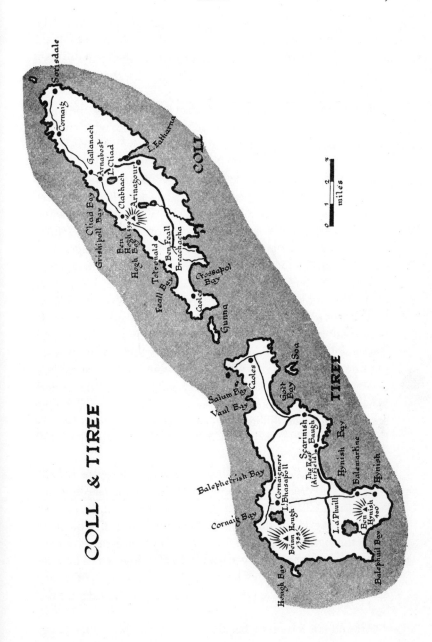

COLL & TIREE

Coll has twenty miles of good road, which crosses the island's centre from Arinagour to link the farms up and down the west coast; south of Arinagour, it runs down the eastern moors to Crossapol Bay. North of Arinagour, the east coast is uninhabited and trackless.

On crossing the central road we can see at once that the entire middle part of Coll is rocky and boggy moorland, which invites no tramping. Where it joins the western machair at Arnabost a ruined school stands on the site of an ancient earth-house. The entrance to the earth-house is under the floor of the school's porch, from which an underground passage runs forty feet south-eastward to an old gravel-pit. Various implements, brooches, pins and a vase have been found within. Written notes on its recent history are held at Arnabost cottage. The name Ar na Bosd means Earth of the Chest (or Coffer), most probably in reference to the concealed earth-house. The people of the Isles took refuge in earth-houses during Viking raids.

The whole west coast has machair, but unlike Uist, where it is continuous, it is here several times interrupted by spurs of low rocky moor running out from the central hills and thrusting out to sea in short headlands. Between the headlands lie a dozen or more bays, nearly all sandy and backed by dunes and machair. The spur-like divisions give a constantly changing scene, every beach different but each flanked by a most beautiful pink and yellow rock. The wide hollows between the spurs appear like green oases, where farmhouses lie.

Only ten of Coll's forty lochs appear on its southern half, and only two drain west. The water is clean but flat-tasting and peaty. Loch Cliad is the biggest, south of Arnabost. Its narrow river, cutting deep through the machair, gives the quickest route through the dunes to Cliad Bay. The shell-sands stretch half a mile, elegantly curved and normally deserted. The outward view here, as everywhere else along the coast, is of empty ocean: at Coll we have come to a true 'Isle on the Edge of the Sea'.

Around the point to Cliad's south-west, this 'outer edge'

atmosphere is felt still more at Grishipoll Bay. Here there is no sand. A broad cat's-paw of gneiss sticks out into blue sea, which roars foaming white across the sparkling pink claws to green grass, which starts the upwards lift of machair to the moor. At the shore-end a tall ruined house stands on the wide turf. I was there on a day of high westerly wind, when black squalls were passing to north and south of Coll, leaving us in blue sky and sun. The walls of clean pale grey, washed by years of storm and zigzagged by cracks in lightning-flash pattern, pointed the fingers of their stacks to a sky wild with storm-cloud tearing east to Mull. Times out of number, as nowhere else in Scotland, the Hebrides disclose in one sharp moment the brevity of a century.

In the hollow across the next spur lies the farm of Clabhach. Its grass falls steeply below to whitest sand, and above rises to Coll's highest hill, Ben Hogh, 339 feet. The summit carries a boulder left stranded by an Ice Age glacier, and so delicately poised on three stones that with small effort it can be rocked.

The road crosses over the Ben's seaward spur and ends at the croft-house of Ballyhaugh. A reed-fringed lochan beside it empties into Hogh Bay, which is like Kiloran in size and shape and quality – the same golden sands are here fringed by rock of pink and yellow granitic gneiss, glittering with mica. On its jagged north arm huge Atlantic rollers crash and leap high in gouts, giving the beach a mixture of shell with pulverized yellow rock, which so wonderfully colours the sand. Among the marram dunes are outcrops of sandstone in process of formation, still coarse and crumbly but bedding down firmly in solid layers, richly yellow.

The Hogh dunes form a wide desert extending more than a mile to the croft-house of Totronald. The track through them is hard to follow near the middle, and towards the end is transfigured in August by banks of bloody cranesbill. The blooms are almost as small as red campions' and the leaves deeply incised.

At Totronald we rejoin the main road. Down the coast thus

far from Cliad Bay are several deserted farmhouses, all of the
same design, square-built in stone of two storeys. They date
from 1852–60 following the clearances, and are unsuitable to
present-day needs. They lie empty through more recent emigrations. The apparent succession of crofts at the head of
western bays (in Coll's south half) are in fact no longer separate
crofts but are farmed as one unit.

The south road ends at the flats of Breachacha (Speckled
Field). Immediately beyond, Feall Bay and Crossapol Bay
pinch in from north and south respectively, forming the 'tail' of
the Caoles peninsula. The isthmus is only half a mile wide, and
filled from shore to shore by marram dunes. Feall Bay is by
general consent the finest of all Coll's bays or beaches. The
sands are golden, the bay goes deeper and wider than Hogh.
Distinction is given by the cliffs of Ben Feall, which rises to 217
feet on the east headland, and by skerries shooting out north
from the west point. Bloody cranesbill redden the marrams
behind. Feall must rank among the two or three foremost bays
of the Hebrides.

Beyond the marram belt, Caoles farm and machair fill the
remainder of Coll to its southernmost tip, where the Sound of
Gunna, only two miles wide, separates Coll from Tiree. But no
ferry-service from this intractable coast is possible. The only
sailing is from Arinagour to Gott Bay, a voyage of eighteen
miles. Thus, for all their closeness, there is little social intercourse between the two islands. On the sound lies the little
island of Gunna, one mile long, on which cattle are grazed from
Caoles. Barnacle and grey lag geese arrive there in winter.
Sheld-duck are numerous in spring, but above all it is beloved
by terns, including the little, Sandwich, and arctic.

On the flats of Breachacha, close by the sea, stands the
MacLeans' fourteenth century castle, and behind it their
eighteenth century Georgian house, a winged box with four
bastions at the upper corners. The inland flats prosper in
cornfields and splendid grass, where large herds of cattle graze.
This Breachacha farm of 6,000 acres is the island's biggest. The

east-coast road to Arinagour runs over moorland at an almost
level one hundred feet. Several crofts spread out of sight along
the coast below. The seaward view is to the hills of Mull, which
look surprisingly close, whereas from Mull Coll appears far
off. Mull now seems to be virtually a part of the mainland.
Here one feels deep in the sea, exposed to all elements.
Yet in unsettled weather Coll is often a good place to be,
for many clouds pass overhead to precipitate on mountainous
Argyll.

The north half of Coll has more continuous and broader
machair extending inland beyond the road, which is half a mile
from the shore. On the moors above are thirty lochs, four of
which drain to the machair. Coot and wigeon are sometimes
seen on the moors, but the once plentiful buzzard appears to be
rare. The Coll machair was formerly paradise for rabbits, which
made deserts of arable fields, for there are no foxes, weasels or
stoats on outer islands. Buzzards and black-backed gulls were
the main predators. The rabbits are gone now, to the gain of all
except the unlucky buzzard.

Gallanach, the first farm northward from Arnabost, is the
second largest in Coll with some four thousand acres in arable
and grazing ground. On so rocky an isle, it is good to see these
wide fields of corn and hay, of green grass and machair covered
with black and brown cattle, and tall barns hay-filled to the roof
Alongside the road both at Gallanach and at Cornaig farther
north, daffodil and tulip are grown for the Hebridean Bulb
Growers of Oban. Several acres are planted. The work gives no
extra local employment, because students are used for the work
of planting and gathering, and although the bulbs are good the
project is thought to be insufficiently profitable.

Behind Gallanach lies a half-mile bay of sand. Beyond
reproach as this may be, it pales before the splendours of the
next series of beaches underneath the hill of A Chroic a mile
north. These splendours are of humble kind. The bay is narrow
and short, but nearer the sea it expands sideways, disclosing
half a dozen secluded coves divided one from another by pink

fingers of rock. The sand is flawless and tawny, the rocks not jaggy; small islets lie offshore. At low tide one can walk a mile south-west from beach to beach – all the way back to Galla-nach. These, to my way of thinking, are the most delightful kinds of bay, even though the big ones like Hogh and Feall are in truth far more spectacular. The birds agree with me. Here one finds sheld-duck, dunlin, and oyster-catchers, gannets and terns. Peculiar to this coastal stretch are large flocks of starlings and sparrows on the machair, whereas on the east coast the chief bird is the long-necked shag – not counting gulls, the mewing of whose young is, throughout the Isles, the principal seashore cry in August.

Beyond A Chroic the road and coast turn eastward to the two farms of Cornaig. They rival Gallanach in their wide spread of corn, hay and barley. Two streams coming off the hills on this stretch of road cut deeply into the machair and are full of small trout. In springtime the north-east half of Coll is thick with primroses.

The road climbs off the machair to twist between the rocky knolls of the last bare land, at length to fall to the shore at Soris-dale, where a tiny whitewashed cottage nestles like a tern on the last rocks. Grey sand spreads below, above there are several cows on the hill, at the back a small hayfield, about the door a scratching of hens, and all around rock ribs and low bleak moorland. It is not, one feels, a place to live. Many years ago there was a crofting community at Sorisdale, but this cot is all that is left – the wisp of peat-smoke from its chimney like a last flicker of life, soon to be snuffed.

Coll in its early days was settled by Norsemen, then fell to Somerled and the Clan Donald Lords of the Isles. They granted the land to the MacLeans, who held Coll till last cen-tury. After the Forty-five the population grew too great for the island, to the detriment of the machair where the cutting of marram caused blowing. MacLean of Coll impoverished him-self buying food for his people. By 1841 the population had mounted to 1,442 and the situation became desperate. MacLean

EIGG
On the jetty at Galmisdale, waiting for the early morning boat

By Tom Weir

SKYE
The Old Man
of Storr

SHIANT ISLES
Columnar basalt

By Tom Weir

SHIANT ISLES Guillemots and razorbills

By Tom Weir

resolved to clear the island, not for sheep but in the best inte-
rests of all concerned, and to lay out the ground as farms.
Between 1841 and 1861, half the people were evicted and settled
in Canada and Australia. MacLean finally sold Coll in 1856.

Well intended as the clearance was, the blow appears to have
been too sharp and sudden, for the society deteriorated in structure and virtually collapsed, emigration not abating to the
present day. The land is good for pasture, not for ploughing, so
the clearance was followed by the recolonization of Coll by
dairy-farmers from Kintyre and Ayrshire. Small farms kept
twenty or thirty cows for milking, the larger sixty or seventy.
Huge quantities of cheese were produced, sweet from the rich
clover on which the cattle fed. Coll cheese became famous – it
was supplied to the House of Commons – but the First World
War took too many men, the milk industry failed, and severe
competition from cheap New Zealand cheese caused a shift to
the breeding of beef cattle.

The West Highland Survey of 1944–50 made a report on
Coll by an expert committee, published in 1955. They reported
that 350 to 400 people could be supported on Coll at a modern
standard of living by dairy-farming. If Coll were instead
ranched for store-cattle, then a dozen families could do the
work, but this community would be too small as a social unit
and would finally disperse. On a Coll farm, without electricity
or much mechanical aid, one man could manage 12–15 dairy
cows, whereas he could manage 120 head of beef cattle. Dairy-
farming would give more work and a bigger gross income to
pay for it. Stock-farming would give more cash per head, but
this would not mean a higher standard of living, because social
life and services would decay. It was thus argued that to preserve the level of population (230 in 1945), dairy-farming was
the only choice.

The expert committee appear to have made a true forecast.
The Coll farmers have persisted in production beef-cattle, of
which have a fine reputation and earn good money, but the
island's population has now fallen to 130. The only hope of an

E

increase in population remains a return to dairy-farming, and the ownership of land by the small farmers themselves. To this the report would add the draining and treatment of moorland with phosphates and shell-sand to improve soil production.

The island now has three owners. There is no poverty and the farmers are prosperous. The stock carried is 1,000 beef cattle, 7,000 sheep and lambs, and 40 or 50 dairy cows and calves. There are twenty large and small farms and ten crofts. There used to be a herring industry at Coll, when large numbers of boats would call at Arinagour from Orkney and Shetland. Fishing was important if only for domestic supply, but all that has ended. Two men fish for lobsters full-time and send the catch to Billingsgate. The last available figures show a catch of 3,775 lobsters fetching £924 gross. But such returns will vary greatly from year to year.

The school at Arinagour has twenty pupils. Most of the people now on Coll are from the mainland, and of Lowland rather than Highland speech. Only a few families still speak Gaelic. As on all other small islands, crime is unknown and no police needed.

The people put some hope for the future in the growth of tourism. At the present time, over a thousand visitors come in summer. The hotel is filled to capacity and there is difficulty getting private accommodation. There is room here for development and for profit, but tourism will not keep Coll alive. The enthusiasm and energy of an island people are best drawn out in developing the island's natural resources, which in Coll are considerable; in such work they achieve the greater satisfaction and (quite incidentally) contribute most to their country's well-being.

TIREE

ON a warm day of June or July, the scent of wild white clover carries over the sea to the Oban steamer approaching Tiree. Not for nothing was this island named Tir Iodh, meaning Land of Corn. It was known for centuries as the 'Granary of the Isles'. And yet, the rock is archaean gneiss, the same as Coll's.

No two islands of the same basic rock, within a couple of miles of each other, could well be so different. Tiree is so flat that standing on the east coast at Baugh I have watched the sun set in the Sea of the Hebrides. The land lifts only a few feet above wave-level. In shape like a Stone Age hammer, head to the west, Tiree is twelve miles long by six wide at the head; the shaft varies from half a mile wide to three. The only two hills are appropriately placed at the ends of the hammer-head: Ben Hynish, 460 feet and Beinn Hough, 388 feet.

Fifteen miles out from Mull, unscreened from weather by other islands or by interior hill ranges, Tiree is a windswept platform. These apparent disadvantages, even including the high winds, have been its salvation, have indeed made it fertile for man and beast, for of all Hebridean islands it is the one most widely affected by shell-sand blown in from its vast beaches. So complete is this sanding that the original character of the gneiss has been transformed into that of a calcareous plain, ploughable and freely draining. In the middle there is still much moss, and in the south-west good loam, but the rest is machair-type land, pre-eminently suitable for stock-raising. Further advantages are a rainfall of 50 inches, neither too much nor too little, and the highest long-term average for sunshine in Great Britain during the spring and early summer: 234 hours in May and 203 hours in June.

Tiree is reached by the Oban steamer, which calls three days a week on the outward run to Lochboisdale in South Uist, and three days on the inward run. There is a daily air service from Glasgow.

Two huge bays, named Hynish and Gott, account for the entire south coast of Tiree save for its rocky eastern peninsula. Between the two is the village of Scarinish (Norse for Seagull Point), widely dispersed but given entity by a small tidal harbour, hotel, butcher, store, and post office. The harbour is nowadays little used, for a new pier has been built in Gott Bay. The hull of an old schooner, named *Mary Stewart*, lies deep-sunk in the harbour sands, with another, less elegant tub alongside. *Mary* was one of the last sailing ships to trade on the west coast. The pier at Gott Bay allows ships to come alongside in all conditions, but the bay itself is not a safe anchorage.

West of Scarinish, a central plain called the Reef runs two miles across the island from Hynish Bay to Balephetrish Bay on the north coast. The Reef was occupied by the R.A.F. during the last war. An appalling mess was left when the base was evacuated. Scott Moncrieff, writing in 1950, reported: 'Tiree was never bombed, but five years after the war it looked more like a bombed area than any bombed area in Britain.' Twenty years after the war, the Reef is still marred by the same ugly Nissen huts, concrete slabs, and walls and sheds. Since the Air Ministry have declined moral responsibility, this ugliness could surely be removed by the County Council with aid from the government, who have invited applications for grants for reclamation and improvement of beauty spots. The Reef in itself is no beauty spot, but Tiree is sufficiently small for the grant to be applicable.

Gains from the war have been the modern aerodrome available for civilian use, electricity, and good roads throughout the island.

Gott Bay has Tiree's biggest single stretch of sand. The

Traigh Mhor extends two and a half miles eastward to the rocks of Soa Isle. The road from Scarinish runs through the short green machair close to the edge of the beach, then out to the far east butt of Caoles, where all is rock and marsh, not unlike Sorisdale in Coll. Long ribs of gneiss break through thin soil, and the coast-line is rocky. This eastern end of Tiree is shaped to a peninsula by the half-mile neck of machair between Gott Bay on the south and the twin bays of Vaul and Salum on the north. Vaul and Salum are finely shaped, deeply curved, and divided only by a long rocky point. Recent archaeological excavations at Dun Mhor Vaul (Fort of the Big Wall) have shown that it dates from the first century B.C.

West from Scarinish, the road circles Hynish Bay, which has two, mile-wide sweeps of sand looking out to Mull and the mainland. At the south end, the crofting community of Balemartine is the island's chief centre of population. Many old black houses still stand here, but are converted to white houses and fully modernized. Some still have the thatch as of old, but most are roofed with bitumen-felt and all are of good appearance. Tiree is studded with fine modern houses, one of the great benefits brought to the Isles by grants from the Department of Agriculture.

The south coast road ends at Hynish. This little village is a curio, for its row of many-chimneyed houses is built of granite from the Ross of Mull. Even its old pier, now silted up with sand, is a massive and elaborate granite structure. Beyond them both rears a tall granite tower. Although occupied, the houses have an oddly deserted air, perhaps because they lie at a road-end on a south headland. They were built around 1844 to house workers building Skerryvore lighthouse. The granite blocks were shipped from Hynish pier. The masons cut all stones for the lighthouse dove-tailed, inter-locking even the granite floors from wall to wall. The Hynish tower was built to allow signal communication with the men working on Skerryvore, which lies twelve miles south-west.

The west coast of Tiree is reached by a road from

Balemartine to Balephuil Bay. The ground inland is marshy and carries huge clumps of irises, but improves on rounding Ben Hynish, until suddenly the brilliant green machair spreads out around the western bay. It has a mile-wide sweep of beach, unusually broad and most gently sloping, so that waves sweep far up to lacquer the sands powder-blue or pearl according to the sky. Skerryvore lighthouse stands up clear to the south; behind the beach, on machair green as a billiard table, Loch a Phuill shines. At the road-end is one of the most delightful little villages of Tiree, a clachan of converted 'black houses', their low walls and rounded corners all shining white, forming a gay huddle with hens and children and cows and dogs all-of-a-tumble.

The Tigh Dubh, or Black House, has often been described as so named from its lack of a chimney, for the fireplace at the middle of the floor vented smoke through a hole in the roof, thus blackening the beams and most else inside. In fact, the original Tigh Geal, or White House, usually had the same smoky central vent. The Tigh Dubh is defined in Gaelic as 'Thatched house whose walls are dry-built *without* cement, and double'. The Tigh Geal is distinguished as 'Thatched house whose walls have their stones *cemented* together. In many parts such houses are now slated'. The black house design is the very best one to cope with Atlantic winds and to stand to frequent hurricanes in winter. They have no corners or gables, and although dry-stone-built have double walls, which in Tiree vary in thickness up to nine feet. The space between is filled with earth, rubble or peat. There are no eaves to the roofs, which are set on the inner wall, not the outer. This roof-design is unique to the black house and has two purposes: storm winds striking the outer walls are shot upwards clear of thatch, on which they get no grip, and the outer walls' tops give a platform both for renewing the thatch, which must be done every two years, and for stopping leaks, which are probably frequent. So effective is this design that sitting inside one hears no wind.

The genuine black house is found today only in the Outer Isles. In Tiree they are now all Tigh Geal with cemented walls, proper chimneys, and the roofs felted or slated.

The west coast has a wide belt of dunes, which continues round the seaward side of Beinn Hough in the north. On top of Beinn Hough are tall wireless masts, which can be seen from every part of the island. The ground inland of the hill is spread with fields of corn and barley, and dotted with cows and sheep grazing on the turf. To its north-east lies the most handsome village of Tiree, Cornaigmore. Everything conspires to give it excellence. It looks out north to Rhum, Eigg and Canna, and north-west to the islands of Barra. Behind it lies Loch Bhasapoll; in front, a perfect sward circling a bay of pure shell-sand. The buildings are of modern design, pre-eminently the school, which is one of five in Tiree and the best-appointed in the Hebrides. All together they give a much-needed demonstration that new house-design can be made to harmonize with an island environment. In the length and breadth of the Inner and Outer Hebrides I have seen no other new housing scheme to match Cornaigmore for fitness. Most of them, needlessly, blot the landscape.

Cornaig Bay (from the Norse Kornvik, meaning Corn Bay) is not named in the one-inch Ordnance Survey map, nor is the village given its site. The one-inch maps for the Hebrides are much out-of-date, and Bartholomew's half-inch sheets should be used if accuracy is required on man-made developments, such as new roads, bridges or villages.

Loch Bhasapoll is famous for its duck. Even gadwall, which are rare on Hebridean islands, come here in winter. They can be distinguished from other duck by their white bellies and black and white wing-patch, which are clearly seen in flight. Tufted duck stay to breed. The fertile arable land draws a large variety of birds. White-fronted geese are common winter visitors, for Tiree is on the migration route, and summer and winter welcomes many voyagers that fail to appear on the coasts of the North Minch. The great open beaches are liked by some waders that appear to be wary of Coll's small ones – greenshank and sanderling, and the bar-tailed godwit, which is like a slenderer version of the curlew, but with straight bill and a reddish head, neck and breast. Terns, which do not favour small islets, swarm on Tiree. The little, arctic, and common terns can be found nesting on blown-out parts of the marram, which are often floored with pebble. Most surprisingly, fulmars breed. In former days they much preferred big sea-cliffs, of which Tiree has none, but their more recent wide spread throughout the Hebrides has led them to accept nesting sites on rocks of fifty feet or less. Tiree snipe-shooting is said to be the best in Europe. Hugh numbers of snipe fly in to the marshes in October. During November a party of four guns may shoot six hundred in a week. All over the island are great flocks of starlings and sparrows.

East of Cornaigmore, the bay of Balephetrish is the biggest on the north coast. The name is from Baile Pheadairich, meaning Township of the Storm-Petrel. These birds have a habit of running lightly over the waves with the aid of their wings, hence the name Petrel after St. Peter. The narrowest strip of marram hems a mile-long beach of silver sand. From here the broad belt of the Reef extends south to Hynish Bay. There used to be a big farm at Balephetrish, but that has long since been broken up into sixteen crofts. In most of the Inner Isles there has been evident a strong tendency to amalgamate crofts into larger units, but not in Tiree, which has thus retained a larger population. The land is tight with crofts, which number nearly three hundred. For this reason the machair is best seen and scented in June or July when overlaid with blossom, not in August when all has been cropped short and green is the one surviving colour.

Tiree has a bloom of its own, which might be unique were it not for Iona, in the brilliance of its light. The burning and tanning effect of its springtime air can be dangerous to un-prepared skin. In this enveloping light fewer shadows are cast than elsewhere. Blue butterflies skim in profusion along the myriad-flowered machair. Encircling all is blue sea, edged by shell-sand as creamy as Tiree milk.

The extreme flatness of the land is most like Holland. In recent years Tiree has seen a most worthy experiment in bulb-production. Early results were promising. Tiree bulbs have been found by the dealers to be of excellent quality, and they still are. But the pilot-scheme, which might well have led to the growth of an important Hebridean industry, develops slowly. Expansion in the Isles has been from 1 acre in 1957 to 22 acres in 1964. Bulbs are supplied to the islanders and marketed by the Hebridean Bulb Growers, Ltd., a co-operative society directed by four growers and five nominees of the Secretary of State. In 1964 the average net return was £500 an acre. But unless a crofter gives his crop the extra effort it needs his return can be disappointing. He may grow his bulbs, send them off to Oban, but get only a tenth of the potential figure, because too many are not of acceptable quality.

A high quality product demands care and attention. The bulb must have well-drained ground – it does not like getting its feet wet. It must be fertilized and thoroughly weeded, the more so as fertilizer encourages weed. A man can be occupied full time on two acres, lifting and replanting an acre each alternate year. Daffodils, which are the principal crop, can be lifted between mid-June and mid-July. Microscopic examination of a section of the bulb is not required before gathering. The bulbs are dried, their longest roots removed, then mechanically graded for size. Large grades are used for the retail trade, medium grades for forcing. Small grades only are washed in warm water to control eelworm, mites and flies, then returned to the growers. These small bulbs are required for planting stock, and any surplus fetches a good price.

Crops can be blighted, as happened in 1963. Bulbs are subject to many diseases and pests, but these can be controlled or eliminated by proper management. It has been shown that this high-value crop fully repays good husbandry: returns for the cultivation of rejuvenated forced daffodils have been the most rewarding of any crop grown in the Highlands. Hence there is much scope for expansion in the Isles, but whether the crofters will choose to make the effort is still uncertain.

Tiree formerly belonged to the MacLeans of Mull, but in 1674 fell to the Campbells of Argyll. The present duke still owns.

Population reached its peak in 1831 with 4,453 people, and has now fallen to little more than 1,000, but has remained fairly steady over the last five years. The decline has been less violent than on most other islands, and has occurred for much the same reasons. Many evicted people squatted by the sea and lived precariously on kelp-burning and fish, but most others emigrated to Canada and Nova Scotia. Fishing was at that time the chief money-earner after farming, and fish a principal food. In the latter part of the nineteenth century, the arrival of steam trawlers from the mainland ended Tiree's fishing industry. They poached within the three-mile limit and ruined the banks. This led to further emigration, but in time the reduction in numbers and the natural fertility of the land, and the break-up of the big farms into crofts between 1910 and 1920, allowed the retention of a large native community in comparative prosperity and happiness. The only commercial fishing now is for lobster, and that on a small scale.

Tiree's principal industry is stock-raising, which depends on the island's chief asset, the machair, which in turn depends on the preservation of marram. The tough roots of the spiky marram bind and stabilize the sand. From that simple beginning a machair develops through a first colonization by small plants like bird's-foot trefoil and hop trefoil. They fix nitrogen and thus create the conditions that allow sixty other flowers to strike root (I have counted over thirty such flowers on one machair in South Uist). Grassland then spreads, cattle and sheep graze, and humans thrive.

Were it not for the humble marram the economy of several islands would collapse. Many acres have been lost to cultivation by human carelessness, such as the over-cutting of the marram for thatching, or excessive rutting of it by cart-wheels, thus allowing the wind to blow out the sand and create dune-deserts. It used to be specially stated in the Duke of Argyll's Tiree leases that if a farmer found a hole in the marram dunes he must plant a bent to fill it.

Machair is deficient in potash, needed to grow white clover, and in cobalt, needed to prevent pine in sheep. The farmers therefore give it heavy dressings of tangle-weed, which is cast up on the beaches in huge quantity after winter storms, and scatter cobalt salt where necessary. Tiree is almost wholly crofted and heavily stocked. The latest available figures give 12,000 sheep and well over 4,000 cattle. Tiree cattle fatten quickly. Approximately 1,200 are exported annually, and 5,000 sheep. Dairy-farming is limited to the supply of domestic needs. Crops grown are largely for winter fodder.

The people of Tiree, like their own land, are in good heart. Most men who leave the island still take to the sea as they have in the past. But the exiles return. Tiree is home.

THE SMALL ISLES

FROM the mainland coast or from sea, Muck, Eigg, Rhum and Canna appear as the most splendid group of all the Hebrides. The strange monolith of the Scuir of Eigg, the six gabbro peaks of Rhum, and the high platform of Canna, are the chief landmarks of the western coast from Ardnamurchan to Skye. They impress the eye as do no other island groups by their boldness of feature. St. Kilda would be one exception, but that lies outside the archipelago. In storm they loom blackly menacing through the cloud-wrack, to emerge at the clearance hard and grey upon steely seas, finally to lie blue but sharp on that uncertain border where the lights of sky and sea coalesce. They seem then the no-man's-land between heaven and earth, belonging to and uniting both, and their clear peaks like frontier megaliths.

Eight miles south of Skye and between ten and twenty-five miles out from Mallaig on the Inverness-shire coast, they form a geographical and social group known as the parish of the Small Isles. They are linked three days a week by MacBrayne's mail and freight steamer from Mallaig. Rhum is the largest but Eigg the principal island, holding half the population of 150, including the parish minister, doctor and an S.C.W.S. store. All have jetties or piers, but only the pier on Canna can take a steamer alongside.

Eigg, Muck and Canna are the most favoured of the four geologically and climatically. Their rock is Tertiary basalt (like Mull) and the soil good. Rainfall is 40 to 60 inches. Rhum on the other hand is of gabbro to the south, where the hills rise 2,500 feet, and in the north of Torridon sandstone, both of

which rocks give poor soil. The island is one of the wettest of
the Hebrides, with a rainfall of 100 inches or more on the hills.
It holds a population little bigger than that of Muck, although
twenty times the size.

Muck (Eilean a' Muic, meaning Isle of the Sow) is the southmost island lying three miles off Eigg. Measuring little more
than two miles by one, it is mostly low but rises at the west end
to a hill of 451 feet. Adjoining it on the north is a tidal islet
named Eilean nan Each (Horse Island). A little harbour to the
south-east is protected at the mouth by skerries, which make
entry troublesome in bad weather. Muck is exceedingly fertile,
and made still more so by shell-sand blown in from the north
coast. Sheep fare unusually well and early crops can be harvested, notably potatoes, which are often ready for market by
the end of May. An energetic owner who farms the land has
made possible a population of 20. His motor-boat comes twice
a week to Eigg to meet the steamer.

Eigg (pronounced Egg) is one of the favoured isles of the
west. Like Muck, a basalt isle of high potential fertility, it is big
enough to have the social services that Muck lacks. It measures
five miles long by three wide, but in the northern third only
half that width. Most of its 5,000 acres are high and hilly moorland. The approach by sea shows that the whole northern part
is ringed by cliffs rising to 900 feet, set well back from the shore
upon steep slopes, which plunge seaward in scree and grass.
But south-eastward the land falls away into farmland. Around
the harbour at Galmisdale, well-wooded slopes swell upwards
to a bare hill-top, on which the Scuir towers higher and bolder
the closer we approach. Dean Monro's famous description of
Dunvegan Castle in Skye as 'ane stark strenth biggit on ane
craig' would apply more aptly to the Scuir of Eigg. It shoots up
like a Dolomite peak, seemingly far bigger than it really is. The
tower is a block of pitchstone lava on the 1,000-foot contour,
rising sheer to 1,289 feet.

The harbour is closed to the south-east, save for one narrow
channel, by the Eilean Chathastail, a rocky island bearing a

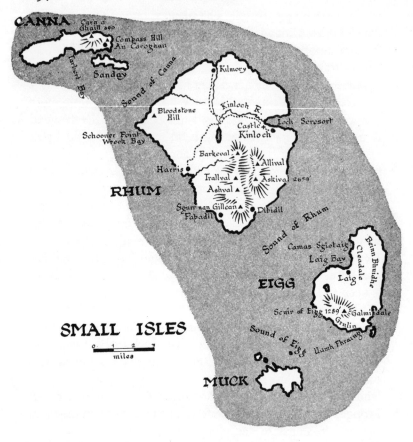

lighthouse and squat round tower, the tomb of some former owner.

The harbour may not be a good one, for the bay shallows at low tide, but it does have a substantial jetty and is much used in summer by yachts. Each night one hears the long-drawn moan of anchor-chains as new arrivals drop hook. Behind the innermost sands a narrow road curves past an old stone pier to a second bay of sand and machair with skerries offshore. The grass verge is lit by yellow silverweed and ragwort, white clover and yarrow, and by dwarf dandelions in dense clusters. The purple thistle stalks among buttercups and daisies and wild thyme. Cattle graze the fields behind, alongside July hay that glows rich yellow, the very hue of the moon when it rises. Above the fields, dense thickets of blackthorn and hazel merge into pine and spruce, which undulate over the hill-slopes.

When the sun goes down, the Scuir stands black on a bright yellow sky, and appears to overhang its base. The outward view is to the coast of Knoydart, Arisaig and Moidart, where the distant peak of Sgòr na Ciche juts horn-like from the head of Loch Nevis. The eight miles of sea between then turns every subtle shade of lilac, pale yellow and blue-grey. Oyster-catchers cry along the shore, where the sands are speckled by worm-casts. At all times the beach is busy with birds, grey wagtails at the dry seaweed, a gang of ringed plovers and dun-lin at the lower beach, and just offshore a couple of eider-duck with young, sometimes steaming about with the determined air of tug-boats, or scooshing and diving near the skerries, occasionally, at high water, coming ashore and waddling fast across sand and rock to the next bay. Each evening curlews begin to cry along the headlands, and always when dusk falls a heron swoops on to the nearest rocks.

From Galmisdale, a good tarmac road winds steeply up through woods and crosses the island's back northwards to Cleadale. The school and post office and store lie mid-way across the moor between the two settlements. The land up there between 200 and 300 feet above the sea is covered in heather and bracken, but trees stand in sheltered spots by the roadside, where harebells grow sparsely and pheasants can be seen or heard. From this northern angle the Scuir is seen to be a long hogsback and the 'tower' to be its eastern edge, curved like a tusk. The name Eigg may thus come from the old Norse Egg, meaning Edge, or from the Gaelic Eag, a Notch (well-marked between the Scuir and the north hills).

The long descent to Laig Bay on the north-west coast reveals one of the most splendid sights of the Hebrides. The great double bay is a mile and a half wide, ringed far back by the high cliffs of Beinn Bhuidhe. Cleadale thus lies in a great amphitheatre between these cliffs and the sands of Laig Bay and Camas Sgiotaig. The crofts stretch to the sea's edge in broad strips of green corn and yellow hay. They form the foreground to the Sound of Rhum, and to the sweep of the five Rhum peaks that now stand close and clear across five miles of blue water.

The crofts undulate across the entire amphitheatre. Most of the houses are clustered at the north side, but some line the main road with small gardens of purple fuchsia and veronica and honeysuckle. Burns falling from the cliffs run through the croft-land, their deep channels lined with blue irises and honeysuckle, everywhere packed tight with flowers. Lanes run out from the houses into the fields, which in summer lie in happy disarray, some in course of reaping or gathering, others of stooking or stacking. They end at the beach itself, on a strip of marram only a yard or two wide.

The sands are broad and fine, pounded by rollers even in calm weather. Splendid as these sands are, their thunder is stolen by the still more famous 'Singing Sands' of Camas Sgiotaig. This bay is reached either by the road through Cleadale or by a walk of one and a half miles along the beach from Laig. The wide blunt point dividing them is of strange formation, spread in flat pavements eroded into pots and fissures and backed by small natural arches and overhangs. The Camas Sgiotaig is of rounded quartz grain, giving a pure white sand with black speckles. It squeals loudly when scuffed by hand, still more loudly to the scuffed foot. A winter storm will sometimes carry away much of the sand, leaving the rock-bed bare, but always the sand is replaced before the spring. This unusual feature (not unique – there is a similar beach on St. Kilda) gives the bay its name – Sgiotaidh means Dispersing. Blue irises and purple bell-heather cap the crags behind.

At the opposite, south-east corner of Eigg is the MacDonald's Cave, the most notorious of the Isles, It lies little more than half a mile west-south-west of Galmisdale jetty, but unless the site were known it would be hard to find, for the entrance passage is low and narrow under a long line of cliffs that face Muck. In the winter of 1577 several MacLeods of Skye were passing Eigg by boat. They came ashore and raped some MacDonald girls. They were caught before they could embark, and although sent home alive were allegedly castrated. Norman, the eleventh chief of the clan MacLeod (a man notoriously cruel even by sixteenth-century standards), sent out his fleet on a punitive expedition. The MacDonalds of Eigg, seeing from afar that they were hopelessly outnumbered, took refuge in the cave, which was big enough to hold the entire population of 395 men, women and children. The MacLeods landed, but failing to find any MacDonalds were obliged to put to sea. Meanwhile, the MacDonalds had sent out a scout. This man was spotted from the departing boats, which promptly put back to Galmisdale. Snow had begun to fall. The scout ran back to the cave and the MacLeods tracked his footprints. But they failed to force an entry. The passage was so low and long that one man could stop hundreds. So they gathered immense quantities of brushwood which they piled and set alight at the narrow mouth. All inside were asphyxiated. Not one survived. The bones were brought out and buried only last century.

The cave lies at the inmost curve of a bay that looks out to Ardnamurchan Point and to Muck. An apron of iris-covered grass falls away from its mouth to the stony shore. The small entrance passage runs in twenty yards, forcing one to crawl when the roof drops to four feet. The main chamber is a hundred yards long, high-roofed, and maybe twenty yards wide. It must easily have held the four hundred MacDonalds. The floor is stony but clean and dry. The inner part is very dark, requiring a torch for movement.

There are several other caves along this stretch of coast, some running fifty yards deep and used by rock-doves. Ravens skim the crags and birds-of-prey hover. A few hundred yards west of the MacDonalds' Cave is the Cathedral Cave. Its huge throat has a high arched roof stretching far in like the nave of a cathedral. This ends at a dry-stone dike, beyond which the cave broadens to an inner chamber, which was used for services during the persecution of the Roman Catholic Church. The priests came here under threat of death to say mass. Stones are still placed side by side along the floor with an aisle between, leading to a short stone wall that may once have been a rough altar-table.

The Scuir, which looks so impossible of ascent from the south and east, can be climbed quite easily from the north side, west of the summit. The summit gives an excellent panorama of the Isles, for it includes most of the Inner Hebrides, the Outer from Barra to Uist, with the Cuillin of Skye and Rhum close at hand, and range upon range of mainland hills.

On the easterly and southerly slopes below the Scuir, Manx shearwaters breed, for the basalt gives easily burrowed soil. The sea-cliffs are favoured by puffins, which at close-quarters look fantastic. Their broad bills, flattened on the vertical plane, are bright red and yellow; a big grey ring circles the cheeks and eyes; the legs are vermilion; the back black and the front white. But despite all this gaiety the bird's expression is mock-solemn, giving it a clown-like appearance. They arrive on Eigg in May, lay one egg, and are gone before the end of August. Choughs bred in Eigg until 1886; hopes of their return have grown since their reappearance at Ardmeanach in Mull.

In 1616 a monastery was founded in Eigg by St. Donnan, but he and his brothers were slain by the people. The monastery was refounded, only to be destroyed by Norsemen. In 1309 Robert the Bruce gifted Eigg to MacDonald of Clanranald. The clan fought in the Forty-five rising, after which Eigg was visited by H.M. Navy: the ships *Terror* and *Furnace* called to arrest Dr. John MacDonald, the brother of Kinlochmoidart. He surrendered to save the islanders. The commander of the *Furnace*, Captain Ferguson, then gave MacDonald his promise that if he would command the islanders to lay down their arms no harm would befall them. When they did so, all suspected of serving Prince Charles Edward were seized, the island was laid waste, the women were raped, and the younger men transported to Jamaica.

In 1826 the MacDonalds were obliged to sell Eigg. The population must then have been far too large, for in 1821 the Small Isles had a population of 1,620, of which Eigg would hold a high proportion. Most of the people lived at Grulin, on the south side of the Scuir. The new owner cleared them to Cleadale and gave the rest of the island to sheep. Grulin became a waste of valueless bracken. Since 1950, Eigg has been successfully farmed by its owners, who graze up to 1,500 ewes and 100 cross-highland cows and their followers. The future of the crofts at Cleadale is thought to be uncertain: as the crofters grow old, will they be replaced by young men? The ground is basaltic loam, which would be appreciated by men from the congested gneiss of some outer isles.

In 1965 the population was 80. Ten children attend the school. From the age of twelve they go to Lochaber High School, Fort William, where they are boarded in hostels. At long school holidays the County Council Education Committee pays full return fares to Eigg. The parents pay at mid-term holidays, and if the ship should fail to sail in foul weather they must board the children at Mallaig. When they leave school, most young men of Eigg go to sea.

By contrast with Eigg, Rhum may seem a desolate land of moor, hill and sea-cliff, yet it never fails to exercise a powerful spell over all who come to know it. The hills rise out of the sea fortress-like to 2,500 feet, in their shape, steepness and cragginess deserving the title of mountains. An almost continuous line of great sea-cliffs runs fifteen miles round the southern and western shores, breached only by the bays of Dibidil, Papadil and Harris. Near Wreck Bay at the western extremity they reach a thousand feet in height. At their base lies a chaos of huge blocks and weird pinnacles, angrily whitened by crashing seas. Only the grey seal can use these wild shores, and their eerie bark can often be heard above the everlasting thunder of waves. The cliff-tops and moors are given to sea-birds and wild goats and red deer.

Rhum is diamond-shaped, measuring eight miles by eight between the farthest points. The mountains all lie in the southern half, where the rock is gabbro like the Cuillin of Skye. In northern Rhum, where the hill-tops fall below a thousand feet, the rock is Torridon sandstone. The west point, where the sea-cliffs are most steep and high, is granite. The island's rock gives poor soil, not good for crofting and ploughable only at Kilmory on the north coast, Harris on the west, and a small area at Kinloch on the east. The castle and village of Kinloch lie at the head of Loch Scresort, the only deep-cut, sheltered bay in the island. It has no steamer-pier, but the jetty is stone-built and big, and steamers can safely lie out in the bay in storm.

The loch runs a-mile east to west and is half a mile wide. The 'castle', in reality a big house of red sandstone, is surrounded by a wood planted eighty years ago. A road from the jetty runs round the bay past the castle gardens and crosses the Kinloch River to the 'village', where there is a post office and shop. A rough road strikes inland up Kinloch Glen to the island's centre, where one branch goes north to Kilmory, and another south-west to Harris. Although no better than cart-tracks these roads give fast walking between the north, east and south parts of the island. There used to be two other west-going tracks, now much effaced by weather, one down Glen Shelleader to Guirdil Bay, the other to Bloodstone Hill at the west point. Bloodstones used to be quarried on the precipitous north side, close below the top, and may be collected on the beach below.

One of the most important tracks on the island runs south from Kinloch down the eastern slopes of Allival and Askival, rising to 750 feet before dropping to Dibidil. Eagles nest on the crags of Glen Dibidil, which strikes deeply into the mountain-range. One side is walled by the steep flanks of Ashval and Sgurr nan Gillean, the other by Askival, 2,659 feet, the highest peak of Rhum. At the head of the glen, Trallval thrusts up its sharp wedge, and out to sea across the Sound of Rhum crouches the hogsback of the Scuir of Eigg. The glen is unique in the isles for mountainous ruggedness, and important for the quick access it gives to the southern ridges, and for its pass over the Bealach an Oir to Glen Harris. In May, the bare slopes of Sgurr nan Gillean come alive to a burst of primroses. The coastal track to the old shooting lodge of Papadil on the south-west bay is in poor shape and hard to follow.

The traverse of the six main peaks gives the best day's mountaineering in the Isles, barring Skye. The start is from Barkeval in the north, then over Allival, 2,365 feet, and south along a sharp, rocky ridge, blocked by a 'gendarme', to Askival. The descent to Bealach an Oir is followed by a rocky scramble over Trallval, 2,300 feet, to Ashval, 2,552 feet, and Sgurr nan Gillean, 2,503 feet. The delight of this day's work is in part the unfailing interest of the ridge itself, but still more the seascapes. The long low line of the Outer Hebrides seems like a dike along the rim of the world. The Cuillin of Skye, now close to the north, break in a massive blue-black cluster out of a broad base like leaf from the top of a pineapple. Down below on the west coast, long Atlantic rollers cream on the Harris shore.

Rhum from the hill-tops looks a wide and spacious island, and is thus truly named: the original Norse Röm öe, 'wide (or spacious) island', was shortened in later years to Ruma, and finally to Rum, but is spelled Rhum by wish of the owners. The evidence of Norse occupation is everywhere apparent in its place-names. On the cession of the Isles by Norway it belonged to MacLean of Coll. By the end of the eighteenth century the population had reached the too large figure of 443. Conditions became intolerable. In 1828 the entire population was shipped to North America and replaced by 8,000 sheep and their shepherds. Towards the end of the nineteenth century, Rhum was bought by John Bullough, a Lancashire engineer, who planted eighty thousand trees at Kinloch and replaced the sheep with deer. His son, Sir George Bullough, built Kinloch Castle in

1900. The workmen, sent from Lancashire to lay out the grounds and build the house, were supplied with kilts while living on the island. The red sandstone was shipped from Arran, the garden soil from Ayrshire. Kinloch was transformed. and peaches and grapes were grown in huge greenhouses. But by the end of the Second World War the red castle had become very much a red elephant.

In 1957, Rhum was bought by the Nature Conservancy and became a Nature Reserve. The Conservancy's long-term object is to recreate the natural characteristics of a Hebridean island by encouraging the richest possible variety of vegetation and wild life, and to make of it a great open-air laboratory for biological and other research. The more valuable contents of the castle were presented by Lady Bullough to the Royal Scottish Museum. The building is now used for the training of scientists, game-wardens and conservation officers. The resident population is ten households. All are employees of the Conservancy, save for one school-mistress.

During the period of heaviest population in the eighteenth century the red deer became almost extinct, but after the island became a deer forest the numbers rose to nearly 1,600 in 1957. When I first visited Rhum in 1948 I saw a white hind at Papadil, the only one of its kind on the island, although the head keeper told me that in former days the island had also had a white stag, which was later shot by a poacher. He knew of only one other white deer in Scotland – a stag in Ross-shire. Since 1957, the Nature Conservancy have been making a special study of red deer population-dynamics and correct herd management. They maintain the number at around 1,500 by culling 240 stags and hinds each year.

Rhum has long been famous for its herd of free-running ponies. The tradition is that they sprang from horses that swam ashore from a wrecked galleon of the Spanish Armada. They are smaller than mainland breeds, but exceedingly strong and hardy. Originally they were dun-coloured with a black eel-streak down the back, but the use of different stallions has produced also chestnut, white, black and grey animals. They move around the island according to season, but broken-in ponies can be seen at Kinloch. The stock is being maintained both to perpetuate a stud of national repute and to provide essential pack-animals for transport of deer-carcases. Any surplus stock is sold.

There are now no sheep on Rhum, but a small herd of dairy-cows is maintained to supply milk. The Conservancy is actively engaged in a programme of tree-planting to provide variety of habitat and to replace lost shelter. Sixty acres have been afforested with species native to the island, and this present total is being increased by about twenty acres a year.

In May the sea-cliffs become alive with puffins. Fulmars, guillemots and razor-bills breed too, but Rhum is above all noted as the breeding ground of Manx shearwaters, which arrive in spring and burrow the mountain-slopes. Despite the name, they do not breed in the Isle of Man. Shearwaters fly in stiff-winged glides first on one wing then the other, showing black and white as the upper and under parts are alternately exposed, often 'shearing' the wave-tops with their wing-tips. They give occasional wing-beats between glides. High up on the mountains, they burrow into grassy ledges on the cliffs and lay one egg at the back of the hole. They stop flying by day when nesting and feed only at night. I have climbed Allival at midnight in May and found the hill-top burbling as if alive from the underground chirpings of many hundreds of birds. As they came and went I could hear the whirr and swish of wings, but rarely glimpsed the bird in the air.

When the young hatch out, the parents stay to fatten them up, then fly off to mid-ocean leaving the young to develop alone. By September, the young birds have grown too hungry to wait longer. They still cannot fly, but off they start to the shore, fluttering down cliffs and waddling over the moors till they reach the sea, where they feed in shallow water. When strong enough to fly they migrate. It is not yet known where the West Highland species go, but in recent years many of the Rhum birds have been ringed, which should finally solve the problem.

On the moors, heather has been severely reduced by past burning and is now only locally dominant. There is no bog myrtle. The moorland is covered mostly with blue moor grass, bents, and fescues. There are few grouse or ptarmigan, and no rabbits, hares or wild cats. Peregrine falcons and merlins breed, and two or three pairs of golden eagles.

The secret of Rhum's spell-binding power is in large part its unmitigated wildness, whereas Canna, which lies two or three miles farther out to the north-west, and which ought (one might think) to be still more desolate, is the best cultivated island of the group. It measures only five miles by one, but has two great advantages. The rock is Tertiary basalt, giving a good soil, and the harbour is excellent. Steamers can call at a well-sheltered pier.

Long and flat-topped, the island lifts high out of the sea to 400 or 500 feet, rising at the east end to 690 feet on Carn a' Ghaill. A more easterly top is named Compass Hill, for ships' compasses are said to be affected by the iron in the rock. Short sea-cliffs ring the island, but fall away at the south-east where the tidal island of Sanday projects a long arm to protect the harbour. The channel between the two dries out on the ebb, leaving only a stream at the west end, narrow enough to be crossed by a long foot-bridge. Fishing boats come in and dry out on a shell-sand beach. The Sanday people fish for cod and lobster, thus their crofts are not worked to the same capacity as land on Canna.

Canna has long been famed for the high quality of its Cheviot sheep. At the east end the ground is southward sloping and in small part sheltered by Sanday. The soil is more fertile than elsewhere and gives early crops. As on Muck, potatoes are saleable by the end of May. The owner has been wise enough to keep a high cattle to sheep ratio, and bracken has not become a menace. The whole island is extraordinarily green for its height and exposure. Despite remoteness, its population of twenty has a firm hold on continued life.

Canna is a breeding station for Manx shearwaters, puffins and guillemots. Some of the guillemots are bridled, having a white eye-ring and streak like a monocle and cord. Grey seals breed on the westerly rocks.

A distinctive feature of the most easterly rocks is an isolated stack named An Coroghan, which rises from the sea a few hundred yards north of the harbour. From its top juts a ruined tower. An irate chief of Clanranald once imprisoned his wife there, hoping, it is alleged, to frustrate her lover, a MacLeod of Skye. The name Coroghan is probably from Corrachan, meaning Fetters.

Six miles south of Canna, and ten miles out from Rhum, are the twin reefs called Oigh-sgeir, or Maiden Rock. They rise only 38 feet out of the sea, and are little more than half a mile long, yet draw to themselves a great number of birds and seals at the breeding season. Hexagonal columns of basalt or pitch-stone project from the islet. Kittiwakes nest on the eight-inch tops of these columns, and large numbers of eider duck and arctic and common terns. The rocks appear to be too low for the guillemot – although it has been known to breed on a ledge near the top of Rockall, which projects 70 feet but is three hundred miles out from the mainland. In past years, pintail duck and teal have both been reported nesting on Oigh-sgeir. Between the columns the sea has cut deep channels, and these are beloved by the grey seal. At the south end, one such channel leads up to a little lagoon, which has often been used as a refuge by small boats and lobster fishers, which can lie in safety while storm-seas thunder on the rocks close beside them, and vast sheets of water, torn off the tops of the breakers, speed overhead to be atomized as a white, fast-travelling fog. This oceanic skerry is a worthy member of the Small Isles parish.

SKYE

'THIS Ile is callit Ellan Skiannach in Irish, that is to say in Inglish the wyngit Ile, be reason it has mony wyngis and pointis lyand furth fra it, throw the dividing of thir foirsaid Lochis.'

Thus spake Sir Donald Monro, the Dean of the Isles, in 1549. Eilean Sgiathanach was the correct Gaelic spelling. To the Norsemen it was Skuyö (pronounced Skya), meaning Isle of Cloud, which is rendered in the Gaelic as Eilean a' Cheo.

Skye is sixty miles long, but what might be its breadth is beyond the ingenuity of man to state. Sea-lochs bite deep into the land, which spreads four wings far out to sea in the great northern peninsulas of Trotternish, Vaternish and Duirinish, and in the southern of Sleat. Thus, for all its bulk – it is the biggest of the Inner Hebrides – Skye has no land more than five miles from the sea. The coasts, which are cliff-bound for the most part, are unique among the principal islands for their lack of shell-sand. Carved as they are by bays innumerable, only four or five of which have sand, and that of blackish colour, they have no true machair. The hinterland stands high in hill and moor. One broad belt in the southern third, pastorally useless, is renowned beyond all else on the island, for there rise the stark and spiky mountains of the Black and Red Cuillin.

South Skye is separated from the mainland by the Sound of Sleat, which narrows at Kyle Rhea to a quarter of a mile, and by Loch Alsh, which narrows at Kyle Akin to half a mile. Both are crossed by car-ferries from the Inverness coast at Glenelg and Kyle of Loch Alsh. Farther south, MacBrayne's car-ferry from Mallaig crosses the Sound of Sleat five miles to Armadale.

A steamer sails daily from Kyle of Loch Alsh to Portree, which is the principal town and harbour. Its sheltered position near the middle of the east coast is enhanced by the long screen of the island of Raasay, four miles out. From Harris on the Outer Hebrides, a car-ferry sails daily to Uig Bay on the west side of Trotternish.

The southern third of Skye lacks good soil. Sleat (pronounced Slate) is mostly Torridon sandstone, giving poor and boggy ground, while the Cuillin are red granite and gabbro, which may be worthless materially but are of high landscape value. They draw more visitors to Skye than any other feature of the land. The northern two-thirds are Tertiary basalt, rising in a prominent spine down the length of the Trotternish Peninsula. This basalt gives Skye its pastoral wealth, for it breaks down to a brown soil on which cattle and sheep thrive. It follows that the majority of the population live in the north and west, and that most of the townships, which number 180, are set in long line upon the coastal strips between hill and shore. Rainfall varies throughout the island from 60 to 80 inches, rising still higher on the Cuillin but diminishing at Trotternish and Vaternish, which being more exposed are much windier. Skye as a whole is bare of trees, but there are sizeable woodlands at private estates, such as Dunvegan and Armadale, and at Forestry Commission plantations comprising 5,000 acres. By far the greater part of Skye is in the hands of crofters and farmers.

A man's first impression of Skye is very much coloured by his line of approach. I have travelled to Skye at every season of the year and by all five lines, and find that each presents a different island. A landing at Armadale in Sleat is like arriving at Craignure in Mull, in wooded Argyll. If we cross instead to Kylerhea we climb at once on to bare, windswept moor; or to Kyleakin, we move north along low coastal strips between hill and sea, aware on either route of a bare, treeless isle, exposed to sea and wind. On the other hand, if we cross from the Outer Isles to Trotternish (far more exposed than south Skye), we are

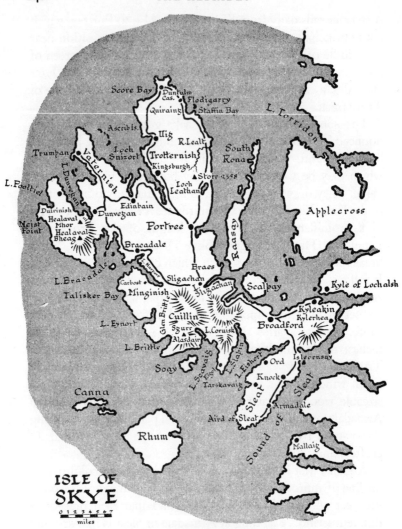

ISLE OF
SKYE

0 1 2 3 4 5 6 7
miles

astonished at the great height to which Skye rises out of the
sea, at the comfortable shelter given by its big hills, at the green
lushness of the grass, the well-stocked gardens and bigger
fields of potato and corn, at the abundance of exotic blooms
along the roads – foxgloves, forsooth, and wild roses! After the

oceanic platforms of the Long Isle, Skye seems like the main-land.

By further contrast to the Gneiss Islands, northern Skye is of rich basaltic loam, and there is no greener place in Skye than Uig Bay. The green coastal fringe circles the whole peninsula. On the east side it narrows between the central spine and great sea-cliffs, broadens at Staffin Bay, and then narrows on the long southward run to Portree. One big river breaches the sea-cliffs – the Lealt, which gives a huge double waterfall at the roadside. South of the Lealt the coastal scene is no less than magnificent. The parallel cliffs of sea and mountain form two steps with a vast green shelf between. The road winds along its outer edge, giving glimpses of a narrower green terrace by the shore. Each turn of the road reveals huge cliffs and capes, whose long tops of short turf stand sharp-edged against the wrinkled sea. Far offshore lie the rocky, honey-coloured islands of South Rona and Raasay.

The cliffs are all of brown basalt, which often takes columnar formation, spectacularly at the Kilt Rock, two miles south of Staffin Bay. These two miles are worth walking along the cliff-tops, which are 350 feet high. The Kilt Rock is named from the tartan-like effect of the vertical columns, which are based on grey Jurassic sediment stratified horizontally. Some of these columns have been eroded out into isolated pinnacles. From many points along the shore in summer, long salmon nets are set running outwards, each ending in an orange bag. The catch is good but the season short.

The central spine of Trotternish comes to a dramatic climax at either end. At the north is the Quiraing, at the south, the Storr. The Quiraing (pronounced Kooraing) is from the old Gaelic Cuith-raing, meaning Pillared Stronghold. It has been caused by a down-slipping of the upper cliffs to form a corrie close under the summit of Meall nan Suireamach, 1,779 feet. Its position can be clearly seen from Loch Langaig to its north. This loch is one of the most beautiful in Skye. It lies in a big green bowl of the hills beside the coastal road. A track leads in and climbs past it to a second bowl or corrie, where peats are cut. Around the two corries, conical knolls swell like giant ant-heaps, forming a belt of foothills to the Quiraing cliffs, which stand square-cut to the sky in a long, pale-grey wall. At the left-hand end rears a row of pinnacles, apart from and below the rim of the main top behind. The narrow valley between is the Quiraing.

Loch Langaig is surrounded by banks of foxgloves and bracken. When the long dusk falls and the wind dies, and provided the fish stop jumping, the water smoothes to a velvet blackness. Then it mirrors the distant pinnacles so clearly that even the dividing breaches are distinct. At the water's edge, big stones dappled black and silver by lichen run out into the shallows. Clumps of rushes between them cast black reflections that lie on the water sharper than the real plants in the air above.

The Quiraing is reached by an inland road that crosses Trotternish from Staffin Bay to Uig. At a height of 500 feet we traverse under the cliffs along a grassy terrace, dry and springy underfoot. On its seaward side, castellated crags seem splendid till we see the still higher spires of the Quiraing. An obelisk named 'The Needle' shoots up to a hundred feet, vertical on all sides save the inner, where it overhangs. A very steep path turns it on the left-hand side to a saddle behind. From there we drop into a grassy corrie, lined along its seaward side by rock towers and pinnacles, and along its inner side by the summit cliffs. No upward escape is possible. We wend our way between hummocks on to a rectangular crag at centre. Its top is a flat meadow, a hundred yards long by forty wide, hence its name 'The Table'. It seems to be set in the hall of a fortress, the outer wall slit by tall windows, through which we look across the sea to the mountains of Wester Ross and Sutherland. Our only company is a couple of ravens, whose croaks resound from tower to tower. A large variety of alpine and rock plants grow on the inner cliffs.

The Quiraing is one of Scotland's many geological freaks, but is no place of gloom (unless in wet cloud). It delights by the gay freshness of its green turf, from which these stark needles spring. They give a dramatic foreground to the flat and prosperous crofts of Staffin, which extend far along the coast below, their vast greenness dotted by white houses, dappled by cloud-shadow, and bordered by the deep blue of the Sound of Raasay. High above these flats, the hill-spine runs twelve miles south to the Storr.

The Storr, 2,358 feet, is the highest hill of Trotternish, but its fame resides in a much lesser eminence, low down on its eastern side. This is the Old Man of Storr, a great pinnacle that can be seen outlined against the sky from far south of Portree, and is a landmark to ships at sea. It is easily reached by climbing several hundred feet up the hillside to the north of Loch Leathan. It balances on the rim of a circular corrie deeply sculpted under the great cliffs of the Storr. These cliffs rise six hundred feet, split by five black gullies into six buttresses, which thus appear as separate towers, all vertical or overhanging. The Gaelic Stor means both high cliff and decayed tooth, peculiarly apt since both apply. The corrie beneath is one of the most wonderful in Scotland. Round its lower rim stands a dozen pinnacles, great and small, several of fantastic shape – one a thin corkscrew of a hundred feet with three keyhole arches in its pillar. Towering over all is the Old Man, one hundred and sixty feet high. It balances precariously, leaning outwards on a rock plinth, which is set on top of a high grassy mound. It is undercut right round its base, where the rock is black, spotted white. The main mass is light grey basalt, heavily weathered and pock-marked. Improbable though it must seem, the Old Man was climbed in 1955 by Don Whillans.

Three lesser pinnacles, including the corkscrew, are grouped close around the Old Man, which stands like the obelisk of Callanish in Lewis above its inner circle. The sight is made startling because all this aspiring rock springs from a corrie so brilliantly green, even flowery where spared by grazing sheep. Ravens croak around the upper buttresses, and buzzards flit among the lower pinnacles.

If we climb on to the summit of the Storr we can see well how Skye got its Gaelic name. Far out to the west lie the vast blue sheets of Loch Snizort, Loch Dunvegan and Loch Bracadale. Loch Snizort stretches a long arm surprisingly close below and less than six miles from Portree Bay. Skye is seen as truly winged – by Trotternish, Vaternish and Duirinish – a land of great peninsulas stretching far out to sea. The central body is quite small, ringed by the road from Portree to Loch Harport, Dunvegan and back to Portree.

In the thirteenth century, Trotternish belonged to Clan Leod under the Lords of the Isles, but after the break-up of the Lordship it was seized by the MacDonalds of Sleat, who ousted the MacLeods from Duntulm Castle on the north-west coast. Donald Gorm of Sleat moved his seat there in 1539, and sixty years of bloody feuding resulted. The ruins still stand on the edge of a sea-cliff at Duntulm Bay and look to Harris and Lewis across the Minch. After the Rising of 1715, Trotternish was forfeited to the Crown and Duntulm fell into disrepair. The fourteenth chief then used much of the stone to rebuild a family home on the flats north of Uig, where St. Columba's loch then lay – now drained to give farmland. The new house was named Monkstadt (Monk's Steading) from an islet's monastery.

It was from Monkstadt that Lady Margaret MacDonald organized the most famous escape of Scottish history – that of Prince Charles Edward from the British army and navy. Her chief agent, Flora MacDonald, was born at Milton in South Uist, but her life's story binds her forever to Skye. She lost her father early and was brought up in Sleat, where her mother had re-married. There she came under the patronage of the chief and his wife, Sir Alexander and Lady Margaret MacDonald, who sent her to school in Edinburgh for three years together with her future husband, Allan MacDonald of Kingsburgh. Flora became the MacDonald's very frequent visitor at Monkstadt.

After Culloden, Lady Margaret acted as hostess to the

The BUTT OF
LEWIS

By Aerofilms and Aero
Pictorial Ltd.

Above: LEWIS   Re-seeded moor
Below: LEWIS   Crofts at Loch Erisort, with lazybeds

By Tom Weir

officers of the Crown searching for the Prince. Her unwearied
efforts to win from them information on the movements of
their forces were entirely successful. The Prince was now in
Benbecula and South Uist with £30,000 on his head. In June,
Lady Margaret discovered that government troops had received
orders thoroughly to comb the Long Isle. She at once informed
her agents there. Flora, then aged twenty-four, simultaneously
set off for South Uist 'to visit her brother at Milton'. She was
met by Captain O'Neill of the Prince's retinue and undertook
to arrange an escape to Skye. She was arrested by troops while
visiting Lady Clanranald, but demanded an interview with the
commander of the Hanoverian force in South Uist – who
happened to be her stepfather. He at once granted her pass-
ports for the return voyage to Skye, made out in favour of
herself and her maid 'Betty Burke'.

The Prince had been hiding in a cave on Rueval, a hill on
Benbecula. On 28th June, he and Flora went to Rossinish, on
Benbecula's riven east coast, and that evening put to sea in an
open boat manned by a crew of five oarsmen. A storm blew up
in the Minch, and after a fearsome night they tried to land for
rest next morning at Vaternish Point, but were fired on by
troops. Rounding the point, they sighted warships but were
able to dodge into a creek until the coast was clear. Despite
these delays they landed at noon that same day on the Trotternish shore below Monkstadt House.

Leaving the Prince, now disguised as Betty Burke, among the
rocks by the shore, Flora entered the house to find Lady
Margaret dining with General Campbell and other army
officers. She had to accept the invitation to sit with them, but
succeeded in passing information to Lady Margaret, who at
once sent MacDonald of Kingsburgh (Allan's father) to the
Prince with food. Prince Charlie spent that night at Kingsburgh House, and after five more days of hazardous travel in
Raasay and Skye, escaped from Elgol to the mainland, and in
September to France. There can hardly be more striking evidence of the loyalty and devotion to the Prince of the simple

F

folk of the Highlands than their utter contempt of that £30,000 reward, then a vast fortune.

News of the Prince's escape from the Isles had broken when the crew of the Benbecula boat were arrested on their return to South Uist. Confession had been forced. Flora, meanwhile, had returned home to Sleat, but nine days later was arrested and taken aboard the *Furnace* under command of the notorious sadist, Captain Ferguson. She was luckily transferred to the *Royal Sovereign* and taken to London, where she was held prisoner in a private house until the passing of the Indemnity Act of 1747. On her release, she found herself the lionness of London, visited by Frederick, Prince of Wales, among many other men of rank. Her admirers raised a fund and presented her with several hundred pounds.

She returned to Skye and married Allan MacDonald, with whom she lived for eight years at Flodigarry (now a hotel) in north-east Trotternish, and by whom she had five sons and two daughters. They removed to Kingsburgh on the death of Allan's mother in 1759. When Dr. Johnson and Boswell paid a call in 1773 they found them in straitened circumstances. Heavy losses in livestock forced them to emigrate to North Carolina. During the American War of Independence, Allan served with the British forces, holding rank as brigade major until he was made prisoner. On his advice, Flora returned to Milton in South Uist. Five years later he rejoined her in Skye, where he took the tack of Peinduin in Trotternish. Flora died in 1790 at the age of sixty-eight and was buried in the churchyard of Kilmuir. Allan, who died two years later, lies beside her.

Their tomb at Kilmuir is sited on high ground overlooking Score Bay. Tourists have broken up the original tombstone and removed all of it in pieces. In its place there has now been raised a tall Celtic cross, which looks across the Minch to Uist. Inscribed on the cross are the words spoken in her praise by Dr. Johnson: 'A name that will be mentioned in history, and if courage and fidelity be virtues, mentioned with honour.'

Portree, at the base of the Trotternish Peninsula, is the

capital of Skye, the finest harbour, and the fairest town. It received its name of Port Righ, or King's Harbour, when James V landed during his tour of the West Highlands. Its present population is 2,000. The old inn, where Flora Mac-Donald took leave of her Prince, is now part of the Royal Hotel. Four roads strike out across Skye from Portree. One goes by way of Loch Snizort twenty-two miles to Loch Dunvegan, which is enclosed by the great wings of Vaternish and Duirinish. The road falls from the Trotternish moors to round two inner arms of Loch Snizort, both well-wooded at their heads. The second, Loch Greshornish, is unusually beautiful on the approach to the village of Edinbain. The fields sloping to the narrow sea-loch are in July flushed pink by seeded hay, and sparkling white from massed banks of ox-eye daisies. Thereafter the road rises and falls across green moors to Dunvegan.

Much of the best natural scenery that Skye can offer, apart from the Cuillin, is concentrated at or around Dunvegan. It is a land of mountain, moor and woodland, seen across foregrounds of rugged shore varied by bays and cliffs, islands and green crofts, thatched steadings and white houses. Less than a mile beyond the village, Dunvegan Castle stands on its crag by the shore. Substantial as it is, the building is not of high architectural value. It is said to be built on the site of a ninth-century Norse fortress, and is one of the oldest inhabited castles in Scotland. For seven hundred years it has been continuously occupied as the home of the MacLeods, of which the present chief is Dame Flora. A part of the castle, and its woods east of the main road, are open to the public. It is a rare pleasure in the Isles to have this chance of walking through scented pine, spruce, larch and cyprus, and to enjoy the sight of deciduous trees in abundance, which here are beech, chestnut, cherry, sycamore and oak. Among the various treasures displayed in the castle is the famous Fairy Flag, which the fairies gifted to the fourth chief. Waved in battle it summons supernatural aid for the Clan Leod. The extremely fragile cloth still retains most delicate beauties of colour.

Vaternish divides Loch Dunvegan from Loch Snizort. Five miles up its west coast, a little peninsula thrusts out west, then curves south to form Ardmore Bay. On a high, windswept plateau above the isthmus stands the ruin of Trumpan Church, the scene of the sequel to the massacre at the cave of Eigg in 1577. Ever since then, the MacDonalds of Clanranald had been seeking revenge. In May 1578, the MacDonalds of Uist sailed across to Skye with a fleet of eight ships. On a Sunday morning, under cover of thick fog, they landed at the north bay of the isthmus below Trumpan. The local people were at church. The invaders barred the door from the outside and set the thatch alight. All inside were burned alive, save for one woman who somehow escaped although her breast had been cut clean off by a swordsman. Wind cleared the fog and men of the district gathered, but they were easily beaten off.

Meantime, the MacLeod at Dunvegan had heard the news. His galleys were quickly manned and sped north. They came into Ardmore Bay on the south side of the isthmus, where the Fairy Flag was unfurled. The MacDonalds withdrew to their boats, only to find them left high and dry by the ebb-tide and already in MacLeod hands. Along the shore ran a long, dry-stone dike, built to screen the crops from the sea. The Mac-Donalds set their backs to it and made a last stand. They were killed to a man along the base of that wall, which was then tumbled on top of them. It has been reported that in big westerly storms, when great seas crash over this rocky shore, the old wall has been breached and bones exposed.

The wall is still there, now low and grassed along the edge of the north beach, which is appropriately of black stone and black sand. Trumpan Church still stands on the hill, pointing one gable to the sky, the other walls being low and broken. At the wide mouth of Loch Dunvegan, islands ride like high-prowed ships, sheltered by the great butt of Dunvegan Head. Ardmore Point has a fine flying buttress, where the sea has bored a big double arch. This is a windy promontory at the best of times. I last tried to go there when a westerly gale stopped me, forcing

me to crawl on hands and knees along its broad ridge. From
there I could see the line of sea-cliff running three miles north
to Vaternish Point: half a dozen rivers pour over these cliffs
and should have been dropping as waterfalls, but the wind was
seizing them and blowing them vertically up, so that they
looked like geysers spouting high above the cliff-tops.

Four miles north of Dunvegan Castle are two beaches of
coral, often wrongly claimed as unique to Skye or Scotland.
They lie at the strait of An Dornell between the Dunvegan
coast and the Lampay islands. The beaches are entirely of coral,
fragmented to a coarse sand and thickly strewn with shells of
every conceivable colour. At low tide, pieces of pink, white
and purple coral, branched and twisted, can easily be gathered
in quantity. They are not made by the polyps of tropical seas,
but by one of the algae called Lithothamnion. This seaweed
grows in cushions several fathoms offshore. Bits broken off by
the sea are cast up to form the beaches. The plant is a most
efficient extractor of lime from sea-water. In former days,
thousands of tons of its product were carted for fertilizing the
fields. This coral is also found in Skye near Staffin, in the
Summer Isles at Tanera Beag, at Erbusaig near Kyle of Loch
Alsh, and at Duncraig Island on Loch Carron.

Duirinish, on the other side of Loch Dunvegan, is a much
bigger wing than Vaternish, with higher hills that give better
protection to its numerous crofting townships. The biggest of
these is spread around Glendale above Loch Pooltiel on the
north-west coast. The crofts lie in a strath of oolitic loam,
which gives good arable land. The hill-grazing too is good, for
the rock is basalt, but cattle and sheep tend to get lost over the
crumbly sea-cliffs, which ring the coast for thirty-five miles
and are grassed to their edges, and thus doubly dangerous.

Duirinish has splendid sea-cliffs at Neist, the most westerly
point of Skye. Neist Point is the north arm of Moonen Bay, but
juts south and carries a lighthouse. At the inner wall of the bay,
Waterstein Head rises vertically out of the sea to 967 feet. A
concrete stair on the crags allows descent for a hundred feet to

a path running out to the lighthouse. From the path under this hillock, we may walk northwards up the coast along the cliff-tops. Shags' nests can be seen on the rock-faces. Fulmars nest there too, solan geese dive offshore, and black rabbits scurry among the boulders. This cliff-top is alive with rabbits, which must please the eagles that keep eyrie a mile to the north above Oisgill Bay.

The lighthouse perches on the brink of a high cliff. The paraffin burner and reflectors, which are mounted on mercury, are turned by gear-wheels moved by a weight, which hangs on a long chain down the centre of the lighthouse. This chain has to be wound up by hand every forty-five minutes. If we go out-side to the upper balcony we find a view embracing the entire Outer Hebrides. The sea below is green and yeasty, and crawls.

The east side of Duirinish, which forms the west shore of Loch Bracadale, has been favoured by the Forestry Commis-sion. They have several new plantations on the hill-slopes of the Varkasaig River beneath Healaval Bheag (MacLeod's Table) and at bays along this coast. Varkasaig Bay has a beach of black sand, which looks south to Rhum and Canna, and across the many-islanded loch to Minginish. The best view in all Duirinish is from the top of Healaval Bheag, 1,601 feet. Its sister, Healaval Mhor, is bigger in bulk but sixty feet shorter. They are famed as 'MacLeod's Tables', and not simply because their tops happen to be flat. The true Table is Healaval Bheag, and how the Table got its name is one of Skye's best stories.

During the first half of the sixteenth century, Alasdair MacLeod was the seventh chief at Dunvegan, and one of the ablest men of his time. As a youth he had led his clan in battle against invading MacDonalds in Duirinish and routed them, but had received an axe-wound between the shoulder-blades. The wound deformed him, so that he was known thereafter as Alasdair Crotach, or Hunchback. He extended Dunvegan and lived there in state. On one of his visits to the royal palace at Edinburgh, when he was dining with King James V, his gracious air and ease of manner discomfited a Lowland earl, who tried to trap this islander into some admission of wonder at the palatial dining hall.

'MacLeod,' said he, 'I'll wager that nowhere in Skye have you clapped eye on a room so big and spacious, nor any with roof so high, or table so rich, or candelabra so brilliant.'

Alasdair Crotach gave him a quick, astonished glance, then for the first time allowed his eye to travel around the room. 'Unsurpassed in Edinburgh, most certainly. But in Skye I could readily show you a room more spacious, a roof still loftier, a table greater and more richly spread, and lights more splendid by far.'

Incredulity sharpened the earl's eye. Enraged, he swore to prove MacLeod false by a visit to Skye. Alasdair Crotach, with a mocking smile, invited him to Skye as his guest.

Some weeks later, news reached Dunvegan that the earl was coming. Great preparations were made. Alasdair Crotach met his guest on the Bracadale road, and led him and his retinue not to the castle but to Healaval Bheag. They arrived on the summit as the sun fell behind the Outer Hebrides. Long thin clouds above the western sea were blazing scarlet and gold. The flat mountain-top, over its whole surface of fifty yards square, was spread with meats and wines. All round the edge stood the chief's clansmen, bearing aloft flambeaux, which they now lit. The chief invited his guests to be seated. When the banquet ended in the early hours of the morning, he pointed to the starry sky and said, 'I ask you to agree with me, sir, that my roof is loftier than Holyrood's, this table greater than any to be found in cities, and my clansmen more splendid than candelabra.'

We may assume that the earl agreed, since he came down alive.

Alasdair was also a patron of the arts, and the first of the MacLeods to patronize the MacCrimmon pipers. He gave them the district of Boreraig, on the north-east shore of Duirinish, where they lived rent-free and without feudal obligation save to train one son for the office of piper to the chief. The

MacCrimmons were thus able to found their college of piping, which became world famous. Nearly all the Highland chiefs sent their pipers to Boreraig to finish their training. By 1770 the value of land had soared. Norman, the nineteenth chief, then took back half the Boreraig farm. So galled was MacCrimmon that he and his family renounced piping and left Boreraig forever.

The site of Alasdair Crotach's banquet is often wrongly given as Healaval Mhor, which is nearer Dunvegan. Its much bigger top is exceedingly wet, marshy and rough. Damp moss would give the only, intolerable seat. From either hill, but especially the dry top of Healaval Bheag, the view is superb. Its two great features are the Cuillin seen across Bracadale Bay, and the Outer Hebrides across the Minch.

The Cuillin, Red and Black, are seen in full length to better advantage than from anywhere else in Scotland, for their fore-ground has no rival. Its huge sheet of gleaming blue is encased by cliffs carved into twenty bays, capes and points. The off-shore islands lie around, blunt-nosed like Moby Dicks. Beyond all towers the long jagged line of the Black Cuillin, their teeth raking the fast-travelling clouds.

Out west the scene is much quieter. There the Outer Hebrides curve in a vast bow round the horizon, a hundred and thirty miles from Barra Head to the Butt of Lewis. All the main isles are clear but change colour with distance: Lewis and Harris dark brown, Berneray rimmed white by sand, North Uist grey and South Uist blue, Eriskay and Barra pale lilac.

The road south from Bracadale leads into the district of Minginish. Its north boundary is Loch Harport, its east the Cuillin. The west coast is worried into great headlands by the bays of Fiskavaig, Talisker, Loch Eynort and Loch Brittle. The land between is high moorland, but the glens trenching it to the bays are fertile at their seaward ends. Fiskavaig, where the sands are black, has the island's best view of MacLeod's Tables across Loch Bracadale. Talisker is a deep, green glen, narrowly enclosed. Its wide black sands are fringed by dirty black cliffs and by one tall basaltic stack. Glen Eynort is very much more pleasant with new Forestry Commission plantations. The loch has a sheltered, inland character, for its twist between hills cuts off the sea-view. The forest has brought Eynort new life in a village of well-designed wooden houses.

Glen Brittle is by far the finest glen of Minginish, broader and more open than the others, its fields well-farmed and fertile – flat enough to be used prior to the last war as an air-strip. The upper part is planted by the Forestry Commission. The sands of the bay are less black than the others of this coast, and the foreshore in summer is heavily congested by campers, nearly all of them climbers. Between Glen Brittle and Sligachan, the seven-mile ridge of the Black Cuillin swings around Coruisk. Their north end is best approached from the inn at Sligachan; the south by motor-boat from Elgol to Loch Coruisk, which best of all shows the shape of the main ridge.

When people think of Skye, the Cuillin are always a main part of any mental image, for they are visible from every district, the island's distinctive scenic backdrop. They remain a backdrop for most people. To the man of exploratory instinct with energy to burn, they disclose at close quarters a mountain scene unique in Britain. The range is naked rock. Its name comes from the old Norse Kjöllen, meaning Keel-shaped Ridges. Other ranges thus named are found in Iceland and Sweden. The derivation from Cu chuill-fhionn (or Cuchullin), meaning Hero of the Fair Hair, is the fanciful work of Gaelic story-tellers.

The peaks are of coarse, crystalline gabbro. This rock, so dear to the heart of mountaineers, has the same chemical composition as the smooth basalt, which they so much dislike – and which is present in the Cuillin in equal surface-quantity. Basalt has cooled rapidly from the lava poured out at the earth's surface. Gabbro has cooled slowly under its cover, but has since been exposed by erosion. Proving more resistant to weather than basalt, it projects in twenty sharp peaks that form a continuous horse-shoe round Loch Coruisk. The ridge is narrow, its corries have been deeply gouged by glaciers, and the rock is bare of grass. The tops are mostly of 3,000 feet and lift to 3,251 feet on Sgurr Alasdair. Few can be climbed without aid of the hands, and since much of the rock is magnetic, compass bearings cannot be relied upon for route-finding in mist. The Cuillin are mountains for mountaineers.

Two summits that can easily be reached by walkers are Bruach na Frithe, 3,143 feet, by way of its north-west ridge from Sligachan, and Sgurr Alasdair by way of the great Stone Shoot of Coire Lagan from Glen Brittle.

The traverse of the main ridge, which gives ten thousand feet of climbing, is the best day's mountaineering in Scotland. I have been along the entire length of that ridge at every season of the year except midwinter, and traversed it at least in part on more than a hundred days. I find the extreme diversity of its scene equalled by no other range. When the skies are clear I am inclined to drift along the ridge, which is then no place for blind-eyed speed, watching and moving by fits and starts. The cliffs stand around in tall-towered battlements that react chameleon-like to every change of sky, turning from black to purple, to blue, grey, pale brown (the natural colour of the rock), rich chocolate, sunset red, and so back to black. The clean slabs take a free and spacious lift, their brown gabbro bending over space with the virgin freshness of green seas breaking white on a skerry.

The Cuillin reach an extreme of bleakness in foul weather. April snow and October sleet have caught me on the ridge encircling Coire a Ghrunnda and translated me to the ninth and inner circle of hell. September gale has flattened me like a pinned beetle on a cliff-face of Sgurr nan Gillean. A May hurricane has torn a tent from above my head at midnight in Coruisk. I have crouched shivering in June on damp rock below the cairn of Garsbheinn, enduring thick wet drizzle, waiting for the dawn-light to let me start along the ridge, and listening to the staccato bark of foxes in lonely Coruisk, where they raised lingering, mournful echoes. Far below me, the flashing light on the island of Soay would momentarily reveal the isle's flat outline on sea ink-black. It was then hard to believe that any humans would choose to live in lands so wretched. An hour or two later, the crowded peaks and pinnacles, black no longer but steely grey in the sunshine, surged up as if eagerly towards the light of a blue sky. With equal extreme emphasis, the Cuillin mourn, rage and rejoice.

Anyone who has not been on the Cuillin in May or June has not, in strict truth, seen Skye at its best. There is then an exquisite quality in the sunlight seen only during the three months after the spring equinox. At this time the Hebridean seas take that royal blue of depth unknown to other seasons. In June from Sgurr Alasdair I have watched the Minch, burnished by light, appear like a slope of polished ice rising gently up to the horizon – so strong an illusion that I wondered the Outer Hebrides did not slide back like curling stones to the mainland. The unfailing Atlantic swell must still have been there, for snatches of foam were frilling the shores of Loch Brittle. Eighty miles north-west, across the back of North Uist, St. Kilda showed as a tiny dot on the skyline.

When clouds are trailing over the tops, and mist writhing between the pinnacles, the savage edge astounds the eye in a series of distorted towers. They impend suddenly and vanish away like grim ghosts. On one such morning, when I was on Sgurr a Mhadaidh between dawn and sunrise, the swirling mist slowly began to sink on every hand until each Cuillin peak thrust a black tip through snow-white cloud. Across still submerged passes, the cloud-sea poured like the seething overfall of Corrievreckan, surging and spinning, falling and rising, as though impelled by a powerful tide. The empty skies changed from grey to cornflower blue, black rock to ashen, and the sun rode up behind the Red Cuillin. At once the cloud-surface flashed to flame. Coruisk like a mountain crucible brimmed with burning silver, and the twenty circling spires flushed faintly pink, For the space of a minute the rocks crimsoned, as suddenly paled, and day had come.

I have mentioned only a few of the penalties and pleasures of exploring the Cuillin – being infinite in variety they are not exhaustible in a man's lifetime – hoping to show that if one is heavy the other is high.

Some very different rewards are won by work in Minginish. From Carbost, by the shores of Loch Harport, comes a most famous product of Skye, Talisker whisky, which my palate prefers before all other pure malts. Talisker is the only distillery in Skye. It was first set up in 1830 by two brothers Macaskill, who were sheep-farmers, and is now owned by the Daluaine Distillery Company. The site remains unchanged and thirty-five men are employed. The ground is still leased from the MacLeods of Dunvegan Castle, and peat still cut from the hills above.

In Scotland there are almost a hundred malt whisky distilleries, each producing one whisky known as a 'single whisky', and no two are alike. Just what determines the flavour of a single whisky (as distinct from a blend) is very much a mystery. It is not the water nor the quantity and quality of the peat used in drying out the malt, or not these alone. Distillers consider that the factors determining flavour and quality are probably a combination of water-character, local climate, the shape of the still, and a host of details in processing. For this reason, they prefer to extend an old distillery, whose whisky has been proved, than to build a new one where the quality of the product is necessarily speculative.

Barley is delivered to Talisker by sea. It is steeped for fifty-eight hours in water drawn from the Carbost burn, then spread four inches deep on a concrete floor to germinate, which breaks the starch. The grain is turned by hand to prevent the felting of the rootlets. Germination must be checked at an early stage, and this is done by re-spreading the now malted barley on a grilled floor and heating it until only 3 per cent water-content remains. The barley is now 'dead'. It has a delicious malt-like flavour when picked off the floor and eaten. From the drying-floor, which is overhung by great pagoda-shaped

funnels, the malt goes into a double roller-mill. The first breaks
the husk, paddles flip it off, and the second rollers crush the
kernel. The meal goes into tubs of hot water where rapid action
by the grain's enzymes on the starch produces sugar. Yeast
joins the mash and hastens fermentation (the insoluble residues
are used for cattle-cake). The resulting wash is cooled through
copper worms and fed into two copper wash-stills. The distil-
late is piped out as 'low wines' (low alcoholic degree) and
returned to another two stills, whence it is finally piped out as
proof spirit. A proof spirit is 57 per cent pure alcohol and 43
per cent water. It leaves the still colourless and is stored in oak
casks to mature over several years. Once bottled, Scotch
whisky does not alter in any way.

I have been asked, especially by Englishmen, 'What are the
best malt whiskies?' or 'What qualities should one look for in
choosing a whisky?' The true answer is that there is no 'best'.
I have tasted thirty single whiskies at one sitting, and been con-
vinced that one cannot be declared 'better' than another. They
differ widely in weight and taste. The most that any man can
justly say is that his palate prefers one to another. Let his palate
be the judge and let him trust it. The 'best' whisky is the one he
best likes.

Three miles up the coast from Carbost is the little township
of Port na Long, whose men work at the distillery. Crofters
from Lewis and Harris came here in 1921, hence much weaving
of tweed is done by the men and knitting by the women. The
small crofts in their open, sunny situation preserve one of the
few remaining scenes of old-time Skye. Another such scene is
at Isleornsay in Sleat. Sleat has the smallest isthmus of any of
the big peninsulas – less than one and a half miles across. On
passing through its bare land we come down the east coast into
mainland scenery at Isleornsay, where there is a lush growth of
hedgeside plants below the trees and hedges. Sleat is weeks
ahead of the rest of the island in crop-growth, for it is much
better sheltered.

Isleornsay has a snug bay between the tidal island of Ornsay and Sleat. An inn stands on a little headland facing the pier, where all is quiet and peaceful, for there is no passing traffic. Between the sea and the main road, a side-road runs a quarter of a mile south. Croft-houses line it, all neat and close and well-painted. Their tiny holdings fall to Camas Croise Bay. The whole forms a piece of old Skye in a delightful backwater. Across the sound, Loch Hourn is guarded by the tall mountains of Ben Sgriol and Ladhar Bheinn.

Three miles south, the bay at Knock was once guarded by Camus Castle, now an ivy-clad stump on a rocky knoll by the shore. Camus was formerly one of the two principal castles of Sleat, the other being Dun Sgathaich on the west coast. It belonged first to the MacLeods, later to the MacDonalds. It says much for the strength of Clan Donald in Sleat that when Sir Donald MacDonald's estates were declared forfeit, because he declined to recognize William of Orange as king, and two warships were sent to bring him to heel in 1690, his men captured the landing party and strung them up on gallows improvised out of oars in front of the castle – and that none the less the MacDonalds have retained Sleat from that day to this.

From Knock four miles south to Armadale the land becomes more heavily wooded, especially around Armadale Castle, until recently Lord MacDonald's seat. The ground in southeast Sleat is glacial drift on gneiss, giving green hills and prosperous farms and crofts. Depopulation has here given larger holdings, but there are numerous small crofts farther south at Aird of Sleat. The high ground of Aird gives splendid views to Mallaig and the mouth of Loch Nevis, and to the miles of white sand lining the Morar coast.

The west coast of Sleat is almost empty, apart from one good crofting township at Tarskavaig, a croft or two at Tokavaig farther north, and a small hotel at Ord, which lies in a backwater with islets offshore. Ord and Tokavaig share one of the most excellent views to be had in all Skye. They look straight across Loch Slapin to the Cuillin. I know of no other low point from which every single peak of the Cuillin main ridge may be seen – all twenty-three of them, followed by Blaven, Clach Glas, and the Red Cuillin. A sunset from Ord can be one of the great sights of Scotland.

At Tokavaig, the bay of red sandstone has an island stack crowned by the ruins of Dun Sgathaich ('Scaich' on recent maps). It was once held by the MacAskills of Skye for the Norse kings of Man, then for the MacLeods, until the MacDonalds took possession. It has been stormed, taken and re-taken in countless clan feuds and rebellions. A deep sea-moat between shore and ruin is still spanned by an arched bridge, which can be crossed with difficulty. The grassy battlements give Sleat's finest view of the Cuillin.

Save for these seaward views, the shores of Sleat seem curiously dead after those of the Argyll islands and Outer Hebrides. The woods along the coastal strip are a pleasant surprise at first. They shelter landbirds: wood-pigeons moan, wood-peckers drill, owls hoot and tits are ubiquitous, but the hinterland is uninteresting and the shores have this strange lifelessness. One misses the oyster-catchers.

The whole of Skye facing the Minch is poor in fauna, by comparison with other islands. But wild-life is far from absent. The islets near Dunvegan are visited by both the Atlantic and common seals. Birds nesting there include shags, gulls and eiders. There are many buzzards, eagles, ravens, and foxes around the hills and cliffs – I have seen four eagles in the air at once close around Sgurr Alasdair. On sea and coast one may notice fulmars, curlews, redshanks, red-throated divers, herons and oyster-catchers. In autumn the cormorant visits. In winter many birds arrive from the Arctic: whooper swans to the fresh-water lochs, great northern divers to Kyle Akin, small flocks of snow-bunting, and barnacle and white-fronted geese.

In prehistoric times, when Skye was joined to the mainland, birch and hazel covered much land now bare. Evidence of early inhabitants are seen in chambered cairns, earth houses tunnelled into the flanks of hills, beehive houses, and duns, of which eighty or ninety have been listed. In 794 Skye was devastated by Norsemen. Around 875, following the revolution in Norway that established Harold Fairhair as king, they came for the first time as immigrants. After Somerled's conquest of the southern Hebrides Norse rule continued in Skye and brought bloody attacks from the mainland. The Norse King of the Isles, Olav the Black, appealed to Norway for aid. King Hakon sailed west over sea in 1263 to meet his doom at Largs. On his southward voyage, his fleet of a hundred and twenty ships anchored off Skye in the strait that has ever since been called Kyle Akin (Hakon's Strait).

On the cession of the Isles to Scotland, Skye was added to the territory of the Lords of the Isles, who made grant to Clan Leod. Leod was son of Olav the Black. Towards the end of the fourteenth century, the Clan Donald took Sleat from the MacLeods by force, consolidated the gain, then seized Trotternish a hundred years later. In 1539 the MacDonald seat was moved from Dun Sgathaich to Duntulm. The next sixty years of clan feuding ended in 1601 after a last battle at Coire na Creiche in the Cuillin. James VI, now concerned for his reputation in London, brought the two parties together in amity, and this lasted.

The population of Skye reached its peak of 23,074 in 1841. Half the people were destitute. The kelp industry had failed, the potato crop had failed and continued to fail in successive years, and the herring fishing failed. Fishing had formerly been a most important industry, but around 1830 the herring seem to have disappeared from the sea-lochs of Skye. Lord MacDonald ruined his estate trying to maintain his wretched people. His affairs had to be placed in the hands of trustees. Sheep-farming was introduced and ruthless factors cleared the people – freely using force to evict them and razing their homes to prevent return. Emigration followed, reducing the population to its present 7,400. The decrease of the last decade has been 12 per cent.

In 1882 there occurred one of the more important events of recent island history. In the district of Braes, on the east side of

Skye, the crofters revolted against the unjust land laws. They evicted by force a Sheriff's officer trying to evict crofters. In the 'Battle of the Braes', which followed, they stoned and fought in hand to hand combat with sixty policemen sent to enforce the eviction order. The people of Skye were now seething with anger. Warships and troops were sent in a vain attempt to over-awe the crofters – who finally won their battle, for Mr. Gladstone began to realize that there had been a gross dereliction of responsible government from London in preceding years. A Royal Commission was appointed under Lord Napier, whose revelation of dire injustices brought the Crofters' Holdings Act of 1886, which gave security of tenure and fair rent.

Since then, the redistribution of land by the Congested Districts Board, and later by the Department of Agriculture, has greatly reduced the number of large owners. Preservation of game has wellnigh ceased. Almost all the hills are grazed and Skye has become one of the most heavily crofted areas of west Scotland. Since the Land Improvement Scheme of 1956, six hundred acres of croft land have been regenerated, reseeded or reclaimed.

Game sport is thus not an ancillary occupation. Work offered in support of crofting includes a wool mill at Portree, and the weaving of tweeds, rugs, and baskets at Kilmuir in north Trotternish and at Port na Long; masonry, building, a diatomite factory, estate work, and the distillery at Carbost; forestry work, which is becoming increasingly important in Minginish and Duirinish; road work, which employs a large number of men – Skye has 250 miles of motor-road; some lobster, prawn, salmon and herring fishing; and tourism.

Tourism has brought much money into Skye. In 1964, a hundred thousand cars and more than a quarter of a million passengers crossed the south ferries. In terms of actual employment, however, forestry and road-making give more work. The flood of summer visitors has brought great changes to Skye. One fairly recent feature, which has changed the appearance of the island very much for the better, is the exterior painting of houses. The bed-and-breakfast houses were painted first to draw tourists, and the rest followed suit. A change for the worse is the dying out of the islesman's traditional generosity and hospitality towards visitors – an inevitable process granted huge numbers of tourists. This process is by no means universal, but it is marked, and is accompanied by a growing disposition to regard the tourist as a subject for plunder. In short, I have witnessed in Skye over recent years a corruption of the people's former standards of behaviour, which in some respects remain higher than those of the mainland – one can leave a car anywhere in Skye unlocked – in others no better. Honesty stays but avarice, 'the spur of industry' (said David Hume), slowly spreads. These observations do not apply to the old people.

Most Skyemen still speak the Gaelic and belong to the Free Church, often called the 'Wee Frees'. The fight that the people have recently made to preserve the Sabbath as a day of rest in face of demands from men of business outside the island, who would provide facilities for tourism on Sundays, deserves sympathy, respect and acceptance. The Skyeman, like other islanders, is radical in politics and conservative in religion. His history shows the good reason.

LEWIS AND HARRIS

THE Outer Hebrides are the oldest-known splinter of Europe. Their rock is almost wholly of archaean gneiss. Forty to fifty miles out from the mainland, they and Skye were probably the original Hav-bred-ey, since the Norsemen would explore them first on rounding Cape Wrath. Today they are often distinguished from the rest of the Hebrides by the name Western Isles, which denotes a political constituency of all seventeen inhabited islands from Barra to Lewis: a unity shown again in their name Long Isle.

The character of the gneiss has determined the distribution of the population. The rock swells in vast moors not far above sea-level, but often rises in hills of 1,000 to 2,000 feet, which reach their highest point and density around Clisham, 2,622 feet, between Lewis and Harris. The moors are so blanketed by peat and congested by freshwater lochs that nearly a quarter of the land-area is under water. The deep peat of the interior is an accumulation of the last seven thousand years, when the warm dry climate prior to 5000 B.C. was succeeded by wet. It is not habitable land. Man lives on the coastal periphery.

The west coast of the Long Isle is lined for almost a hundred and thirty miles by shell-sand, rather scantily in Lewis. This one feature has been of the most vital importance to the life of the islands. Behind the marram dunes lies the calcareous machair, which forms in the southern half from North Uist to Barra a continuous strip of grassland from a few hundred yards to two miles deep, much of it arable. It supports a strong population. The Uists and Barra have only one third of the land area of Lewis and Harris, which is the biggest island of the Hebrides, but have more grazing ground and nearly as much tillage; yet Lewis and Harris have almost thrice their population.

The explanation is that the men of Lewis, having relatively little machair, have been faced with a sharper challenge than those of the south, whose way of life is almost entirely agricultural. The men of the north have had to find alternative ways of livelihood, and so well have they risen to that challenge, especially in weaving and fishing, that Lewis and Harris carry a population of 24,600 – far greater than their crofting could possibly maintain.

In sharp contrast to the west coast, the east flank of the Long Isle is the grimmest of the Hebrides – stark rock frenetically torn. Yet this too is well inhabited, especially in Lewis and Harris, for the west coast has few harbours, the east coast many, encouraging fishing if not agriculture. Granted the townships based on fishing, there has followed weaving, knitting and tillage by lazybedding – the most elaborate and best of its kind in Scotland today.

Rainfall varies from 40 to 60 inches, being highest around the hills of the Harris-Lewis boundary, and lowest at Ness in the north. The outstanding climatic feature is wind.

Lewis and Harris are divided not by sea but a county boundary: Lewis to the county of Ross and Harris to Inverness. There are three lines of approach: by daily plane from Glasgow to Stornoway; by week-day steamer from Mallaig to Stornoway; and by week-day car-ferry from Uig in Skye to Loch Tarbert in Harris. The latter allows a sea-approach of only twenty-seven miles as against nearly one hundred from Mallaig – a matter of some moment on a stormy Minch.

Sailing out from Uig of Skye, we pass three groups of islands: the Ascribs in Loch Snizort, the Fladdachuain off North Skye, and the Shiants close to Harris – all Tertiary basalt capped with friable soil, therefore thronged by burrowing puffins. On closer approach to East Loch Tarbert the Shiant Islands claim our attention. The three Shiants lie twelve miles north, yet take the eye with their great cliffs, which on the north side rise to 500 feet in Scotland's most impressive array of hexagonal columns. More than a thousand guillemots nest on the Shiants, and the puffinry is one of Scotland's biggest.

Athwart the entrance to East Loch Tarbert lies Scalpay Island. It was once the centre of a thriving herring fishery; it is still heavily inhabited and its western bays busy with boats engaged in white fishing. Any visitor new to the Outer Isles will now be astonished that so much bare rock, scarcely tufted with heather, can harbour numerous human lives. The landscape here and all around Tarbert is lunar. Tiny though it is, Tarbert is a most pleasant village and the people smiling and friendly. The only town in the Outer Hebrides is Stornoway.

LEWIS

Before turning to Stornoway, we do best to see the real Lewis in which it is set. The long approach through the Harris hills by the shores of Loch Seaforth gives a first glimpse of that extraordinary feature of the Outer Hebrides, the black moor of Lewis. Its dark brown peat-bog is bespattered with several hundred lochs, especially around Loch Erisort. When the sky is bright they scintillate, intensely blue on the stark moor; when the sky is full of windy cloud they glint whitely, or in rain lie black and fathomless, weird or brilliant as weather dictates. They give the land its name, for Lewis, called 'the Lews' by the people, derives from Leogach (pronounced Looach) meaning marshy. Depressingly grim as the scene can often be, yet when flooded by sun and seen from the moor's centre, say on the Glen Mor Barvas road, which crosses the island from Stornoway to the west coast, its rolling immensity and vast skyscapes display a Hebridean majesty unique of its kind.

The moor is by no means entirely sterile. Apart from the excellent fishing to be had on many of its lochs, there are green slopes and hollows where a few cattle can be grazed in summer.

These are the shielings, often with tiny huts alongside, which can be seen from the roadways. Earlier, in May and June, the moors are busy with peat-cutters and lifters. Wisps of blue smoke may be seen curling from the fires, where old black pots boil potatoes and herring for lunch. A good man can cut a thousand peats a day, or a year's supply in fifteen to twenty days. The women lift and gather using creels to carry from the banks to the roadsides. Hard as the work is, and expensive in time, it makes an important social occasion, which the people enjoy.

Peat-cutting over the centuries near the crofting townships has laid bare boulder-clay, which is called skinned ground. Usually this becomes part of the common grazing, but when treated with shell-sand (lime) and seaweed it has made good soil.

Townships spread all the way up the west coast from the great bay of Loch Roag to the Butt. The infrequent sandy beaches, like Dalmore and Dalbeg, lie in bays ringed by cliffs, which prevent the beneficial inward blowing of sand. These cliff-tops offer delightful walking on short springy turf. Blue spring squills and primroses spread among the grass. Grey lag and barnacle geese come down in winter, but not in great number. Promontories allow close-up views of shags and fulmars nesting on the pink and grey rock. The fields around the bays are whitened by daisies, and sometimes blackened by flocks of starlings where a ruined house gives them shelter. Their enemy the hoodie-crow will sometimes pick out one bird and pursue it relentlessly from cliff to cliff across the bay while it soars and plummets in vain, finally to drop exhausted into the water, often there to be snatched by a gull from under the hoodie's beak.

The townships lie on the mile-wide strip between moorland road and sea. Nearly all the names have the Norse ring: Callanish, Carloway, Shawbost, Bragar, Arnol, Brue, Barvas, Shader, Borve and so on all the way to Ness at the Butt. The numerous houses stand widely spaced on their green crofts in chaotic disarray of site and design. The new and the old stand together in striking contrast and giving a tumble-down effect. The new white houses, mostly built by the crofters themselves, are uniform in grey-cemented walls of two storeys, roofed in composite slate, or corrugated iron, or bitumen felt. Alongside them lie the old thatched black houses, now used as byres or weaving sheds. Many are modernized, inhabited by old folk who have been unable to build anew. They have electricity, and tap-water laid on to a post outside the front door. Great stacks of peat form a useful windbreak beside each house. The air is scented with the reek of the fires. The crofts are long and narrow, and nowadays well-fenced. They are so many and so small that we are at first astounded that so many people can live off so little land – until we see at the roadside dumps of woven tweed awaiting transport to the mills at Stornoway, where the tweed is finished, or the bundles of yarn awaiting collection by the crofter-weavers.

Compared with Skye townships, those of Lewis are stark, unpainted, and to the unaccustomed eye, ugly When white-washed and painted they are transformed, as can be seen by the gay aspect of Balallan on the shore of Loch Erisort. For the most part the Lewis crofter has no time as yet for frills like paintwork or tourism. He feels that a man's work is on land or sea. Catering is for women, and the women are busy enough on croft and house. The Department of Agriculture has offered him loans for building tourist-chalets, but the Lewisman has thus far not responded.

One of the most exciting developments of the last decade is the resolution with which Lewismen have reclaimed moorland by reseeding. In 1956, when the Crofters' Commission introduced their Land Improvement Scheme, inviting crofters to apply for grants, the work was undertaken most enthusiastically in Lewis. Throughout the Highlands, 22,000 acres have been reclaimed from the moors, and 12,000 of these in Lewis alone. The best example is seen at Garynahine, near the head of Loch Roag. When travelling down the west coast, one is startled to come on this green oasis, which suddenly lights up the black moor.

Surface seeding is effected by cutting a few inches of the topmost matt by machine or spade, then spreading to each acre 10 tons of shell-sand, 5 cwt. of nitrous phosphate, and 3 cwt. of balanced fertilizer. Clover, timothy, fescue and rye are sown, and if the area is not too large sheep are turned in to trample it down. Bacteria and worms complete the work by creating soil, which after some years of grazing can be ploughed. The ground is potentially good. The owner at Garynahine told me that he could graze on moorland one ewe to eight acres. When that ground was reseeded he could graze four ewes and their lambs to one acre. Cattle and sheep, he said, gave the best balance of stock: cattle to crop the long grass, sheep to eat it down further; but they must be moved on before they bite too close. Grazing could and should be heavy if it were controlled.

It would appear that crofters have small hope of getting new moorland to reseed. Much of it is in the hands of absentee landlords and syndicates, who use it for shooting and fishing.

Most of the west coast lobster fishing is done from the island of Great Bernera on Loch Roag. Bernera is connected to Lewis by bridge. Its main body is typical gneiss moor, with lazybed cultivation around the crofts inland. The bays are splendidly sheltered. Lobster fishing has for many years been efficient and profitable, but decreasing catches in 1964 have caused some anxiety. It may yet prove that this trouble has come of overfishing the smaller lobster. The popular size in London has long been 1½ lb. – Englishmen like to see the red shells on their plates. Other and lesser tribes will accept a larger lobster at a lower price, and in former days 10 lb. lobsters were taken off the Hebridean coasts. A return to that policy would grant respite to overfished sheltered coasts, but would need bigger boats to fish remoter rocks.

Northward from Loch Roag the land becomes ever more flat and windblasted towards Ness, which although a true Atlantic promontory is greener than most of Lewis. From

Swanibost we can see two miles north to the Eye of the Needle, a great sea-bore through the Roinn a' Roidh, whose cliff juts out near the Butt. On the east side of the Butt, Port of Ness has a little harbour and strong breakwater where lobster-boats are moored. Over the last four centuries the men of Ness have made an annual expedition to the gannetry of Sula Sgeir, an oceanic rock forty miles north. The gannet has been a source of food for islanders from earliest times, but Sula Sgeir is now the only gannetry from which birds are still harvested. The men go out in early September, sea permitting, and take some three thousand young birds or 'gugas' at the stage where they are still on the nest but have been deserted by their parents.

From the Port of Ness, croft-houses stretch two miles across the island to Eoropie on the west side of the Butt. Machair spreads behind the wide sands of its bay, and green turf along the cliff-tops to the north. The tall lighthouse at the Butt is of red brick, standing on a cliff that spreads talons of gneiss far out into crashing seas. The walk southward on the windy cliff-tops can be most exhilarating. The fascination of the brink draws us along deep-cut bays, where jutting spurs are colonized by nesting fulmars in June. Half a mile south of the lighthouse is Luchruban, or Pigmy's Isle, which was alleged in days far distant to have been inhabited by a pigmy people. The small bones found there have since been shown to be those of birds and small mammals, probably the food of an anchorite who had lived in a stone cell on the summit. The tidal island is a piece of the original main cliff, which has been eaten off by the sea. The deep moat between can be reached by a scree gully and the rocky wall of the island easily climbed.

The top is flat and thickly cushioned in sea-pinks, which even in high wind scent the June air. The old cell is still there, its low stone walls forming a narrow rectangle. It looks to the Butt along half a mile of riven coast, where Atlantic rollers seethe among the reefs and skerries and hordes of gulls wheel screaming. The nearer cliffs bear a colony of two dozen black shags, exhibiting their acrobatic ability to perch for hours on steep sharp edges, yet always at ease. Their heads gleam green in the sun, and their chicks jostle on the ledges.

The Outer Hebrides, especially the Uists, abound in ancient monuments: chambered cairns, duns, brochs, standing stones, sun-circles, beehives, earth-houses and wheel-houses, and churches. They offer great opportunities for fresh discovery by excavation, but many have been despoiled for house and wall building. In Lewis, the megaliths of Callanish rank next to those of Stonehenge as the most important in Britain. They date from 1500 B.C. and mark the site of the largest Teampull na Greine (Temple of the Sun) in the whole of Scotland. The stones stand like a petrified forest on the flat top of a peninsula, which thrusts into East Loch Roag. The site is sun-flooded and windy, with a fine view to the Harris hills and down Loch Roag. The design is that of the Celtic Cross. Thirty-nine gneiss monoliths are set in cruciform shape with encircling 'glory', and aligned from north to south. The Great Avenue approaching the circle from the north is ninety yards long by nine wide, marked out by stones six feet high (thirty-eight were counted in 1831, of which less than half remain). The circle is of thirteen bigger stones set at thirty-seven feet diameter around a central monolith seventeen feet tall. At the outer circumference, four stones are aligned to radiate east, four south, and four west. In 1831 there was an outer circle of twenty-one yards' diameter, but this has since vanished. In 1857–58 the site was excavated by Sir James Matheson, who removed five feet of peat to reveal a chambered cairn beside the central pillar, probably a neolithic communal tomb. The Druids were sun-worshippers and would use the site for that purpose; for the rest, all is conjecture. Herodotus, Eratosthenes and other early Greek scholars refer to the Callanish stones as 'The Great Winged Temple of the Northern Isles'.

Six miles north of Callanish, on top of a knoll above Loch Carloway, is the best-preserved broch of the Hebrides. It still stands high in double drystone walls spiralled by interior passages, by which one may climb to the top or to a window facing the inner court. The walls have a dull green patina, and the stones overlap to give a gentle beehive shape. The gateway is four feet high. Set into the wall by its side is a low guard-chamber barely three feet high. Duns were usually built to fifty feet with no windows in the outer walls. Details of their defensive purpose are conjectural. Dun Carloway is dated to the first four centuries A.D., and would therefore be built by the Picts. The site gives fine views across Loch Carloway to the hills of Uig and Gallan Head.

The most beautiful coast-scene in Lewis is around Uig and Valtos, where Gallan Head divides Loch Roag from Camus Uig to its south-west. In extreme contrast to its flanking coast, the headland is high bleak moorland, not only ugly in itself but crowned by long-range radar apparatus of the R.A.F. Three miles inland, it is traversed from coast to coast by the remarkable formation of Glen Valtos, long and narrow, flat and twisting, with escarpment walls like a frontier nulla in Tibet. From its east end, the road climbs a hill into new country totally opposed to the rocky moorland preceding. All around is short, green turf, which falls from a school on the hill-top to the flawless sands of Camus na Clibhe, where rollers surge in from the open Atlantic. In all Lewis, here is the most lovely spot in which to receive an education – clean, sunny, airy, sandy, full of light. The road falls east to Valtos village, where forty houses cluster in a grassy corrie by the shores of outer Loch Roag. From the beach, prongs of gneiss run out through brilliant green sea towards the islands of Pabaidh Mhor and Vacsay.

Valtos still has one genuine black house in occupation. Its golden thatch is blackened at centre by peat-reek, for there is no chimney. At one or two other townships, such as Arnol, I have found the original black house still inhabited. The owners are most diffident. Unlike the rest of the people of Lewis, whose age-old tradition of generous hospitality towards strangers has remained unaffected to the present day, they will suffer no conversation. They are unhappy to be seen living in black houses when all their neighbours occupy modern white houses.

The original name Tigh Dubh meant dark house rather than black, for the drystone walls had darker appearance than the cemented, which could be whitewashed (the original Tigh Geal, or White House, was just as black inside). One end of a black house is always higher than the other, and both roofs and floors slope accordingly and markedly. The reason is that for many centuries man and beast shared the same roof and the low end was the cow's. In early days there was no inside partition between the byre and living-room, for men scrupled to shut out the cow from a view of the fire. These old houses may not have been too clean, but they were (and are) much warmer and of better appearance than modern buildings.

The other houses at Valtos are of plain modern design, their sheds noisy from the clack of looms. July is the best time to enjoy Valtos, when the rolling knolls of its steep fields are a blaze of wild flowers, seen best of all from a boat out on the bay. Across a green headland to its south-east lies the Traigh na Beiridhe, a mile-long sweep of sand. I have walked on most of the western shell-sands of the Outer and Inner Hebrides, and nowhere else have I seen shell of such pure quality, white even when one digs deep down, brilliantly white on the surface yet with every colour of the rainbow displayed. The unbroken shells are dark pink or light, purple or lilac, orange or lemon, but always a pearly white on the underside and of quite extreme fragility, crumbling between the fingers when touched.

Returning to Glen Valtos, we move west to the many bays of Camus Uig. The ground behind them is lark-loud machair, bright with flowers like Valtos. The Lewis hills across the main bay are bared gneiss, the water between tawny at the nearer shallows, greening farther out, then deepening to dark mauve – all layered like the soft hues of a pigeon's neck. Not even Iona has so much water colour so delicately shaded.

When the tide is low one can walk right across the strand to Ardroil on the south side. Among the sands of Ardroil were

found in 1831 the famous walrus ivory chessmen, now in the
Scottish National Museum in Edinburgh, and in the British
Museum. They were found by a herdsman, according to local
tradition, when his cow dug her horns in a dune. More than
seventy ivories were collected, kings, queens, bishops and
knights exquisitely carved, not in identical sameness but each
piece given individual character with a full play of inventive
detail. There seems to be no doubt that the craftsman was
Norse.

Twenty miles west of Gallan Head lies a cluster of seven
islets and twenty skerries called the Flannan Isles or the Seven
Hunters. They belong to Lewis and for a thousand years have
been put to use. They still hold the ruins of an eighth-century
chapel dedicated to St. Flannan. Later they held a stock of wild
sheep, for although the islets are cliff-bound, good grass grows
on the flat tops. In the sixteenth century MacLeod of Lewis
used to send out men and hounds on annual sheep-hunting
expeditions. Over hundreds of years the men of Lewis culled
sea-birds and eggs as on Sula Sgeir, and up to recent times
grazed fifty sheep.

They are still inhabited: the main island has a lighthouse.
Soon after it was built the three keepers vanished. It is pre-
sumed that great waves swept them off the cliff. Leach's fork-
tailed petrel breed on the Flannans, fulmar too, and great
numbers of puffin.

The east coast of Lewis realizes our vision of typical gneiss
country. So many lochs swarm in the myriads of rocky hollows
that the whole parish extending from near Stornoway to the
Harris frontier at Loch Seaforth is named Lochs. Added to their
number are long sea-lochs penetrating far in from the coast –
Loch Leurbost, Loch Erisort, Loch Sealg and Loch Seaforth
among the greater. The townships along their rocky shores are
usually sited in grassy hollows, reflecting green in lengths of
still, gleaming water, which after the heavy swell and crashing
seas of the windy west look so smooth. The air too is still, full
of the warm smell of the moors that roll inland as a low plateau.

There is less stillness around the villages, where land-birds' song gives pleasant change from the west: rock-doves cooing on the lazybeds by the shores of Leurbost, blackbirds and larks singing, and along the street a clatter of looms and hens and children.

Loch Erisort has a new seaweed factory at Keose. It was opened in 1965, the first in Lewis, for the work is centred in Uist. It employs men from all parts of Lewis in gathering tangle in winter and rock weed in summer, with an expected production of 1,000 tons of milled weed a year. At the head of the loch around Balallan there is much lazybedding, although this has to be seen at its best in Harris. Long strips of marsh marigold grow lush in the dividing troughs, and big iris-patches on the bog. Gay Balallan on its black moor is even able to rejoice in a sprinkling of rowan and willow trees.

The biggest wood of the Long Isle is at Stornoway Burgh. On buying Lewis in 1844, Sir James Matheson built Lews Castle facing the harbour; Lady Matheson afterward⸳ planted several hundred acres, mostly with conifers varied by deciduous trees and flanked by massed banks of rhododendrons. The castle is now a technical college training 130 boys.

Stornoway is a clean, sprawling town of 5,250 inhabitants and a still greater concourse of sea-gulls. It shelters under the wing of the Eye Peninsula, which stretches ten miles into the North Minch. When Martin Martin wrote of Stornoway in 1695 it had only sixty families, but this small township had an excellent natural harbour, two miles long by a mile wide. The seas outside were rich in fish, and Hebridean herring are of the finest quality in Europe. Stornoway thus developed into the main centre of the Scottish herring industry. In 1912 it had a population of 4,000, and a fleet of a thousand wherries (sailing boats). Despite the arrival of East Coast steam drifters, prosperity lasted until the depression of 1929. The two principal export markets for cured herring, Germany and Russia, closed their doors in the nineteen-thirties, but the privilege of dealing the death-blow was reserved to the British Government: they

sanctioned the winter dumping of Norwegian herring at East
Coast ports. The Stornoway curing stations closed down.

White fishing declined when steam trawlers illegally swept
the banks, destroying gear and forcing the local line fishers to
beach their boats. The two wars completed these disasters. In
the first especially, vigorous young men were drained away in
disproportion to the size of the Lews, and boats and quays fell
into disrepair.

In 1918, Lord Leverhulme bought the island and planned a
development of herring fishery with a large canning factory at
Stornoway, a proposal that proved to be in advance of the
times. The men of the Lews are bred to a toughly masculine
attitude to life. They refused support to plans that appeared to
mean a forfeiture of their independence – for that is how they
thought of wage-earning in a factory under a business tycoon,
high-principled though he might be. Lewismen move with a
deliberation that is often mistaken for indolence by a main-
lander ignorant of the breed. Two things they have never
lacked are resilient energy and abundant courage. They suffered
an initial apathy on the decline of the herring fishery, but the
sense of defeat has since been banished by the development of
lobster and prawn fishing and a revival of white fishing. They
have put much capital into modern domestic looms. Since the
Second World War the tweed-weaving industry has flourished
exceedingly. Spinning and finishing is centred at five Stornoway mills, which deliver yarn daily to crofter-weavers in most
villages of Lewis and many in Harris.

A tweed wins the distinctive Orb trade-mark of Harris
Tweed only if it meets the following definition: 'A tweed made
from pure virgin wool, produced in Scotland, spun, dyed, and
finished in the Outer Hebrides, and hand-woven by the
Islanders at their own homes in the Islands of Lewis, Harris,
Uist, Barra, and their several purtenancies, and all known as the
Outer Hebrides.' The annual production of Harris Tweed in
1964 was six million yards, worth nearly £4,000,000. Three-
quarters is exported, much of it to the United States.

LEWIS
Stacking peats by
Loch Erisort

By Tom Weir

ST. KILDA   The cliff of Conachair

By Tom Weir

The industry consumes a third of the Scottish wool clip. It employs 1,000 workers at the Stornoway mills and 1,500 weavers throughout the Isles. A man can weave in a week 2½ tweeds (one tweed is 80 yards by 28½ inches), earning approximately £7 a tweed according to design. Further expansion of the industry is expected following the judgment by Lord Hunter (1964) upholding the definition of Harris Tweed and thus excluding mainland producers.

In 1963 the Department of Agriculture and Fisheries completed a Fishery Training Scheme for the Outer Hebrides by providing a fleet of twelve boats (each costing £15,000) for fisherman-owners, and giving them training in handling modern equipment. The men repay 70 per cent of the cost over a period of twenty years. So successful has this scheme proved that the Highlands and Islands Development Board has continued it vigorously. The fish landings at Stornoway in 1964 were herring value £72,000, white fish £25,600 and prawns £74,000. These were from boats of all ports using Stornoway. In 1964 Stornoway had ten of the modern white fish boats. Now it has thirty, which also make landings on the mainland, notably at Gairloch for the Aberdeen market, of no less value than the landings at Stornoway. The town has a large lobster pond, a fish processing factory, and a cold storage depot.

The aerodrome lies two miles east of the town-centre at Melbost, on the way out to the Eye Peninsula. A N.A.T.O. base at the airport has brought new traffic to the harbour. Eye, which is locally called Point, is bare flat moor in the main part, but with good soil on the coast of Broad Bay, and many crofts. Broad Bay has splendid sands in a series of northward-running beaches at Melbost, Coll and Gress. The townships behind them are like most others but with fields much richer in flowers. Unlike the small crofting villages of the Highlands, the Lewis townships often carry populations of 500 and more. Tolsta at the far north point of Broad Bay has nearly 1,000. The proliferation of small independent crofts (four acres and a cow) has resulted in the absurdity of Stornoway's having to import her milk-supply from the mainland.

North of Tolsta Head lies the Traigh Mhor, two miles of sand on which the rollers break in ranks of a dozen at once. Its Garry Bay is the best beach of eastern Lewis. Seas crash green on three pinnacles, which stand together on the sands. On the southmost stack, which is bored by a natural arch, fulmars nest despite many visitors. Behind the bay lies a deeply sheltered corrie floored by green machair and bearing a lochan fringed by rushes. The river Geiraha flowing from it to the sea gives the bay its name.

The people of Lewis have a larger share of the Norse in their blood than other Celtic islesmen. When Norway ceded the Hebrides, Olav the Black's son Leod founded dynasties through his two sons Torquil and Tormod. Tormod MacLeod founded the Harris and Skye clans, and Torquil the Lewis. The MacKenzies of Kintail seized Lewis in 1610 (Harris remained with the MacLeods), and sold to Sir James Matheson, a rich East India merchant, in 1844. It passed to Lord Leverhulme in 1918, and when sold a few years later was broken up into many different estates.

The population of Lewis reached its peak of nearly 30,000 in 1911. Thereafter it fell by emigration to its present 21,550. There had been no earlier clearances like those of Uist and Barra – Lewis was fortunate in its owners – but economic pressures were too great to sustain the old numbers. It remains a well-knit society: the Gaelic tongue is universally spoken, roads are good, communications by bus frequent and easy; the countryside is thoroughly toured by vans from town carrying food and other supplies, and even by a mobile bank. The townships run football teams, dance-bands, concerts and clubs. The lack of big-scale ancillary industries means that each year many young folk leave to seek their living abroad or on the mainland. A great number of young men enter the Merchant Navy.

A unique feature of Outer Hebridean society is the curb on division of labour and the consequent wide range of men's skills: crofters are builders, fishermen, mechanics, weavers – they can turn their hands to anything. It seems obvious that specialization would bring the trades to higher efficiency with bigger output and earnings. Crofts could then be enlarged by amalgamation, becoming economically viable in themselves. Against this, it is argued that life is more varied, interesting and refreshing where specialization is modified. The islander is wedded to his land: in his case, would not the divorce for a money-gain impoverish health and spirit? I would say yes, were it not that unemployment is high in winter.

A relay station brought television to the Lewis townships in 1965. The effect might well be made the subject of a sociological study. In Lewis we have the only community in western Europe who lead a simple country life and yet whose people are thoroughly well educated – their general knowledge is wide, for they are well-read and imaginative; the number of both sexes who graduate at universities (especially in Arts and Medicine) being higher in proportion to population than elsewhere in Britain.

The 'Stornoway Saturday Night', when men from the dry outlands come in to drink hard, is more than balanced by weighty virtues. The age-old courtesy, generosity and hospitality of the country people is intact. Their regard for the religion of the Free Church is strong. They love their land. Many people wonder what will be the effect of television on the young, when they see the more luxurious mainland life, with its demonstration that lax moral standards do not involve material poverty or, in the short run, retributive misfortune. Will they lose their standards? Will their religion waste a way? Will their famed generosity dwindle as they grow avaricious?

Any such fears would underestimate the adult Outer Islander, who is highly intelligent, and no man's fool. But what of the young? A study would be worth making.

HARRIS

A broad rampart of hills divides Harris from Lewis. The boundary comes near the head of Loch Seaforth, from which the Forest of Harris surges west to the sea in four great waves, the troughs between being three glens aligned north to south. The first and greatest wave rises 2,622 feet on Clisham, the highest mountain of the Outer Hebrides. All are treeless deer forest. They long formed a roadless barrier between Lewis and Harris, so that the two have always been regarded as different islands. Their history has differed in detail, they are quite unlike scenically (Harris is machair on the west, naked rock on the east), and the people are different, in appearance, in character, even in their Gaelic speech, which is softer.

Harris itself is very nearly two islands. The north is pinched off from the south by the isthmus of Tarbert (meaning a neck of land where boats can be dragged across from sea to sea), which is here only half a mile wide. North Harris is well seen from the top of Clisham, an ascent easily made from the highest point of the Stornoway-Tarbert road through the great glen.

The summit-view on a clear day extends from near Cape Wrath down the mainland to the Cuillin, and out west to the farthest outpost of Harris, St. Kilda, sixty miles distant. Apart from red deer, ravens, and a few pairs of golden eagles, the Forest of Harris is uninhabited save by a few clachans along the shores of West Loch Tarbert. The switchback road to the most westerly point of Husinish is the longest thirteen miles in the Outer Isles, relieved along the narrow way by the waterfall at Amhuinnsuidhe House, where shoals of salmon may be seen leaping in late June and early July.

The four houses of Husinish stand on the isthmus of a little, windswept peninsula. The ground is all machair, for the south bay has a splendid sweep of shell-sand. On the peninsula's west side low cliffs of pink gneiss are colonized by nesting fulmars, shags, guillemots and rock-doves. A jetty on the north

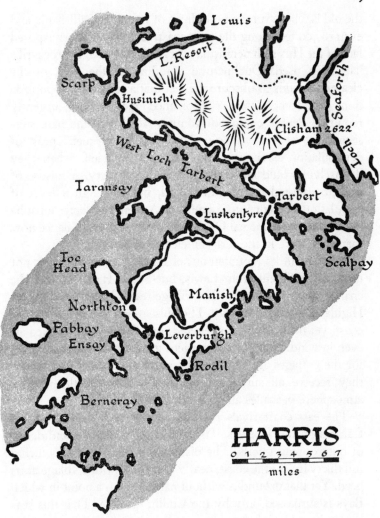

bay serves Scarp half a mile offshore. Remote as that island is,
thirty or forty people still live there, a few in black houses and
all crofters. They no longer fish lobster. Once it bore a heavy
population: throughout Harris before the clearances the pres-
sure of population was excessive. At Husinish one can still see

the old lazybeds running hundreds of feet up the hill-flank, and even to 500 feet along the west coast. Out on the most exposed face of the Husinish peninsula every strip between the rock-ribs had been used. Our natural emotion on the evils of the clearances tends to obscure the fact that a reduction of population (by some other well-planned means) was urgently required. People could not continue to live at the bare subsistence level of these old days. Yet many men speak of depopulation as though that were bad in itself, when they themselves would not consent to suffer poverty. A misuse of land to cause depopulation is bad, but too high a level of population may constitute a misuse. A point of balance must be found, and the principal Outer Islands are nearer a balance now than they were in the early nineteenth century.

Apart from its mountainous character, North Harris is not markedly different from Lewis, but South Harris is, and the change starts at Tarbert. The village seems homely and 'West Highland' after Stornoway. The hills stretch nakedly along the coast, yet the position is sheltered; one feels a more relaxed air even in wind. Many of the gardens grow flowers in profusion, for the cottages are sited on the north side of the bay where they receive all sun from the south. This gentler, milder atmosphere pervades all of South Harris.

The east coast rivals the black moor as one of the freak features of the Hebrides. The land is the greatest island desert of outcropping gneiss. The district is called Bays, of which a full thirty indent the coast, nearly every one with a village at its head. Yet that ground is without natural soil – a point in which Bays is surpassed only by the Cuillin of Skye. That this seaboard should be inhabited by humans seems at first not to make sense. Many were forced by the clearances to seek their livelihood here (or in the west on high ground only). They had not even soil enough to bury their dead, who had to be carried overland to the machair of the west coast. Alongside the road across the island to Luskentyre may be seen numerous cairns, which mark the points where the coffins were rested. Far from perishing in this rock waste, these resolute people mastered it, their triumph being so complete that to this day it is well inhabited.

The numerous bays and inlets made excellent harbours for small boats and snug sites for villages. The inshore fishing was good and the hinterland studded with trout lochs. The women wove and spun; and men and women together created their own soil for tillage. They built up platforms of peat in the hollows of the rock to give drainage, then spread these with seaweed carried up from the shores in creels. On the lazybeds thus formed they planted potatoes (which had been brought to the Outer Isles in 1752) and oats. These patches were only a few yards long, spades and heuks (sickles) the only tools for their cultivation, but long sustained industry has made them fertile. The sight is deeply moving, compelling respect.

The road into Bays from Tarbert meanders through a maze of lochs, the only line of division between one and another being often the road itself. The clachans on the sea-bays – Scada bay, Goose bay, Cluer, Stockinish, among others – are brightened by the tiny, snake-like lines of potatoes and oats, and by the marsh marigolds and irises in the ditches alongside. Unlike the Lewis townships, several cultivate gardens of flowers, conspicuously red-hot pokers and lupins. Rowing boats for the lobster fishing lie in the bays; beyond, the Minch spreads sparkling blue to the north point of Skye.

Stockinish has a big pond for storing lobsters, which are re-fished in the autumn. South of Loch Stockinish, the bays come thick and fast around Manish – Geocrab, Beacravik, Manish, Flodabay, Finsbay. The most astonishing lazybedding is at Beacravik. Every thinnest trough between the long gneiss ribs has black earth, richly manured and cared-for over the succeeding generations. But no longer do the people have to rely entirely on their own produce. Their lifeline is the S.C.W.S., whose vans serve the whole east coast. Many gardens rise to a stunted tree – a rowan, a blasted sycamore, pine, willow or ash; one or two have a rose bush or a spray-stricken rhododendron.

The east coast comes to its southmost point at Rodil, where the church of St. Clement stands on a hillock close to the village. St. Clement's fame is not historical, but rests on its architectural merit. No one knows who was St. Clement or who built the church, which was first mentioned by Dean Monro in 1549. The most likely builder would be one of the early MacLeod chiefs of Dunvegan (who also held Harris), for Rodil was long their burial place. Alasdair Crotach, the seventh chief, repaired it early in the sixteenth century, or perhaps rebuilt it on the site of an earlier church. Nearly twenty years before he died, he caused a tomb to be prepared for himself in the choir. Some unknown craftsman has made of it one of the finest works of art in the Outer Isles. A restoration was made in 1873 by the Countess of Dunmore, whose husband had bought the island.

The plan is cruciform, with nave, transepts and miniature choir. At the west end a square, battlemented tower stands 56 feet. The walls are built of local gneiss. Sandstone dressings were imported from Carsaig; effigies of knights and wall decorations are of jet black schist a-glitter with quartz-grain. The tomb of Alasdair Crotach is set in an arched recess in the south wall. On the outer face of the arch, eight engraved panels depict apostles and angels to either side of a keystone Holy Trinity. These are formal and not so perfectly sharp as the Twelve panels on the inner wall of the tomb; three rows depict a Sun in Glory flanked by trumpeting angels, a ship and castle (both MacLeod arms), the Virgin and child flanked by St. Clement and a bishop, a hunting scene, three stags, St. Michael and Satan weighing souls, and a Latin inscription declaring that the tomb was prepared by Alexander MacLeod of Dunvegan in 1528. The tombstone is an armoured knight carved in black schist. The whole is of unpretentious simplicity, yet a work of good design and beauty.

The south coast of Harris is seamed from Rodil to Toe Head

in the west by three long green straths that flow into each other, interrupted at mid-point by a double sea-loch, which the road divides. On the seaward side is the enclosed loch of the Obbe, on the inland side Loch Steiseval, fed by higher hill-lochs. The township of Obbe has been renamed Leverburgh in honour of Lord Leverhulme, who in 1923 planned to transform it into a big fishing port. He built piers and jetties, kippering sheds and houses, new roads and a fleet of trawlers. In 1924 the first landings were huge; men had to be brought in from the mainland to help in curing and packing. He built a whaling station on West Loch Tarbert, a spinning mill in Bays at Geo-crab, and had many other plans when he died in 1925. His executors abandoned all and a most promising enterprise came to nothing.

The Sound of Harris divides Harris from North Uist. Seven miles wide, it bears nearly threescore islands, all of which – even those close in to Uist – belong to Harris. Many of them are grazed by sheep and some by cattle owned by the south coast farmers, notably the two big islands close to the Obbe, Ensay and Killegray. The only inhabited island is Berne-ray near the Uist shore, and reached from there by Newton ferry. It is well populated by crofters and lobster fishers. Close to its north the very fertile hump of Pabbay is run as one stock farm and (surprisingly) carries a small herd of red deer. A mile off its north shore, Shillay is a breeding station for Atlantic seals. Although just half a mile long it rears up to 265 feet at the north end, but falls low at the south to the breeding ground at Ard an Laoigh, where the late autumn pups lie in scores out of reach of the heavy swell. A convenient time to visit is late Sep-tember, when a motor-boat goes out to Shillay from Lever-burgh to bring in sheep and lambs for the winter. The only safe landing point is a sandy beach on the south-east shore.

In summer the waters of the sound teem with mackerel and huge catches are made. Sea-birds nest on all the islands, which in winter draw long-tailed duck and large flocks of barnacle and grey lag geese.

The west coast of Harris is shaped as one huge bay between the distant point of Husinish and Toe Head. Within its arms lies the big island of Taransay, whose population is five. From Luskentyre to Toe Head stretches an eight-mile strip of coastal green, scalloped by eight sandy bays, each with machair and divided from its neighbour by hill-spurs that end on the shore as rock. The green strip lies largely to seaward of the road; inland the ground swells immediately in rocky but grassy hills.

One of the wonders of this coast is the Traigh Luskentyre at the north end – a tongue of sand two miles long by a mile wide when the tide is out. In May and June the saltings at the head are reddened over an immense area by sea-pinks – thick enough to graze sheep and cattle although not a blade of grass grows among them. The south side of the strand is bounded by Corran Seilebost, a desert of marram dunes teeming with rabbits; the north side by the dunes and crofts of Luskentyre – crofts richer in their land than at any other village of Harris. The flowers grow thicker on the machair, the air is warmer, the grass greener and more plentiful, cows are more numerous, and the eggs the largest I have ever known to come out of hens. People who have not seen machair have difficulty in appreciating that although the crofters call it 'grass', it grows not grass but flowers; in July and August, on good machair like Luskentyre's, so dense is the blossom that when cows are turned on to it the milk becomes scented and tastes flower-sweet; and not only this, the cows' breath too is scented.

When the sea floods the Traigh Luskentyre the water lies green as Iona serpentine, yet alive with light. On the ebb, lagoons left in deep channels of the strand give fine sea-trout fishing. Between tides, the sands stay golden in cool weather, but in summer heat dry out to pure white, hot to the bare foot. From hour to hour as from month to month change is continuous, and in the fine weather of June magical – a land as far removed from the industrial conurbations as heaven from hell. I have stood on the machair of Luskentyre under a crescent moon and watched the seas of the Sound of Taransay still blue at midnight, the sky likewise, and heard cuckoos calling, and one irrepressible lark still trilling.

In Harris and Lewis the commonest bird is the starling. In Lewis they roost in all the old black houses. In Harris there are few black houses but even more starling. They abound on the machairs in small flocks of a dozen or twenty behind these near-perfect beaches that scoop the coast to Toe Head – Rosamel, Seilebost, Nisabost, Iar, Borve, Scarasta. In autumn, the sea off Nisabost is busy with scoters, mergansers, long-tailed duck, and divers.

The most rewarding day I have ever spent on Harris was at Toe Head in June. This peninsula runs out three and a half miles, hunching itself up into a hill of 1,201 feet called Chaipaval, which throws a final spur to the rocks of Toe Head, where fulmars nest. Chaipaval is linked to the township of Northton by an isthmus of sea-level machair, which narrows to three hundred yards with sandy bays to either side, but especially the north side – a strand two miles long from shore to sea.

I walked out along the isthmus from Northton on a sunny but windy afternoon. The first few hundred yards were sown with potatoes. Everywhere larks sang, but all other birds came in a curiously well-defined succession: first a flock of rock-doves gleaning the potato-patch; then some forty starlings in a tight flock among the irises filling a swamp; then peewits crying on the first true machair, which was entirely whitened by daisies; and finally, when I climbed on to the lowest slopes of Chaipaval, I found the ground colonized by dove-grey birds with black eyebars; they flitted from rock to rock disclosing white rumps and uttering a metallic *chack-chack* – they were wheatears.

The top of Chaipaval may be half the height of Clisham but I found it a superior watch-tower, for the nearer scene is the best of the Outer Hebrides. Between the Cuillin and St. Kilda one hundred miles of sea crawled darkly blue and white-capped. Closer below flowed the Sound of Harris mazed by islands: Berneray like a flat green saucer rimmed white by its beaches,

Shillay happily seal-like, even to a spray of whiskers where the
sea broke on its nose, scores of skerries, each one a maritime
maypole ringed by dancing light, and behind them all the dark
hills of Uist. In the opposite direction the Sound of Taransay
flooded north to Husinish. Chain-links of dazzling sand
embossed the shores.

When I came down to the isthmus the machair took me by
surprise: snow-white on my way up, it was now flushed as
though with sea-pinks – then I saw that the daisies had simply
closed their cups as cloud blew over and the wind sharpened.

St. Kilda, in the parish of Harris, has had no permanent
population since 1930, when the people were evacuated to the
mainland. Numbers had shrunk from 200 in 1695 to 30. Their
society had become an anachronism in modern Britain, where
standards of living had risen to create a gulf too wide to be
bridged. The wild life population remains of exceeding interest and the seven islands have become a Nature Reserve.
Their rock scenery is the most startling of the Hebrides. On
Hirta, the principal island, the granite cliffs of Conachair rise to
1,397 feet – the tallest sea-cliff in the British Isles (the Kame of
Foula in the Shetlands is more sheer for a height of 1,220 feet).
Four miles off Hirta, Boreray is cliffed to 1,245 feet. Alongside
it, fangs of naked gabbro project out of the sea to 544 feet at
Stac Lee and to 627 feet at Stac an Armin. These three islands
hold the world's greatest gannetry – 45,000 pairs. Fulmars
throughout the group number 30,000, but the most common
bird of all is the puffin. On Hirta, the St. Kilda wren and long-
tailed field-mouse are unique species. Unique too are the wild
Soay sheep, possibly of Scandinavian origin, brought by the
Vikings more than a thousand years ago (if they did not find
them resident). One 'inhabitant' who never lived there was
Saint Kilda: the name first appears in print as an error in a sixteenth-century map. The correct name, Hirta, may derive from
the Norse word Hirdö (pronounced Hirtha) meaning Herd
Island. Owned for centuries by the MacLeods of Harris and
Skye, St. Kilda was finally sold and in 1957 gifted by the

Marquis of Bute to the National Trust for Scotland, who lease it to the Nature Conservancy. The R.A.F. and Army maintain a small radar station on Hirta to track rockets fired from the range on South Uist.

Harris stayed in the possession of the MacLeods from the Norwegian cession of the Isles in the thirteenth century till they sold to the Earl of Dunmore in 1834. The Long Isle had fallen into a state of great distress and poverty in common with the rest of the Hebrides and for the same reasons. The practical sympathy of Lady Dunmore was aroused. Harris had long been famed for the excellence of the crofters' tweed-weaving, but the cloth was produced mainly for home use or the local market. Lady Dunsmore organized the sale of the first Harris tweeds in London, and her enthusiastic activities were responsible for the early development of the Harris tweed industry. From that small beginning the market gradually and greatly expanded. In 1877 the commercial weaving of tweed spread south to South Uist and Barra, then north in 1881 to Lochs in Lewis, finally to Uig, Stornoway, and the whole west coast, until it is now chiefly centred in Lewis.

In 1918, when Harris was sold to Lord Leverhulme, the best land was held mainly by tenant farmers from the mainland. On Lord Leverhulme's death in 1925, the island was broken up into several estates. Large areas were made croft-land, thus allowing the native people to return to the west coast from which they had been so long debarred. Today, most of the people are crofters and lobster fishers, with weaving and knitting as ancillary industries. The population reached its maximum of 5,427 in 1911. In 1965 it was 3,050. Seafaring and the mainland claim large numbers of the young.

16

NORTH AND SOUTH UIST

FIVE main straits split the Outer Hebrides. The most decisive gulf is that made by the Sound of Harris: it divides the northern isles of Lewis and Harris from the southern of North Uist, Benbecula, South Uist, Eriskay and Barra. Sea communication between Harris and North Uist is poor in summer, but worse in winter when Messrs. MacBrayne cut down the ferry service. Thus the Protestants of North Uist have more ties with South Uist, which is Roman Catholic, than with the northern isles. South of the Sound of Harris the work of the isles is more completely agricultural, for here we enter the true machair lands of the west.

NORTH UIST

North Uist measures twelve miles by sixteen between its farthest points. The eastern half is one half water – a labyrinth of freshwater lochs behind a shattered seaboard. Two sea-lochs almost cut the island through from east to west. These are Loch Maddy, with harbour, pier and village on its south shore, and Loch Eport, which leaves an isthmus at the west end only a quarter of a mile wide. The north and west coasts are gouged in three vast and sandy bays, each with big tidal islands, the farms on which are accessible on the ebb across broad strands. The hinterland is low moor, lifting to central hills of several hundred feet. The highest hills fringe the south-east coast: North Lee, 823 feet, South Lee, 920 feet, and Eaval, 1,138 feet.

These may not be high, but like the pyramids of Egypt they dominate flat desert and look finer than figures suggest. To anyone coming from Lewis and Harris, the chief feature here is greenness. After Lewisian black even the middle moors look greenish and the grass incomparably richer. The land supports a population of 1,850, at which it remains steady after a decline from 5,000 in 1821.

North Uist is reached by daily air service from Glasgow to Benbecula, and from Stornoway by the same plane on its return flight. Since Benbecula is linked to both the Uists by road-bridge, North Uist is thus also accessible by the thrice weekly steamer from Oban to Lochboisdale in South Uist. The direct route is by car-ferry from Uig in Skye (and Tarbert in Harris) to Lochmaddy.

Lochmaddy is the island's principal village with a population of 400, several shops, a bank, hotel, and cottage hospital. Being more scattered than Tarbert of Harris it has a less benign aspect. In the outskirts at Sponish stands the seaweed factory of Alginate Industries, Ltd., where weed is dried over coal fires, milled to a fine meal, and sent to the mainland for processing.

North Uist is ringed by a forty-mile road, which by-passes the south-east water-waste. A circuit of this excellent road by car or bus reveals almost nothing of North Uist. The townships all lie far off at the end of side-lanes, the best bays and beaches are hidden, the road omits all the centres of island life. Misguided tourists might speed round the ring in an hour by car and say, 'We've seen it.'

The first important side-road branches north to the Newton Peninsula across a broad isthmus between Loch Maddy and the Vallaquie strand. This northern farmland is screened eastward by the hill of Beinn Mhor, and flanked westward by the first of these vast strands that run all the way down the coast to Barra. At once we see their beneficial influence in the wider fields grazed by cattle far more numerous than in Lewis and Harris. A mile beyond the farm and hotel of Newton the road ends at

NORTH UIST

a little village on the bay of Port nan Long, which faces Berneray a mile offshore. A byroad swings east around an emerald machair, then crosses the north point to a jetty on Port nam Ban, whence a passenger ferry plies across the sound to Berneray.

Between this jetty and Lochmaddy lorries trundle back and forth all summer, for Port nam Ban is a collecting point for the seaweed factory. The crofters turn out as they find time to cut rock weed (ascophyllum – which they call 'black weed') from the neighbouring islands by motor-boat. They cut with sickles and tow the weed back in 'rafts' which are immense flat masses each held by one floating rope-loop. These are hauled into shallow water, and when the tide ebbs pitchforked into lorries, thence to the mill. For this work the men are paid 22s. 6d. a wet ton (four tons of wet make a ton of dry). Some cutters will bring in four or five tons in a day but tide and weather forbid daily work; a team of two men can average twenty tons in a good week.

Three islands now have factories: Lewis, North Uist, and South Uist (at North Boisdale). Benbecula and Tiree are additional collecting points.

In winter, vast quantities of tangle weed (laminaria) are cast up on the western beaches of North and South Uist. From time immemorial the islesmen have swooped down by horse and cart, and now by lorry, to gather in the tangle for fertilizing the machair. In the late eighteenth and early nineteenth centuries they spread the tangle along the shores to dry in the spring winds, and burned it for kelp. They are thus well used to the work, but remembering the disasters on the collapse of the kelp trade they naturally doubted the success of a new seaweed enterprise when it opened at Boisdale in 1943, and were slow to co-operate with Alginate Industries. But this difficulty had been overcome by 1947. The crofters and the company work in harmony to mutual profit. In North and South Uist the company employs 200 part-time collectors and 40 to 50 men full time in the factories. The company pays £9 a ton for the air-dried tangle, which is processed on the mainland at Oban and Girvan.

The final product is a chemical, whose properties are jelling, thickening and stabilizing, which can be used in a wide range of industries: food (puddings, ices, jellies, etc.), textiles, paper, ceramics, and welding. Exports valued at over a million pounds, representing two thirds of the company's product, are made annually to fifty-three countries around the world, including Russia. North Uist's share is £30,000 a year paid in wages.

In the evenings at Port nan Long the hillside is heavily speckled by sheep, which come down from the upper slopes of Beinn Mhor to lie like quartzite boulders in every hollow, pure white against bright green. The hill rises to 625 feet above Newton. Its ascent is obligatory on a first visit to North Uist, for the loch-scene from the top is one of Scotland's most fantastic. Eaval, the highest hill down south (1,138 feet), is almost entirely surrounded by water and hard to reach, but Beinn Mhor is climbed in thirty-five minutes; it offers the further reward of a pair of golden eagles, whose eyrie may be inspected at close quarters.

The extreme contrast between west and east is seen from Beinn Mhor at a glance. Curling one after the other far down that west coast, white sands divide a sea of peacock blues and greens from cattle-thronged machair. The eastern half is shattered land, like a shell-cratered Passchendaele, ten miles long by five wide. Loch Scadavay at the centre is a labyrinthine freak without match in Scotland. Although its total area is only one and three-quarter square miles, the shore line stretches fifty. At least a hundred and twenty-five islands break the surface. Coot may be seen on these lochs – the only black waterbird with a white forehead, trailing its legs in heavy flight.

Beinn Mhor has two tops. On the south slope of the north top, Beinn Bhreac, the eagles' eyrie is sited on a sunwarmed crag where a lone rowan tree grows out of the rock. The massive nest is of heather on a broad ledge like a rock-garden, bearing roses, ferns, biting stonecrop and honeysuckle – surely the most comfortable eyrie in the Isles.

From the jetty at Port nam Ban a mail ferry crosses every morning to Berneray; a sail of twenty minutes to the harbour at Bays Loch. The island, three miles by one and a half, is divided lengthwise by Loch Bhruist and its outflow. The east half is broken by three bays and four hills, while the west is entirely flat and unbayed, fringed by one long strand. The nine-mile round of Berneray's shore line is one of the most wholly delightful walks in the Hebrides.

The people, numbering 180, live in villages at the back of the eastern bays of Loch Borve, Poll an Oir, and Bays Loch, the latter being the chief. The jobs are crofting and lobster fishing. No weaving is now done. Berneray is the greenest of the Hebrides, hence there is no peat, which a few men cut on the smaller Harris islands and gather by boat. Everyone burns coal and calor gas. White houses are much in the majority, some built in stone and equal to the best of Harris and Lewis. The many black houses have been modernized and the people are proud of them. The cementing of the outer walls, the wood-panelling and flooring of the interior, the installation of chimneyed fireplaces and kitchenettes, the retention of marram thatch, all these have given them excellent appearance inside and out. Especially fine examples may be seen around Risgarry, near the school on the east point of Bays Loch.

From Risgarry a fine beach shoots a mile north to Sand Hill headland, whence the first daisy machair may be walked to the start of the great western strand. Directly above, Moor Hill rises to 300 feet and demands to be climbed for its view across the scatter of islands in the Sound of Harris. Pabbay, the big hump two miles across the sound, was once the granary of Harris and is still farmed. Close under the hill the broad blue waters of Loch Bhruist glitter on green flats. Whooper swans come down there in winter, and a solitary red deer may sometimes be seen – it swam across the sound from Pabbay in the winter of 1963.

The west coast is uninhabited. I first walked its four-mile beach on a cloudless June day. In such conditions sun-glasses are essential – the dazzle from so much white sand could cause conjunctivitis. A tremendous Atlantic swell comes in, piling up in long green walls. Immaculate as the beach normally is, it may sometimes be fouled by tarry globules formed by condensation of oil jettisoned by ships at sea. This affliction is suffered from time to time by all western sands.

At the south end a machair like a tongue of flame licks east to Loch Borve. Set alight by the sun, every living thing upon it glows in its own colour: slow cows and quick calves, glossy black and chestnut, graze in herds over pastures shining white or yellow where rolling daisy-beds alternate with buttercup. The windy air is charged with clover-reek till the machair ends upon the sands of Loch Borve. The bottle-necked bag of the strand dries on the ebb, when it may be crossed to a roadway running up the coast back to Bays Loch.

After the superb beaches of Berneray, the strands of North Uist's north coast may seem disappointing, gigantic though they are. When the tide is out, the strands of Vallaquie and Vallay run out two miles from foreshore to sea, which seems a long way to walk when the sands are dull of colour, not shell. Wide saltings fringe them, but their flanking promontories run out to dunes and shell beaches. Sollas, the principal township of this coast, stands on the east shore of the Vallay strand. The west shore ends on Griminish Point, which has the most interesting natural arch of the Long Isle.

The approach is made through Scalpaig farm on its west side. Swans and waterlilies grace two lochans, and red clover the grass. Low cliffs stretch half a mile north to the point. On these accessible rocks, fulmars nest in niches barely 25 feet above the sea, and will fly off leaving the single white egg at one's feet. Near the point the cliffs rise higher and the fulmars thicken. From the top, I have been able to photograph a bird, which declined to budge off its nest, from a range of under ten feet.

Two creeks breach the headland to either side. The arch, which is some thirty feet high, bores a hundred and fifty yards through the headland from one creek to the other. Neither is accessible save by boat, but a great cavity on the headland's back allows a descent into the arch itself. Rock-doves fly out. The bore has a double twist, which makes play with the light. The central cavity shelters great numbers of flowers and birds. A few hundred yards east of Griminish Point an ancient dun gives remarkable vistas up and down the coast and out to St. Kilda, all the islands of which are clearly seen to either side of Haskeir.

Farther down the west coast are the island's principal communities, Tigharry, Hougharry, and Paible where a new bulb-growing industry has developed. All are set between clusters of freshwater lochs and the sandy beaches of mile-wide bays. They have a better appearance than other Long Island townships. Unlike the raw-looking houses of Lewis, which are flanked by relatively poor grass and black moor, the Uist cottages are mellow, the villages more compact, embellished all around by rich machair and blue sea. More land is tilled for crops. Eight miles west the sea is humped by the sand-swamped reefs of the Monach Isles, now uninhabited. The lighthouse had also to be closed when they were evacuated in 1942. The empty houses are used in summer by lobster fishermen from North Uist, and by nesting herons.

North Uist has numerous prehistoric buildings. One most worth examining is the chambered cairn of Barpa Langass on the southern moor. It lies on the lower slope of Beinn Langass near the head of Loch Eport. This stone mound, 18 feet high by 72 feet in diameter, is a fine example of a Neolithic tumulus, or burial chamber. One of its several cells is still intact and left open to inspection. One may crawl in under a big lintel.

BENBECULA

Benbecula is very much the Cinderella of the Isles. Travellers tend to hurry over it *en route* to North or South Uist. Seven miles in diameter, it serves as a circular stepping-stone between the two. The tidal strands of the North and South Fords once gave adventurous crossings. When travellers lacked detailed knowledge of the route, or were careless, many lives were lost. Both fords are now bridged.

Benbecula is nearly as flat as Tiree. At only three points does it rise above 100 feet. The east side is all fragmented rock and watery maze, the rest bog and moor save for the western sands and machair. Administratively the island belongs to South Uist, for it has no town or harbour of importance, but the north-western flats have an airfield at Bailivanich. Many new houses and huts have recently sprung up around it to accommodate Service personnel and probably stores for the South Uist rocket range, which lies only nine miles south as the crow flies.

Benbecula is one of the most wind-smitten islands on a coast that holds the British record (the Shetlands are less windy than the northern Hebrides). Winter gales seem well-nigh continuous; even in summer life on that west coast is bedevilled by the unrelenting blow. Tourist literature describing beaches here as fabulous say no less than truth, but small use can be made of them. The most hardened crofters have described their life to me as 'like living on the deck of a ship'. But their Norse blood must still be strong, for they are not dismayed. 'Och,' said one, 'it iss not so bad. We haff some shelter under the lee of Rockall.'

Days of calm are known. The three west coast beaches are all good, but the smaller Culla Bay in the middle is excellent. Being wide but deeply curved it gives more shelter and sense of seclusion than the straight strands to north and south. The machair is thick with yellow pansies, the sky with larks, the air with the scent of clover; restless eiders lead trains of a dozen chicks back and forth between rock and shore. The bay has a liveliness unknown to many greater and exposed strands. At the roadside behind the bay stands the old grey stone house of Nunton, formerly the residence of Clanranald.

The highest hill, Rueval, 409 feet, stands close to the island's middle. It is easily reached from the central road by a track leading into the moor, where the people come to cut peats. From the summit Benbecula looks like a well-fired crumpet pitted with holes by the hundred, the east edge nibbled away at Rossinish and the west creamily curved. The shallow seas out west are at first green then lilac in a broad band to the ten fathom line, which lies three and a half miles offshore, thereafter indigo. To either side the spikes of the Cuillin of Skye and St. Kilda prick up from distant horizons.

About 150 feet down the south-east slope of the hill, a line of low crags bulges over a shallow recess. This is Prince Charlie's Cave, where he and one companion waited two days, from 25th to 26th June, 1746, for Flora MacDonald to prepare his escape from the Hanoverian forces, which were slowly but surely closing in on him. She went to Nunton to get from Lady Clanranald the clothing required to disguise him as 'Betty Burke', while boatmen were gathering on the east coast to row them over the sea to Skye. On the night of 28th June they sailed out of Rossinish.

SOUTH UIST

South Uist is the Hebridean machair island par excellence. Mountain and moor fill the eastern half, where the sharp ridges of Hecla and Beinn Mhor rise to nearly 2,000 feet, and where three fine sea-lochs pierce the coast at Skiport, Eynort, and Boisdale. The island's peculiar character is given by its west coast. Unbroken machair and vast shell-sand beaches extend twenty miles down its full length. Between machair and moor, again down the full length, are spread a host of lochs, great and small, abounding in birds, brown trout, salmon and waterlilies. South Uist is the angler's Mecca, as the Cuillin is the climber's; her trout lochs are favoured by H.M. the Queen. On one day in September 1964 an angler caught on Loch Barr nine salmon weighing over sixty-three pounds. This may well be a local record, but it demonstrates the quality of the fishing. Everywhere is some kind of abundance.

Access to South Uist proper may be had either to the south end by way of the thrice weekly steamer from Oban to Lochboisdale, or from the north by two routes: car-ferry from Skye or Harris to Lochmaddy of North Uist, or by air to Benbecula, thence south by road.

The main road striking through the island from north to south holds a remarkably straight course along the flat lands between moor and machair. The villages and townships nearly all lie off this road on the rocky grassland where the machair has acquired humus and begun to merge into the peaty hinterland. It is thus possible to drive right through South Uist without seeing the coast, which lies between one and two miles west, or seeing its crofts and villages, or its chief glory, a flowered machair of scope incomparable, save perhaps for the Hosta machair of North Uist. Awaiting our exploration are thirty side-roads striking west into this machair land, and six more east-bound to the moors and sea-lochs.

Three-quarters of a mile south of the South Ford our first important diversion goes west to the Iachdar machair. Halfway along, a thatched cottage museum has recently been opened to exhibit the old tools of husbandry, like the caschrom or foot-plough, spinning wheels and looms, kitchenware and the ancient dress. The dress was sensible: pinned to the wall are three skirts worn by women in the fields, the first of red flannel, the second black with thin red stripes, the third of rough tweed made voluminous to be pulled up around the head and shoulders in rain. Odds and ends range from neolithic arrowheads to the inevitable 'piece of Prince Charlie's

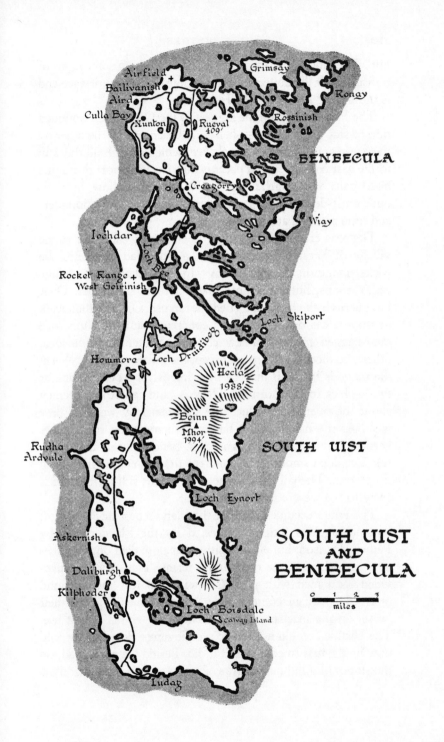

Airfield
Bailivanish
Aird
Culla Bay
Nunton
Rueval
409'

Grimsay
Ronay
Rossinish

BENBECULA

Creagorry

Wiay

Iochdar

Loch Bee

Rocket Range
West Geirinish

Loch Skiport

Houmore
Loch Druidibeg

Hecla
1988'

Beinn
Mhor
1994'

SOUTH UIST

Rudha
Ardvule

Loch Eynort

Askernish

SOUTH UIST
AND
BENBECULA

Daliburgh
Kilphoder

Loch Boisdale
Calvay Island

0 1 2 3
miles

Ludag

kilt'. The museum in its early phase is exhibiting some items of no value, but the collection can become of real importance and is the first of its kind in the Hebrides.

The Iachdar flats are the biggest of the Outer Isles, bounded on one side by the longest shell-sand beach and on the other by the greatest inland water, Loch Bee, which spreads all the way to the east coast, where it decants into Loch Skiport through a flood-gate. Set on such flat ground it remains shallow through-out (waist-deep), but has good trout fishing; even flounders and lithe come in at the spring tides.

The road crosses the centre of Loch Bee by causeway to the village of West Geirinish, where a side-road runs into the rocket range on the machair. A wired enclosure at the fringe cages troops, huts, transport, sheds and mobile cranes. Over long periods the launching site is not in use. One can then walk or drive a car on to it along a concrete roadway. Numerous sand-bagged pits and a few concrete shelters dot the area, otherwise there is little to see except the buttercup blaze. When the range is in use it may be used intensively, even at one or two o'clock in the morning. There is (and can be) no secrecy about the operations, which the Uistmen may watch if they wish. At the first burst of flame and smoke the rocket rises vertically, then gradually leans over, pencil-shaped and grace-ful. A sudden smoke-puff – and the first jet-engine fires, then the second. The tail glows. The rocket leans still further and is away to the west, controlled by radar.

The range occupies some of the island's best machair land. Its opening was bitterly contested by the islanders led by Father Morrison, but all opposition has now died out. Service-men and islanders are on friendly terms. The range has pro-vided local men with jobs. Crofters who lost their ground received adequate compensation – and can still graze their beasts on the machair when the launching-site is out of use. The Uistmen would not like to see the range closed and would now be the first to complain if it did. Beside the main road, on the slopes of a hill named Rueval, there stands a tall madonna

and child sculpted in white granite by Hew Lorimer, R.S.A.
The child is raised to the shoulder, his hand uplifted in bene-
diction, and both faces are turned to the rocket range as though
blessing man's operations there. The gesture now appropriately renders local feeling, but one suspects that the sculp-
tor's original object was different.

One mile south, a side-road strikes east alongside Loch
Druidibeg towards Loch Skiport on the east coast. Since 1958,
Loch Druidibeg has been a Nature Reserve managed by the
Nature Conservancy. Approximately two miles long by one
wide, its wild convolutions, heavily islanded, are most beautifully shaped and set. Hecla and Beinn Mhor tower craggily
behind. The north shore is fringed at the middle by spruce,
pine, red rhododendron in massive clumps, golden whin, and
some monkey puzzles. The Reserve is valuable as an excellent
example of varied Hebridean habitat. It includes machair,
machair lochs, and the peaty hinterland of Loch Druidibeg
itself. The loch is the main breeding ground in Britain of the
native grey lag goose, which nests on the islets. The grey lag
(as a breeding species) is rare on the mainland, but still breeds
in small numbers on Lewis, North Uist and Benbecula. In June
one may stand by the loch and see not one, but when the gos-
lings are fully fledged the geese lead them out to the nurseries
on the machair lochs. In autumn the sky can be noisy with
young birds flying to and fro between loch and machair. Later
on, in winter, they (and the livestock) lose command of the
machair to barnacle and white-fronted geese.

In South Uist, in fact throughout the Long Isle, the lochs
have such an extremely wide range of site and shape that most
kinds of waterbird find a home: tidal lochs and mountain tarns,
peaty lochs and clear, shallow and deep, clear and islanded,
rounded and riven, set on machair, moor, rock, and arable
ground. We can find on them the arctic skua, black-throated
diver, heron, tufted duck, eider, mallard, wigeon, merganser,
swan, teal, coot, sheld-duck, shoveler, geese and many others.
The skua is one of the fast flyers, and to no small extent lives

on fish that she forces other birds to drop in the course of her ruthless pursuit.

The seaward strands have the usual summer birds, but still more come to them in winter, such as bar-tailed godwit, sanderling, brent goose, redshank and greenshank, even snow-bunting and raven. Purple sandpiper and turnstone may appear where reefs breach the sand.

East of Druidibeg the ground becomes rocky to the head of Loch Skiport. The old pier there, which used to supply Ben-becula, is no longer used. Both here and at the head of Loch Eynort, which is reached by another side-road half-way down the island, the land is well-sheltered by the hills but carries only a few scattered crofts. Lobster fishing is done from all three eastern lochs. The Long Isle accounts for 40 per cent of the Scottish west coast lobster catch (almost half a million), of which the Uist and Barra men take nearly double that of Lewis and Harris.

At the island's centre a road forks west to Ormaclett Castle, home of the Clanranald family before they moved to Nunton, then forks south to the village of Bornish. Here is the real South Uist, the heart not seen from the main road. The tracks running in are often poor and rough, but the villages have a workmanlike character on excellent sites. The machairs are broad (a mile wide at Bornish). Rougher ground borders the moor and this buffer-strip bears the chain of lochans that shine along the machair's edge. They are thronged by swans and geese, trout, reeds, and waterlilies.

South Uist is Roman Catholic country and the church at Bornish is one of the best of its kind. The exterior could not be plainer. The inside is of splendid gneiss left bare like the wood of the pews. Nowhere is there decoration, save behind the altar where a huge green drapery falls from roof to floor. High on the draped wall a great wooden cross bears the nailed Christ. In one alcove Mary stands robed in blue and gold. The simple dignity of the whole is most unusual.

Bornish lies behind the Rudha Ardvule, the most westerly

point of South Uist and one of the more delightful promontories of the Outer Hebrides. The flat point cups a lochan which is linked to the sea at the true point by a shingle beach. The Bornish people say that the shingle was once swept away in a storm to uncover an old stone causeway. This might well have been of Norse construction; the lochan would then be made to give the only haven along the entire coast. To either side, the bays curve mile upon sandy mile, interrupted by slight rock points only at several-mile intervals.

One midsummer's day I walked out to Rudha Ardvule from Loch Bornish, a mile across the machair, treading a thick-pile carpet of yellow pansy, trefoil, buttercup and red clover. The bays close in to the point were alive with sheld-duck, one shepherding eight chicks, but even more so with eiders. Fluffy dots speckled the water where the ducklings went *whooshing* and scuttering. Scattered around the turf by the lochan were many puffs of brown eider-down, all that remained of ducklings torn to bits by birds of prey. There were eider too on Loch Ardvule, and probably other duck, but when they saw me they hastily swam into the reeds. Two swans joined them there, glowing softly white through a golden veil. One of the rarer island plants found here is purple loosestrife, about two feet high with bright red spikes. The lochan, so wonderful a place for bird-watching, draws wildfowlers. Many of the barnacle geese are shot when they come down in winter.

Flora MacDonald's birth-place lies close-by at Milton, two miles south on the undulating buffer strip. The low ruined walls bear a cairn and bronze plate. Near them stands a disused thatched cottage, which probably gives a good idea of Flora's as it once was. The site is saved from dereliction only by a modern croft-house with trimmings of children, peat-stack, and hens. Milton has a wide outlook over moors to the eastern mountains, but is hardly worth a visit save for sentimental reasons.

Two miles south of Milton, a golf course stretches behind the dunes from Askernish House to the Pictish wheel-house at

Kilpheder. Whether one is interested or not in golf or archaeology, that two-mile machair is to be enjoyed for its own sake: it has an archetypal quality, a claim that could not be made for the other two. All three are easily surveyed at once if the approach is made through Daliburgh (where the main road branches off to Lochboisdale) to the Kilpheder road-fork a mile farther. The side-road twists through Kilpheder township to end at the wheel-house on the dunes. The house is sunk below ground as an open pit with grass floor. Dry-stone walls, six feet high, make a perfect circle ten yards in diameter, from which short stone spokes converge to form chambers. On the landward side, an eight yards' entrance passage with stone steps leads down. Starlings inhabit. The archaeologists appear to know very little about wheel-houses, which belong to the Hebrides, the Northern Isles, and West Scotland. They are thought to date from around A.D. 200 to 500, and thus to be Pictish, not Scottish.

I had a tantalizing experience one thirsty day when I walked the beach from the wheel-house four miles north on firm white shell-sand. Great waves came thundering up the sands to leave a thick piping of creamy foam, which wound in unbroken line several miles long. The foam lay like jelly shuddering to the wind, warm to the hand, and of exactly the colour of Guinness.

Behind the beach is a little marram, then come the dunes, almost mountainous but green in long-established grass; behind these lies the Askernish golf course. The greens are cut, their turf fairly good, but the fairways are true machair grazed by cows – a sea of buttercups, clover and daisies, an undulating, rolling sea, flushed pink or yellow where the flowers merge and thicken, greening where they spread and fade away, only to thicken again at some other trough. It makes a glorious sight to which larks sing praise. But a man would have to be rich in golf balls to finish a round.

On the other side of the island, an exhilarating ridge-walk may be enjoyed along the summit spine of Beinn Mhor, 1,994 feet, to Hecla, 1,820 feet. If the start is made from the main road at Loch Dòbhrain, the round involves less than 4,000 feet of ascent in ten miles. Beinn Mhor has a fine range of gneiss cliffs running east from the summit. They stand in 800-foot buttresses above Coire Hellisdale and give good rock-climbing.

On the south slopes of Beinn Mhor above inner Loch Eynort, is the shallow glen of Allt Volagir, famous for its small woodland where bluebells, wood-sorrel, primroses and violets grow beneath hazel and birch. Later in the year foxgloves appear (I have never seen them on the west coast) with herb-robert, bugle and wild thyme. Nearly eight hundred species of plants have been listed in the Outer Isles, and a surprisingly large number of native trees (a naturalist will be properly indignant if one calls the isles treeless). Such a list will state the truth yet mislead the unwary. It will include apparently normal flora such as honeysuckle, several kinds of rose, aspen, holly and silver birch. Yet one may journey from the Butt to Barra Head and see none of them. Most trees that we do see are stunted. The flora of the Isles gives extreme pleasure; we observe them more keenly and feel the pleasure more sharply than we would on the mainland by reason of their unexpectedness in lands so exposed, and their vividness of colour in air so clean.

The island's main centre of population is the south land around Daliburgh and Boisdale. Loch Boisdale, spattered with islets, runs in nearly four miles from its outer headlands. A splintered peninsula projects into the loch and carries Lochboisdale village, with harbour, pier, and a good hotel. Farther inland, the townships of Daliburgh and North Boisdale form the larger settlement flanking the main north-south road, on which the seaweed factory is situated. The road continues south on flat croft-land to the rocky bays of the south coast, where it ends at Ludag. From the jetty at Ludag a daily ferry service plies across the sound to Eriskay.

ERISKAY

The name of Eriskay is internationally renowned out of proportion to the island's size or importance – in consequence of a Love Lilt. Within Scotland, Eriskay is held in high esteem for its own sake and that of its people. Its rocky back emerges out of the broad sound between Barra and South Uist, one mile and a quarter off the Uist shore. Less than three miles long by one and a half wide, Eriskay is much the same size as Iona, but has thrice Iona's population – this despite its greater remoteness and lack of soil, for Eriskay is one of the most barren of Scottish islands. It is worked by a vigorous community of 300 people, who like their neighbours on Barra and South Uist are Roman Catholic.

The island belongs to South Uist. Its whole eastern and southern parts are rocky moor. The north and south halves have each one prominent hill, Ben Stack 403 feet, which overlooks the Sound of Barra, and Ben Scrien, 609 feet, which overlooks the Sound of Eriskay. Between the two, the east coast has one deep-thrusting harbour and a score of houses. The island's only road runs from there to the west and north coasts, the latter holding the principal settlement and a small harbour with stone quay. This north-west side has a little soil made fertile over the last century, although everywhere its ribs project. The grass patches brighten the scene even on dull misty days – a brightness enhanced by the red roofs of the houses. Few thatched cottages remain. Most are concreted stone, roofs slated dark blue or painted red, some walls whitewashed, some not; there is variety and colour.

An interesting time to visit Eriskay is the end of June at the start of the school holidays. The teenagers home from Fort William are out from the crofts with ponies and panniers to bring in the peats. They gather from the lower slopes of Ben Scrien. The deep peat has been worked out long since and only the turfy top peat remains. They say it burns well on their

THE SEA OF
THE
HEBRIDES

By Tom Weir

Above: ERISKAY   Calystega Soldanella on the Prince's Beach

By W. H. Murray

Below: GREY ATLANTIC SEAL   Pup

By Tom Weir

forced-draught stoves, but all burn coal in addition. Most surprisingly, they buy more cheaply than mainland householders: each May they take a whole year's supply delivered by puffer.

Sheep graze the upper hill-slopes; on the lower they and their lambs and the cows are tethered, grazing under strict control. What soil there is seems good and suitable for lazybedding, as witnessed by a few well-grown strips of potato and oat, but hardly any lazybedding is done. Crops grown are the minimum needed by way of reserve. The men are fishers. A one-day visitor is likely to see mostly children and old folk, for all the young men will be out at the prawn, or herring, or lobster fishing. At present they find the prawn and lobster markets lucrative.

The women are famed for their knitting. A few specialize in gossamer shawls or in oiled wool jerseys, both for mainland sale. Eriskay fishing jerseys are navy-blue or black, made with symbolic patterns unique to the island: sails, waves, harbour-steps, intertwining lines of mutual love, and others. They take a long time to knit, hence cost ten guineas each (marketed by Highland Home Industries), but their expectation of life is fifteen years.

Too small to hold its young, the island none the less retains all it can employ, and thrives. Most youths go to sea, and the girls to work on the mainland.

Eriskay and its seascape are seen to great advantage from Ben Scrien – half an hour takes one to the top. A quarter of a mile off the north-east point, Calvay Island pops its head out of the Sound of Eriskay. In all neighbouring isles men still drink a toast 'To the man who could not see Calvay', for here it was that the *Politician* struck and foundered in February 1941 with 20,000 cases of whisky aboard. The fiery cross never sped through the isles for the Forty-five so fast as that news. The salvage operation by the islemen, as described in Compton Mackenzie's *Whisky Galore*, is in many respects a diplomatic understatement of events that really occurred.

From Ben Scrien we can see how shallow are the seas around.

H

In calm weather the sandy bottom is visible extending past
Calvay to South Uist and across to Barra at the Traigh Mhor.
Everywhere the sand gives the sea a luminous green colour,
turning to mauves or blues where weed lies or wind ruffles. The
north-west coast of Eriskay has three shell-sand bays. From
the top of the Ben we should descend to the south one, for this
is the Coilleag a Phrionnsa, the Prince's Beach, where Charles
Edward Stewart made his first landing on Scottish soil. It is a
lonely but spacious shore. Half a mile of white sand sweeps to
the rocks at either end. Across the wide sound the Barra hills
rise high, sometimes shrinking away, remote and misty, at
others shrugging the cloud off their shoulders to loom large,
never at any time a flat backdrop but receding in planes, inviting our exploration.

A bank of marram separates the beach from steep grass lifting
high behind. On the marram fringe, near the centre, grows the
pale pink sea-convolvulus (calystega soldanella) said to have
been sown by Prince Charlie when he landed from France. It
grows nowhere else in the Isles except Vatersay, near Barra.
The leaf is small and heart-shaped and the flower a relatively
large trumpet.

There were few people on Eriskay when Prince Charlie
landed in 1745. South Uist, Eriskay and Benbecula belonged
then to the MacDonalds of Clanranald, who also held Eigg and
Canna, until they sold to Colonel Gordon of Cluny in 1838.
Colonel Gordon, the most heartless landowner ever known in
the Outer Hebrides, evicted large numbers of crofters from
South Uist, which had then a population of more than 7,000, to
make way for sheep. Whole communities were cleared from
the east coast, which had the best hill-grazing around Loch
Eynort, and dispersed to Benbecula, to offshore islets, or to
North America. He committed Barra to the same fate. Many
families had then to live in caves or turf huts by the shores,
others were given a few acres each on Eriskay – that being

valueless land, too barren to feed sheep. To these outcasts the sea had been kinder than man. On South Uist the crofters were able to take matters into their own hands. Before and after 1914 they raided the big farms, thus forcing the intervention of the Board of Agriculture, which gave them holdings.

The population of South Uist, including Benbecula and Eriskay, is now 3,650.

17

BARRA

NOT one island but twenty, the Barra group trails off into the Atlantic, giving to the Outer Hebrides a crocodile tail of south-ward running islets. Ten of the group are sizeable: five have been inhabited during this century, now but two – Barra and its near neighbour Vatersay. The remainder have proved too far, small, and exposed to retain human life in a world of rapidly rising standards.

Barra measures eight miles from north to south by four wide, including in its length the narrow northern peninsula of Eoli-garry, which runs out two miles to Scurrival Point. Even so, Barra is bigger than all the other islands of its parish put to-gether, and much taller. Its south coast rises to 1,260 feet on the grassy hill of Heaval. The bird's-eye view from that top shows the island's unique setting and physical character. The whole interior is seen to be grassily bare and mountainous, the whole coastline heavily bayed from sandy west to rock-bound east. Scurrival Point is a feature of much importance. On its back it bears the hill of Eoligarry, 338 feet, on its flanks sand, sand in vast quantity, filling full the great hollow of the south-east waist, endowing Barra with its famous cockle strand, the Traigh Mhor, used as a landing ground by British European Airways.

Our view across the cockle strand extends north-east to a dozen islets on the Sound of Barra, and beyond Eriskay to the purple humps of Beinn Mhor on South Uist. But the scene unique to Barra lies in the opposite direction. South-westwards an archipelago of nine islands zigzags fourteen miles to Barra Head. The principal are Vatersay, Sandray, Pabbay, Mingulay,

and Berneray, the last often named Barra Head from its south
butt. They curl south, each island rising well above 500 feet,
each with an individual distinction. They trace a pattern that
seems to epitomize the Hebridean scene, their double twist
leading on the eye to that oceanic salient, where the Atlantic
thunders on the last cliff.

The archipelago has a worthy foreground in Castle Bay.
Around it circles the island's principal village, given character
by Kisimul Castle on its rock a hundred and fifty yards offshore. Although facing south, the bay and its pier are well
sheltered by a long arm of Vatersay, and by the cirque of hills
behind.

The name Barra is thought by many people to come from
Finbar, a Celtic saint of the sixth century. It might equally well
derive from the old Norse Barr, meaning the coarse barley (or
north English bere) grown in the isles. Prehistoric remains,
such as sun-circles, indicate that Barra has known man for four
thousand years; thus 'Barra' could have an origin long lost in
the mist of prehistory – or be a recent name as first suggested.

Approach to Barra is by sea or air. Between April and September Heron aircraft fly daily from Glasgow to the Traigh
Mhor; in winter thrice weekly. The sea-route is from Oban by
MacBrayne's steamer, which calls three days a week (by way
of Coll and Tiree) *en route* for Lochboisdale.

The present population is 1,350, settled mainly on the south
coast at Castlebay and the east coast at Northbay. Smaller
crofting communities lie in the west at Borve and Greian, and
at Eoligarry in the north, to which the island's ring-road sends
an offshoot. Castlebay is the capital, with harbour and pier,
several shops, two hotels and a post office dispensing all
services from bike-and-boat-hiring to news on most activities from ceilidhs to trout fishing. All around are tokens
of the township's former standing as a fishing centre – the
ruinous sites of twenty curing stations, which ring the bay,
substantial stone houses that front the main road, and most
prominently the big tower of the Roman Catholic church. The

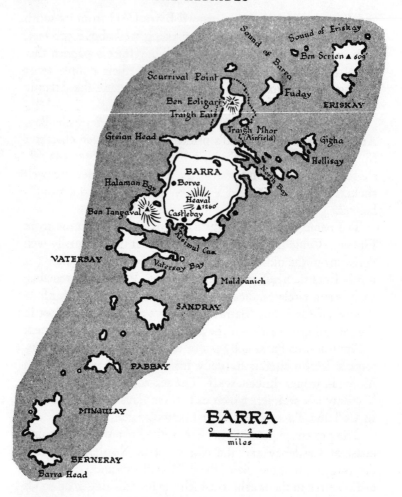

islet-castle from which the MacNeil ruled the waves, stands aloof.

Traditionally, the Kisimul rock bore a castle from the eleventh century, but the present building dates from the fif- teenth. It was restored between 1938 and 1959 by the forty- fifth chief, Robert Lister MacNeil, a commuting architect who works in the United States and lives at Kisimul from May to September each year. When the steamer calls at Castlebay it almost scrapes the barnacles off the castle-rock, but all that can be seen are the blank windowless walls of its square tower. They enclose an inner house, which for its perfect shelter from Hebridean wind forfeits the Hebridean view.

In the sixteenth century, when the Isles were in turmoil, the MacNeils of Barra had a fearsome reputation as sea-rovers. Rory MacNeil, surnamed 'The Turbulent', carried his raids to Ireland, and committed acts of piracy on English shipping, which moved Queen Elizabeth to demand his head of James VI. James summoned him to Edinburgh. Rory had sense enough to refuse. James then commissioned MacKenzie of Kintail to fetch him in by hook or by crook. Kintail chose the hook. He made an ostensibly friendly visit to Kisimul, invited Rory and his armed retinue aboard ship, and wined them well. At the finish, Rory's men preceded him ashore, whereupon Kintail hoisted sail and slipped out to sea with his prisoner.

MacNeil was hastened before King James at Edinburgh and tried for his life. James bent angry brows, and as mere formality prior to a death-sentence put the question, Why had McNeil seized a ship of England and killed the queen's subjects? – knowing full well that the piracy had no political significance and was simply a filling of MacNeil coffers. Rory had commanding presence, and though his head seemed ripe to roll off his shoulders he held it high while it was there.

'I had felt justified,' said he, 'in taking toll on the ships of a queen who had beheaded Your Majesty's mother.'

The unexpected answer struck James dumb. He ended a heavy silence by announcing his royal pardon. And then, to give Elizabeth some semblance of satisfaction, he forfeited the MacNeil's estates, transferring them by happy arrangement to Kintail who promptly passed them back to MacNeil.

In the days of their great power and boisterous humour, the chiefs posted a trumpeter on the battlements every night to sound a fanfare and to proclaim, 'Hear, O ye people, and listen,

O ye nations. The great MacNeil of Barra having finished his meal, the princes of the earth may dine.'

The MacNeils abandoned Kisimul in 1747 when they moved to Eoligarry. In 1838 financial adversity forced them to sell the island, and Barra saw them no more till the return of the present chief a hundred years later.

The road to the west coast from Castlebay runs through a green glen, where yellow flags grow in the marshes, to two lochans at Tangusdale. These and other hill lochans have been stocked with trout. From Tangusdale, where a perfume factory has been opened, dunes roll towards the sands of Halaman Bay, the first of five excellent beaches along the west coast. In August small blue butterfles flit among a profusion of machair flowers. In June the land is the larks'.

Half a mile north, the crofts of Borve nestle in a broad strath, where the Heaval-Hartival massif turns open-armed towards Borve Point. The flat ground looks the most fertile on Barra, but is rivalled farther up the coast by the hillier Greian, where there is a small Protestant settlement (brought in by last century's proprietors). They now seem a peculiarly isolated community. Beyond Borve Point, two parabolas of sand terminate in a seals' benefit of rock-claws at the Greian end. The headland cliffs are colonized by shags, fulmars, guillemots and gulls. Some of the Greian men raid the cliffs for the eggs, which they eat, using the dark yellow yoke of the sea-gulls' eggs for pancakes. More abhorrently, they shoot peewits for the pot. The people are very conscious of their minority status ('Are you one of us?' they will ask). A high religious earnestness combines oddly with a most pawky humour and openly disclosed love of the usqueba'. Many a tale is still told of the *Politician* – of that year when Tir nan Og came to Barra and men drank deep of the water of life.

The remarkable feature of Barra's ring-road is the continually changing scene at each curve of coast: no unusual thing in the Hebrides, but nowhere else do the changes come so fast. The west seems all light and sun and colour after the duller

south (closer in to the hills), but the changeful scene continues
when we strike east to the head of North Bay, which thrusts
two thin arms into the land. We turn north to the Traigh Mhor.
Close by the road, a little glen is crowded with pine, sycamore
and chestnut. The pine-scent is strong and would be unique in
the Outer Isles were it not for Lews Castle.

At the Traigh Mhor the hills fall behind and the whole scene
opens out. The cockle strand is dead flat, a mile wide and long
at the ebb. Cattle and ponies graze along the shore. Near the
inner bay at Vaslain stands a small cockle factory, owned by a
Cumberland firm, where the cockles are cleaned, crushed and
exported as shell-grit for harling houses and for poultry-feed.
The work employs half a dozen men. Live cockles used to be
gathered for export to England until the high freight charges
killed the industry. Recently the work has been restarted by a
local co-operative group called the Traigh Mhor Guild. The
men collect and boil the cockles, then send them off to the
Crofters' Agency at Oban for sale on the British fish market.
These Barra cockles are large and succulent, the best available
in Britain, but at the time of writing are being undercut by the
dumping of inferior quality cockles from Holland. The industry might employ a dozen to twenty men were it given a chance
to establish itself, as it should by virtue of quality, if not
strangled at birth.

Perhaps nowhere in the United Kingdom is an airfield run
with so little fuss as in Barra. A small wooden hut on the innermost shore is the only installation. When the daily Heron is
due, a staff of three or four men is all that appears, including
two men who drive a fire-engine out from Northbay to the
strand. Behind the hut, a narrow rampart of dunes divides the
Traigh Mhor from the perfect sands of the Traigh Eais on the
west coast. The Eoligarry Peninsula is thus near to being a
tidal island, following a collapse of the marram-bondage on the
isthmus caused by livestock, rabbits and wind. Across the narrow neck, the hill of Ben Eoligarry rises to 338 feet. From top
to bottom it is heavily clothed in primroses, the widest and

thickest bank of its kind in Scotland. In springtime the hill becomes one of the minor wonders of the Isles. In midsummer the lower south slope has a great mass of stonecrop, the biggest bank I have ever seen, standing out brilliantly yellow on exposed sand. The summit reveals the peculiarly graceful sculpting of the peninsula at four huge strands, which completely encase it save for the north-thrusting rock of Scurrival Point. On the north-east flats, the crofts of Eoligarry spread green to the Sound of Fuday.

Southward to Castle Bay, the east coast is entirely rocky, riven and bayed. Every bit of marshy ground is bursting with yellow flags, and wherever possible the rocks are cultivated by lazybedding. The township of Northbay ranks in size next to Castlebay, but is free of hotels and tearooms, pubs and recreation grounds. A small factory makes spectacle frames. Lobster boats lie moored in the creeks. This east coast road can be a painful surprise to the walker or cyclist accustomed to flat islands. It is exceedingly hilly, winds from bay to rocky bay, and finally climbs several hundred feet up the shoulder of Heaval before plunging to Castlebay.

Barra houses are more like those of Skye than any others of the Long Isle. Design is plain but walls are whitewashed and painted. Most houses go gay in red and green roofs and with small, flower-crowded gardens, in which purple veronica predominates. One does miss the peat-reek of the northerly isles. Barra never had much peat, and that has nearly all been worked out. The people burn coal.

Barra repeats in miniature the history of the Hebrides. On the cession of the Isles by Norway, the MacNeils held Barra from the Donald Kings and Lords of the Isles until 1493, thereafter by their own strength, which finally failed them in 1838 when they sold out to Colonel Gordon of Cluny. Whatever their faults, the MacNeil chiefs had truly been as fathers to their people. Martin Martin wrote in 1695: 'When a tenant's wife dies in this or adjacent islands, he then addresses himself to MacNeil of Barra representing his loss and at the same time desires that he would be pleased to recommend a wife to him, without which he cannot manage his affairs, nor beget followers to MacNeil, which would prove a public loss to him. . . . MacNeil finds out a suitable match for him; and the woman's name being told him, immediately he goes to her, carrying with him a bottle of strong waters for their entertainment at marriage, which is then consummated.'

When a tenant died, the widow was likewise found a husband by MacNeil. If a tenant lost his cows by any misfortune, MacNeil supplied him with a like number. When tenants grew too old to till the ground, MacNeil took such old men into his own family and maintained them all their life after.

Colonel Gordon, who had also bought South Uist, decided in 1851 that the smallholding system was yielding him insufficient rent. Worse still, potato blight had stricken the Isles. With aid of a government grant, he brought in transport ships, landed police and press-gangs, evicted every crofter (confiscating stock and property), and forcibly transported a large but unstated number to Canada. The population dropped by eight hundred that year to 1,853. The landless survivors grew in number over the years. They appealed to the new owner, Lady Gordon Cathcart, for a grant of land; they offered fair rent; they were starving, and they received no reply – Lady Gordon Cathcart visited Barra once in the fifty-four years she owned it – until, alarmed perhaps by the Battle of the Braes in Skye and Gladstone's appointment of a Royal Commission, she made a small grant of land in Eoligarry. The people were desperate. Men from Mingulay and Castlebay raided her Vatersay farm in 1906 and stayed as squatters. Some were imprisoned, but the furore forced a reluctant government to act. In 1909 they bought Vatersay for £6,250. Similar land-raids were made on the Eoligarry farm in 1914, and finally in 1919, when the whole became croft-land.

Towards the end of the nineteenth century Castlebay began to grow as a fishing port. The abundant herring in the Barra seas brought in East Coast drifters; soon the Barra men began to acquire boats of their own; at the full development several hundred boats were out nightly. When in harbour, packed gunwale to gunwale, they formed a pontoon on which it was possible to cross from Castlebay to Vatersay. The quays were then all bustle, resounding to the smack of coopers' hammers, noisy with the laughter and song of girls gutting and curing fish for the German and Russian markets, the loading and unloading of cargo boats and the screaming of thousands of gulls. Work would go on all day and sometimes all night after a heavy catch. The population of Barra rose to its maximum of 2,620 in 1911. Thereafter the decline set in as described for Stornoway. During the two wars the remaining boats fell into disrepair. An attempt was made to restart in 1945 but no market could be found. Now the quays are deserted, the sheds vanished away, and no more curing is done at Castlebay. The drifters sail direct to the mainland road- and rail-heads at Mallaig, Gairloch, Ullapool and Oban.

The lasting strength of Barra is still its croft-land. Although no weaving is done, sheep stock has been trebled and a good income is earned from the sale of wool to the tweed industry of Lewis and Harris. Lobster fishing on the Barra islands remains excellent. Ancillary industries include the cockle trade, roadwork, quay-side work at Castlebay and Lochboisdale, and summer tourism. Each spring there is an emigration of girls to west mainland hotels, and spring or summer an immigration of young men home on two weeks' leave between voyages. Large numbers of men serve with the merchant navy. Their wives and families have often preferred to live on the mainland rather than stay on their Barra crofts. The consequent drop in population (25 per cent in the last seven years) may prove advantageous, for the island has been over-populated for its size. The community remains big enough to retain the social facilities that hold a permanent population: good schools and houses, roads, halls for meetings, sports' grounds, an airfield, telephones, and a healthy Church in close contact with its people and promoting their social intercourse. Everyone speaks Gaelic. An electricity supply has been promised for 1965.

A Barra Development Committee was formed in 1965. Their plan is to create new employment through a Trust fund, which is raised by appeal to the island's own people both at home and abroad. Their immediate aim is to buy two second-hand fishing boats, and then to foster other, employment-giving projects. A similar body was formed in 1964 in Vatersay, where the need is dire. The two have now joined forces.

A matter of no small moment is the service given to shipping in distress on these rock-strewn seas by the crew of the Barra lifeboat. In winter especially, often in high-velocity winds giving storm-conditions that would appal anyone not born and bred an outer islander, the men are called to ships that may be foundering on rocks fifteen or fifty miles away. The explosion of the maroons, which summon the lifeboat's crew, may be heard at midnight or at two or three in the morning, but within half an hour that lifeboat is heading out to sea.

The social life of the Gael is intense. The dour silent 'Highlander' is a creation of fiction, or else an East Coast or Lowland immigrant. Not only is free communication in the nature of the Gael, it has been cultivated over generations by the ceilidh. In the long winter nights, when the Isles used to be cut off from the mainland world, the people would gather round the peat fire in each other's black houses to enjoy song and story, music and poetry, and hear the sagas and folk-tales of the race. The recounting of these sagas developed in men retentive memories, fluent oral composition, and most correct speech, for all these won praise. They quite incidentally inspired in the young a love of the virtues extolled: hospitality, courtesy, and self-forgetful courage.

The traditional ceilidh has nearly died out in the Isles. The modern concert, organized in a village hall in summer to extract money from visitors (for some worthy cause), is no ceilidh however named. In the Protestant islands, the evangelical revival of the early nineteenth century, which resulted in the dominance of the Free Church, caused the disappearance of song and story as an artistic expression – damned by the clergy as untruth and vanity. In our own times they condemn dancing and piping – even at Duirinish in Skye, once the world's principal centre of the art – as tending to immorality. Prohibitions so extreme have an ill effect on the life and spirit of young people.

The Catholic islanders take a broader outlook on life. A summer Sunday on Barra is startlingly different from the breathless peace of Lewis. After Mass the people enjoy themselves. The café opens at Castlebay; motor-boats sail to Pabbay, Sandray or Mingulay; Barra may be playing Eriskay on the football pitch and a film may be showing at night. In this relaxed atmosphere the ceilidh flourished longer in South Uist and Barra than elsewhere. The clergy have thought it life-sustaining. South Uist has long usurped Skye's position as the heart and home of island piping, and with Barra is by far the richest source of the old folk-tales.

The nine isles south of Barra were once known as the Bishop's Isles, belonging to the Bishop of the Isles *de jure* although to MacNeil *de facto*. Vatersay, second largest of the Barra group, alone remains inhabited with a population of 95 (240 in 1931). It is virtually two islands connected by a narrow belt of dunes, shaped thus like a ham-bone, two miles long by two wide at each end. The long eastern point has a jetty facing Castlebay. Distributed among the island's forty houses are twenty crofts of four acres each, but too few people remain to work them all. The social situation is instructive. Vatersay is conveniently close to Castlebay and should have as firm a hold on continuing life as Eriskay. It has a good road, a sea full of fish, a school that takes children up to the eleven-plus examination, after which they go to Castlebay (returning at weekends), and the crofters breed sheep and cattle for mainland sale: yet only four men fish, the only crops are potatoes and oats, the number of children at school rapidly dwindles – twenty in 1962, ten in 1964 – and the few children under school age are expected to

be the last. Vatersay appears to be a dying island from which most would depart if they could. Numbers have fallen below the marginal level that allows internal vigour and social liveliness, hence communal effort may collapse. The people have made a last effort to avoid evacuation by forming a Vatersay Development Committee. They are seeking new sources of employment, such as the export of shell sand, which being 90 per cent calcium carbonate would be ideal for agricultural use. If such efforts fail the island will probably end up as it was prior to 1908, a single farm run from Barra.

Mingulay (Bird Island) is the penultimate isle of the Barra group and the third largest. Ten miles out from Castlebay, and measuring only two miles by one, it held a population of 140 at the turn of the century. Mingulay's name is famed for its boat song, which although so different from the Eriskay love lilt has the same exquisite beauty. In 1908, when the people moved as land-raiders to Vatersay, they left a township still to be seen derelict on the east coast. The land behind rises high at each end in hills, 891 feet in the south, 735 feet in the north. The latter, Macphee's Hill, was so named after MacNeil of Barra sent out a boat to discover why no word had come from Mingulay over a long period. One of the crew, Macphee, was put ashore and found everyone dead of the plague (probably typhus). When he reported back to the boat the crew refused to have him aboard, and the unlucky man had to spend a year on the island alone. Despite all, he survived, and day after day used to climb that north hill to watch for the relief ship. When Mingulay was resettled the MacNeil made him a grant of land.

One famed feature of the island is the 750-foot sea-cliff on its south-west side, the home of countless sea-birds. Close inshore stand the stacks of Arnamul, Lianamul, and Gunamul, the latter connected to the main island by a natural arch through which a boat may sail. The rocks are a main breeding station for guillemots and kittiwakes, and the upper slopes for puffins. This abundant bird-life draws naturalists in annual expeditions.

Half a mile south of Mingulay, Berneray rears up to its final buttress at Barra Head. Most lonely of the Barra Isles, it had a population of 6 in 1930; now like Mingulay it is given over to puffins, guillemots and kittiwakes, and to fulmars since 1899, the year of their first southward move from St. Kilda or North Rona. The extreme west point is the highest, where cliffs of 630 feet take the brunt of gigantic seas. There is no shallow water to break the blow. It is a place of storm, of unceasing wind, where the surf is blown over the cliff-top in gale and small fish are found in the grass. Sir Archibald Geikie, a Director-General of the Geological Survey, records a hurricane that slowly moved a block of gneiss weighing forty-two tons across five feet of ground. At the brink of the great cliff stands the last outpost of man, the Barra Head light, carried on its tower 683 feet above high water.

Ships can see that light flash and fade, flash and fade across thirty-five miles of black Atlantic, warning and welcoming: Here rise the isles of archaean gneiss, storm defying and ship wrecking, life giving and life taking, the Isles on the Edge of the Sea where men are welcome – if they are hard in body and in spirit tenacious. No lesser men may hold the Hebrides.

APPENDIX I

Chapter 1. THE ISLES ON THE EDGE OF THE SEA

Page 1. Havbredey. In A.D. 129 a small Roman fleet circumnavigated Britain. The commander brought back a name for the Hebrides which Ptolemy rendered as Ebudae or Hebudes (in themselves meaningless). The Romans had most probably heard the local name Havbredey, for evidence is strong that Lewis and Harris were then occupied by Norsemen. (The *recorded* Viking invasions came later). *Hav* means Sea. *Bred* means Edge. *Ey* means Island. Havbredey thus means Isle on the Edge of the Sea, or Coastal Island. The plural is Havbredeyjar.

Chapter 2. WEST OVER SEA

Page 8. Alban. Scotland's early name lasted until nearly A.D. 1000. The word is the plural of the Gaelic Alb, meaning Mountain, and is now best rendered as Highlands.

Chapter 4. COLONSAY AND ORONSAY

Page 48. MacPhee. The name is one of the oldest surviving Celtic surnames. Originally Mac Dubh Sith (Son of the Dark Fairy), it became MacDuffie, MacFie, MacPhee, and even Shea and Shaw. The MacPhees of Colonsay were the right-hand men of the Lords of the Isles. The last chief went down with his chief, Sir James of Clan Donald, in 1615.

Chapter 5. JURA

Page 58. Beinn an Oir. The mistranslation as Mountain of Gold is made by users of school dictionaries. The ancient meaning of Oir was Boundary. Probably this was one of the boundaries that also split Iona, Mull, and Colonsay at the time King Cairbre of the House of Riada in Northern Ireland ruled this area, almost certainly by treaty with the Picts of Alban.

Chapter 8. The Isles of the Sea

Page 78. Muirbolc Mar (Adamnan). *Muir* means Sea. *Bolc* or *Bolg* means Pouch or Bag. *Mar* (an old form of *Mor*) means Great or Big. The literal translation is thus Great Bag of the Sea, which is best rendered in English as Great Arm of the Sea.

Chapter 9. Iona

Page 81. Iona. The suggestion sometimes made by writers that Iona derives from a Gaelic word Ishona has no sound basis. I Sona *could* mean Blessed Isle – but the dominant S sound would never have been dropped.

Page 81. I-Chaluim-cille. The name can be wrongly translated as Island of Calum's Cell. If that were done the Gaelic would have to read I Chille Chaluim. Dwelly makes it clear in his dictionary that Cille was tacked on to the names of highly esteemed ecclesiastics in recognition of their founding chapels or churches. Thus Columba was sometimes named Calum-cille. The simplest modern way to render the high distinction of Cille is by 'Saint'.

Chapter 10. Mull

Page 99. Spanish galleon. There are several differing accounts of the way this ship was sunk.

Page 109. Fingal's Cave. Fingal was the Scottish form of the name Fionn MacCoul, a famous Celtic warrior whose life was devoted to driving the 'Men of Lochlann' (Norsemen) out of the Hebrides. He was finally killed in battle near the river Boyne in A.D. 283. The word Fionn was not the adjective meaning Fair, but the noun meaning Chief. The Scottish name Fingal was derived from the title Fionn na Ghal, 'Chief of Valour'.

Chapter 13. THE SMALL ISLES

Page 135. Eigg. The name is thought by some to derive from the Norse Egöe, meaning Oak Island. The early presence of scrub oak in sufficient quantity to support the name is doubtful.

Page 137. MacDonald's cave. There are several differing accounts of the offence given to the MacDonalds by the MacLeods.

In 1577 the people would not use the title of MacDonald or MacLeod as surname, for that was reserved to the chief alone. Their use of MacDonald as surname became early permissible on the death in 1626 of the last MacDhomhnuill, Sir James of Dunyvaig and Islay.

Page 141. Rhum. The correct pronunciation is Room and the correct spelling is Rüm. The island is mentioned in the *Annals of Ulster* (676) as Ruim, used thus in the genitive form (e.g., Beccan Ruim = St. Beccan of Rüm). The island was renamed Rhum by the family of Bullough, who being English would be unaware that there is no Rh prefix in Gaelic ancient or modern. The present spelling is thus an abortion. The Ordnance Survey adopts (I think mistakenly) place-name spellings that landowners prefer. The name Rhum thus appears on O.S. maps and has become widely accepted.

Chapter 14. SKYE

Page 146. Skye. The Norse word Skuy is pronounced as the English Sky and means Cloud. Lacking aeroplane, map, or compass, the Vikings would certainly not see Skye as having outstretched wings. They would see it, like most sailors since, heavily capped in cloud. The Vikings named islands from prominent landmarks and general appearances, which made useful sailing directions. There is no good way to spell a sound like Skye in the Gaelic, hence 'Eilean a' Cheo' for Isle of Mist.

Page 159. MacCrimmon. A school of piping in Skye much older than the MacCrimmons' was the MacArthurs'. They were brought to Islay as hereditary pipers to the Lords of the Isles and given the lands of Proaig on the east coast near 'MacArthur's Head.'

Chapter 15. LEWIS AND HARRIS

Page 173. Lewis. The name is usually written nowadays in the Gaelic as Leodhas, although recorded in R. A. Armstrong's *Gaelic Dictionary* of 1825 as Leoghas. The derivation would thus be from an original Eilean Leogach (Marshy Island) to Leoghas, and now to Leodhas (pronounced Leuas).

Page 179. Temple of the Sun at Callanish. The early Celts worshipped Bel, the Sun God. Their invariable symbol of eternity and of Bel was the circle. This sacred symbol was carried forward on to the early Celtic crosses.

Pages 172 *and* 190. Lazybeds. These beds are made, principally for growing potatoes, by sowing the seeds on the surface and covering them with earth dug out of trenches alongside. The beds are rarely more than 6 feet wide or less than 3 feet. The method provides soil and drainage where both are otherwise insufficient. The usual crops thus grown in the Isles are oat, barley, hay, and corn. The lazybeds of east Harris do not conform to this description; they are lazybeds with a difference (p. 191): no troughs can be excavated alongside. The beds are built up on bare rock.

Page 196. St. Kilda. The early name, Hirta, would almost certainly derive from the old Norse HIRÐA, with the soft Ð pronounced Th as in 'The'. The word means 'to herd sheep.' HIRÐÖ would thus be Herd Island.

On the main island, still called Hirta, there is a well. The old Norse for well is Kelda. The Gaels who followed the Norsemen, not knowing the meaning of Kelda, probably thought the name honoured a saint and called it Tiobar Childa (which they imagined meant Kelda's Well). The error was perpetuated when the group of islands appeared on the first printed map of Scotland in the sixteenth century as St. Kilder.

APPENDIX II

A SHORT BIBLIOGRAPHY

ADAMNAN. *Life of St. Columba* (7th century). 1961.

ATKINSON, R. *Island Going.* 1949.

BOSWELL, JAMES. *A Journal of a Tour to the Hebrides with Samuel Johnson,* 1785.

BUDGE, DONALD. *Jura.* 1960.

CAMPBELL, J. LORNE. *Book of Barra.* 1936. Stories from South Uist. 1961.

DARLING, F. FRASER. *West Highland Survey.* 1955.

DARLING, F. FRASER and J. MORTON BOYD. *The Highlands and Islands.* 1965.

DOMHNULL GRUAMACH. *The House of Islay.* 1962. *The Foundations Of Islay* (2 vols.) 1965.

DWELLY, EDWARD. *Illustrated Gaelic Dictionary.* 1949.

GARNETT, T. *The Highlands of Scotland.* 1880.

GEDDES, A. *Isle of Lewis and Harris.* 1955.

GEIKIE, A. *Scenery of Scotland,* 1865.

GREGORY, D. *History of the Western Highlands and Isles of Scotland.* 1881.

HUMBLE, B. H. *The Cuillin of Skye.* 1952.

LODER, JOHN DE VERE. *Colonsay and Oronsay.* 1935.

MACCORMICK, JOHN. *Island of Mull.* 1923.

MACCULLOCH, J. *Description of the Western Islands of Scotland.* 1819. *The Highlands and Western Isles of Scotland.* 1824.

MACGREGOR, A. A. *The Western Isles.*

MACKENZIE, COMPTON. *Whisky Galore.* 1947.

MACKENZIE, W. C. *Short History of the Scottish Highlands.* 1906. Book of the Lews. 1919.

MACNEIL OF BARRA. *Castle in the Sea.* 1964.

MARTIN MARTIN. *Description of the Western Islands of Scotland,* 1695. 1934.

MILLER, HUGH. *Cruise of the* Betsy. 1858.

MONCRIEFF, GEORGE SCOTT. *The Scottish Islands.* 1952–61.

MONRO, DONALD. *A Description of the Western Isles of Scotland,* 1549. 1934.

MUNRO, R. W. *Monro's Western Isles of Scotland.* 1961.

NICOLSON, A. *History of Skye.* 1930.

PATENT OFFICE. Reports of Patent Cases: No. 16, 1964. (Harris Tweed).

PENNANT, THOMAS. *Tours in Scotland* (2 vols.) 1771–75.

SCOTTISH MOUNTAINEERING CLUB. *The Islands of Scotland. The Island of Skye.*

STEELE, T. *Life and Death of St. Kilda.* 1965.

STEVEN, CAMPBELL. *The Island Hills.* 1955.

THIRD STATISTICAL ACCOUNT OF SCOTLAND. *Argyll.* 1964.

Index